Praise for *The Practical Writer*

"*The Practical Writer* is a superb companion for the writing life, gathering together in one volume the best possible guidance for writers. Loaded with down-to-earth advice and insights, it covers just about everything from the mystery of the creative act to the mystery of publication."
— Sue Monk Kidd, author of *The Secret Life of Bees*

"Think of *The Practical Writer* as a five-star writers' conference, minus the salad bar and the steep enrollment fee. It anticipates and serves the needs of the beginner, the scribe just entering the publishing maze, and the seasoned veteran of the printed word. Along with sound advice on the craft and business of writing, it has helpful appendices that give poets and prose writers leads on grants, resources, and safe harbors. *The Practical Writer* is solid, serviceable, and valuable—a treasure trove."
— Wally Lamb, author of *She's Come Undone* and *I Know This Much Is True*

"The information and insights here will help you win a writer's best rewards. And because the book comes from *Poets & Writers*, you can rely on it for good reading as well as valuable advice."
— Judith Appelbaum, author of *How to Get Happily Published* and managing director of Sensible Solutions, Inc.

"It's a gem of a guide! The advice it offers is wise and realistic. I wish it had been around when I began my writing career."
— Susan Isaacs, author of *Shining Through* and *Long Time No See*

"An 'up periscope' onto myriad aspects of the writers' world, *The Practical Writer* will prove an essential addition to any writer's library. A wonderful companion in the trenches, for pro and tyro alike."
— Janet Fitch, author of *White Oleander*

PENGUIN BOOKS

THE PRACTICAL WRITER

THERESE EIBEN became editor of *Poets & Writers Magazine*, which is published by the nonprofit organization Poets & Writers, Inc., in January 1998. She has also worked as an independent researcher for Time, Inc., primarily for *Fortune* magazine, and as an editor of nonfiction and fiction for Dembner Books, an independent publisher. She holds a master's degree in creative writing from Brown University and a BA in English from Dickinson College. Her work has appeared in both business and literary venues, including *Fortune,* Time, Inc. Home Entertainment Series, the British Broadcasting Corporation, *Artfolio, Alaska Quarterly Review,* and *Poets & Writers Magazine.* She lives in New York.

MARY GANNON, deputy editor, has worked for *Poets & Writers Magazine* since 1996. She has taught writing as a faculty associate at Arizona State University in Tempe, where she received her master of fine arts degree in poetry. She received her BA from Skidmore College. Her articles have appeared in *Poets & Writers Magazine,* and her book reviews in the *Pittsburgh-Post Gazette* and *Chelsea Magazine.* Her poetry has been published in the *Antioch Review, Hayden's Ferry Review, Louisville Review, Paris Review, Passages North, Washington Square,* and *SHADE.* She has served as a judge for various literary awards and grants given by such organizations as the Academy of American Poets, the Colorado Council for the Arts, the Massachusetts Cultural Council, and the Bronx Council for the Arts. She volunteers for PageTurners, a program affiliated with the Inner City Scholarship Fund that brings writers to schools in New York City. She lives in Brooklyn, New York.

For information about Poets & Writers, Inc.,
please see pages 351–52.

The Practical Writer

From Inspiration to Publication

Edited by **Therese Eiben** and **Mary Gannon,**

with the staff of Poets&Writers Magazine

PENGUIN BOOKS

PENGUIN BOOKS
Published by the Penguin Group
Penguin Group (USA) Inc., 375 Hudson Street,
   New York, New York 10014, U.S.A.
Penguin Books Ltd, 80 Strand,
   London WC2R 0RL, England
Penguin Books Australia Ltd, 250 Camberwell Road,
   Camberwell, Victoria 3124, Australia
Penguin Books Canada Ltd, 10 Alcorn Avenue,
   Toronto, Ontario, Canada M4V 3B2
Penguin Books India (P) Ltd, 11 Community Centre,
   Panchsheel Park, New Delhi – 110 017, India
Penguin Books (N.Z.) Ltd, Cnr Rosedale and Airborne Roads,
   Albany, Auckland, New Zealand
Penguin Books (South Africa) (Pty) Ltd, 24 Sturdee Avenue,
   Rosebank, Johannesburg 2196, South Africa

Penguin Books Ltd, Registered Offices:
80 Strand, London WC2R 0RL, England

First published in Penguin Books 2004

10 9 8 7 6 5 4 3 2 1

LIBRARY OF CONGRESS CATALOGING-IN-PUBLICATION DATA
The practical writer : from inspiration to publication / edited by Therese Eiben
   and Mary Gannon, with the staff of Poets & Writers magazine.
      p.   cm.
      Some contributions were originally published in Poets & writers magazine.
      ISBN 0-14-200400-6
      1. Authorship.   I. Eiben, Therese.   II. Gannon, Mary, 1967–   III. Poets &
   writers.
      PN137.P73 2004
      808'.02—dc22   2003060878

Printed in the United States of America
Set in Janson Text with Gill Sans and Clarendon Light
Designed by Sabrina Bowers

Acknowledgments

Most of the essays in this book are by those devoted authors whose writing distinguishes *Poets & Writers Magazine* as a prominent publication in the literary field. We thank them, and all of the contributors, for their fine efforts on our behalf.

We have the good fortune to have a dedicated and talented editorial staff, whose hard work on the magazine contributed to the conception and shaping of many of the essays included in this book. We thank managing editor Suzanne Pettypiece for her technological wizardry, associate editor Kevin Larimer for his intellectual rigor, and former managing editor Jim Andrews for his creative thinking. We also are grateful to Joel Bernstein and Tom Cherwin for their exacting eye, Hillery Stone for her editorial and administrative excellence, not to mention her good nature, and Rachel Sussman for parachuting in when she was most needed.

We thank our editor Caroline White for her unflagging enthusiasm for this project, and agent Brian DeFiore for his good counsel.

Poets & Writers Magazine is published by Poets & Writers, Inc., whose founder, executive director Elliot Figman, and board of directors we thank for their ongoing support and leadership.

Contents

SECTION I

Concepts of Craft:
Imagination's Many Forms

Contents

SECTION 2

Initial Contact:
Getting Your Work off Your Desk
and onto Someone Else's

SECTION 3

Building Your Team:
How to Work Well with Publishing Professionals

Contents

SECTION 4

Meeting Your Public
(and Getting Them to Buy Your Book)

SECTION 5

Jobs in the Field:
Lots of Reward, Little Pay

Afterword

Appendices

Introduction

From Inspiration to Publication

The poet Alberto Rios came by the offices of *Poets & Writers Magazine* several years ago, visiting from Arizona State University, where he teaches. He had come to town to participate in a tribute to the New Generation of Mexican Poets, a trip that coincided with one of the World Series Championship parades New York City hosted in the '90s. When we saw him he was toting Yankee caps and T-shirts, and he told us a story about the first game he had attended at Yankee Stadium, twenty years before. The Kansas City Royals were hot then; somewhere in the middle innings George Brett connected with a pitch that sent a ball arcing toward the upper deck where the young poet sat. Rios described the suspended moment he shared with the ball: So perfect was its trajectory, he knew without doubt that he could have caught it simply by opening his mouth. He and the ball were one . . . until a jumble of fans intervened.

That story has stayed with us since, in part because of the poet's enviable ability to build a monument to a moment, and in part because the arc that baseball traveled describes the trajectory a writer travels to bring a creative work into being: from the private moment of communion between author and idea to the sometimes frustrated process of making the work public. *The Practical Writer: From Inspiration to Publication* is intended to ease some of the difficulties writers can encounter in transit, but even more important, to help writers recognize the value of each stage of the journey. Certainly publication is part of the writing process, but it is by no means the only worthwhile aspect of it. A writer who values the creative process, who never loses the awe of bringing something new into existence, who understands that the silence of the writing studio is as meaningful as the buzz of a publication party, *that* writer is one who will lead a rewarding literary life.

The Practical Writer is divided into five sections, five points on the arc a writer travels from inspiration through marketing and publication. In the first section, "Concepts of Craft," you'll find seven essays on imagination's many forms. Helen Benedict, a journalism professor at Columbia University, tells how it is possible to get closer to the truth by writing fiction than by writing fact. The poet Gregory Orr explains how he turned to memoir after thirty years of writing lyric poetry—and why. Journalist Michael Depp makes an eloquent case for the elegant essay, following what Howard Norman calls "the meandering line of clarifying thought." In an, *er*, revealing essay, former director of the University of Houston's creative writing program Julie Checkoway shares what she learned about narrative from a Victoria's Secret catalogue. Fiction writer David Long writes about the power of specificity in his article "Stuff." In his essay on revision, poet Jeffrey Skinner addresses the creativity that emerges between drafts. And novelist Nicholas Weinstock writes about the trouble both he and F. Scott Fitzgerald had with titles.

The second section, "Initial Contact," focuses on getting your short stories and poems off your desk and onto someone else's. First, David Hamilton, editor of the *Iowa Review*, offers a proposal for knowing when a story or poem is done (don't stick a fork in it). Amy Holman, the former publishing seminars director for Poets & Writers, Inc., advises on submission strategy, protocol, and the best ways to avoid making it easy for an editor to reject your work. Natalie Danford, series editor for *Best New American Voices*, reviews the range of literary and little magazines that are accepting new work from new writers, and surveys contests that are important to enter. *Poets & Writers Magazine* contributing editor Joanna Smith Rakoff provides a comprehensive overview of the glossies—the eight high-circulation magazines that pay a living wage to fiction writers. *Atlantic Monthly* (one of the eight) editor C. Michael Curtis lets you in on important advice on how to read the rejection letters you will inevitably collect (no good writer escapes them). Scott Bane, an expert on nonprofit foundations, helps you apply for a grant.

The essays in section three, "Building Your Team," address the best ways to work well with publishing professionals. Literary agent Noah

Lukeman offers a step-by-step guide on how to land an agent for your manuscript. The general counsel for the Authors Guild, Kay Murray, walks you through a book contract so that you understand what you are signing . . . and what you shouldn't sign. Betsy Lerner, agent, former editor, and author of *The Forest for the Trees: An Editor's Advice to Writers*, has a clear sight line on what a writer should expect from an editor, as well as what not to expect. Publisher and writer Sol Stein (*Stein on Writing*) dispels the myth of the "midlist" author, and offers an insider's perspective on why it was created in the first place. Michael Taeckens, publicity director of Algonquin Books, lays out a publicity primer for new authors—ways to help your publisher's publicist, and ways to make her job really, really hard. A consultant to booksellers across the country and abroad, Kate Whouley wrote the book—*Manual on Bookselling* (ABA, 1996)—on the subject. In her article, she instructs authors on how to make friends with bookstore owners and managers, a writer's most direct link to people who buy books. Novelist and publishing journalist M.J. Rose explores the gray area between what your editor and publicist are saying and what they really mean.

The whole point of publishing is to go public, right? Well, the essays in section four offer strategies to make the most of meeting your public, and tell you what to do when you're face to face, or when they are in your face online. Story Line Press publisher Robert McDowell writes about tactics small press authors and poets (those who don't have big publicity machines behind them) can use. Journalist Catherine Wald helps you organize an online publicity campaign. Jacqueline Deval, a book publicity expert with more than twenty years' experience at four major houses, walks you through the etiquette of a bookstore reading and signing. Poet Tom Bradley has tips on how to read with conviction. R. Eirik Ott takes an indie approach on selling his poems.

Section five offers essays on jobs in the field. Rebecca Wolff, founding editor of *Fence*, narrates the little-pay, lots-of-reward undertaking of starting a literary journal. Guy Shahar, founding editor of the *Cortland Review*, does the same, but for an online-only journal. Fran Gordon, founder of the PAGE reading series at the National Arts Club in New York, discusses how to do something similar where you live. Novelist Melvin Jules Bukiet, who was surprised to find himself proprietor of the KGB Bar, writes about how it became a literary watering hole. Novelist Hilma Wolitzer, a teacher of creative writing for thirty years, shares her secret of giving your own work primacy, even when you're busy with the work of your students.

The appendices are also full of important information for writers. Every page confirms that there is a national network of writers, a community waiting for you to join—through conferences, workshops, literary journals, small presses, and national and regional literary organizations.

Poets & Writers Magazine (originally called *Coda*) has been helping emerging and established writers since the 1970s. Its readers—a literary lineage that includes Billy Collins, Rita Dove, Clarence Major, and William Styron—know it as the only comprehensive clearinghouse for pertinent, trustworthy, and legitimate information about publishing and grant opportunities. Its writers—those whose articles have distinguished the magazine—come from all walks of literary life. Many of them are established poets, novelists, and essayists; others are agents, editors, and publishers.

The Practical Writer gathers the guidance thirty-one writers offer from various vantage points on the trajectory of the writer's life. Collectively, their essays address much of the experience, observation, and insight that has helped shape the national literary community and conversation, both of which we hope you'll join. We also hope their words provide good company along the sometimes lonely, often puzzling, always rewarding journey of a committed writer.

—THERESE EIBEN, MARY GANNON,
and the staff of *Poets & Writers Magazine*

SECTION I

Concepts of Craft:

Imagination's Many Forms

Fiction vs. Nonfiction:
Wherein Lies the Truth?

by Helen Benedict

Helen Benedict is a professor of journalism at Columbia University. She is also the author of three novels and four volumes of nonfiction.

I teach in a prominent journalism school and recently I committed heresy: I published a novel. It was about a Dominican American teenage mother and was written in the voice of the girl herself. Immediately, my students wanted to know why I had treated this subject as fiction. Why didn't I just go out and write about a real teenage mother, the way they would have done? Why did I let them down, the suggestion seemed to be, by making things up?

Then I shocked them even further. I told them that I had chosen fiction because I believed it could get me nearer to the truth.

The kind of truth I am talking about is the subjective truth of what it means to be a human being in the world. It is the substance of what happens to people not just on the outside, but within: the longings, the moral decisions, the defiance, suffering, pain, and triumphs of the human soul.

This sort of truth has always been the subject matter of fiction, because it is hidden from the public eye. It lies in secrets and private experiences. It rests in the silences that follow broken-off words and truncated sentences, and in the spaces between bouts of self-awareness. It hides in the blanks on a reporter's tape recorder, behind the door after the journalist leaves, and inside the mind where no interviewer can go.

Fiction steps in where the ordinary articulateness of human beings fails. It gives the human soul a voice.

But if these truths about the human condition are so hidden, my students might ask, how does a fiction writer get to them?

Through research, a lifetime of experience, analysis, and, above all, the imagination.

Had I written *Bad Angel* about a real teenage mother, my ability to get at the truth of her experience would have been restricted by all sorts of factors: her sense of privacy, the limits of her ability to express and examine herself, my obligation not to expose her every fault to the world, my inability to know what she was thinking unless she told me, and my uncertainty about how much of what she did tell me was honest. Even had I interviewed her for years, I would have been limited by what she chose to say and whether she knew how to say it, as well as by my fear of exploiting her. I would have always been the white journalist trying to peek into her world, and she would have always been the Other, the way the poor and dark-skinned so often are presented in the press. In short, I would never have been able to understand her enough to write in her voice or from her point of view.

I saw these limitations reflected in the many books of interviews with teenage mothers I read to research my novel. These girls were happy to talk about why they got pregnant and whether they would stay in school, but not one admitted to feeling loneliness, despair, rage, or even irritation with her baby, let alone to neglecting or abusing the child. Yet I knew that teenage mothers often do abuse their babies. I also knew, as a mother and former teenager myself, that motherhood cannot exist without moments of blinding rage, and that teenagehood is inevitably accompanied by loneliness and moods. Furthermore, I knew that being a teenager and being a mother are inherently contradictory: The first is self-absorbed, the second by necessity self-sacrificing. Yet this conflict was not even touched upon by any of the girls interviewed for the books I read. Why? Because the girls either could not or would not admit to these feelings. As a fiction writer, however, I could.

A case in point: Could Vladimir Nabokov have exposed the dark and tortured soul of his obsessive nymphet-lover if he had merely interviewed a Humbert Humbert? I happen to have read dozens of interviews with rapists and child molesters conducted in prisons, and none of them touched the understanding Nabokov achieved with *Lolita*. Instead of giving us sociological jargon about pedophilia, a psychological profile of arrested development, or quotes from some therapy-saturated child molester ("Yeah, I felt her up 'cause my dad abused me when I was five"), he gives us Humbert Humbert's soul, with all its blights and beauties, its fury and remorse.

"I stood listening to that musical vibration [of children at play] from my lofty slope, to those flashes of separate cries with a kind of demure murmur for background, and then I knew that the hopelessly poignant thing was not Lolita's absence from my side, but the absence of her voice from that concord."

In that one sentence, Nabokov gives us the epiphanic moment when Humbert Humbert realizes that he has irreparably robbed Lolita of her childhood. But this is no confessional at a prison therapy session, offered up in the hope of winning parole. This is a poignant and intelligent revelation, H.H.'s first and only moment of true unselfishness. By giving us this sentence, with all the weight of what has come before it, Nabokov uses his knowledge of human nature to make us simultaneously sympathize with and abhor H.H.—he makes us understand him much more profoundly than could any interviewer. And the way he does it is the way the best fiction writers always do it—he conjures us, through the power of his language and imagination, inside Humbert Humbert, so that we cannot stand aloof and condemn him without thought or insight. We cannot dehumanize him because Nabokov makes us become him, forcing us to see all the facets of his personality: the monstrous and the poignant, the insufferable and the pathetic. And in doing so, Nabokov makes us just that little bit more human ourselves.

For several centuries now, readers have appreciated this magicianlike ability of writers to get us inside characters and at certain truths. We have looked to writers from Shakespeare to Tolstoy for moral and philosophical guidance, and for critical evaluations of ourselves and our societies. Jonathan Swift, Charles Dickens, Emile Zola, John Steinbeck, and Upton Sinclair are among many authors whose fiction has changed the way we view social injustice, for example; a few books have even changed laws. Jane Austen, Virginia Woolf, James Joyce, James

Baldwin, Samuel Beckett—these and a multitude of others have held up mirrors to the human soul that have altered our thinking and the way we see and create our art. Until this era, novelists have held a respected role as examiners of society and investigators of the human psyche, as thinkers from whom we learn certain kinds of truths and honesty that no other form of writing can offer.

But something, alas, has changed. Readers are no longer willing to take an author so seriously. Many readers seem to have lost the patience or the willingness to look to fiction for moral, philosophical, or even social truths. If this were simply part of the general post-1960s rebellion against authority, there would be less to lament, but the problem is that millions of readers are turning instead to self-help books, memoirs, or nonfiction, as if these forms contain better truths than fiction. All a book has to do is claim to be fact to be given the kind of attention that almost no literary novel can command anymore. Serious fiction is losing respect, and sales to boot. Many readers would rather see a reporter interview a teenage mother than see a novelist create one. Others seem to consider cold facts about how a computer works more important than the troubling mysteries of the human psyche. The novel and its unique access to the truths of the human soul have fallen with a crash.

The reasons for this fall are many. It is partly the fault of deconstructionism, mixed in with Freudianism, which destroyed the mystique of the author and put critics on the throne. Suddenly, authors became hapless beings batted about by the tides of fashion, formalism, cultural traditions, and their own circumstances. Whatever messages they tried to impart were probably unconscious, certainly unintended: The poor saps would be the last to know.

Then came our current Information Age, in which people are driven to feel so inadequate and ignorant that they are afraid to spend time reading anything but hard fact. This, coupled with the twenty-first century version of a lifestyle—work twelve hours a day, spend your leisure time at the gym, and forgo sleep—has given people the illusion that reading fiction is an expendable luxury. Who has time for the subtleties of fiction when the Web, television, movies, radio, newspapers, and a torrent of nonfiction books all promise to fill us with the facts we need to join rush hour on the information highway? I see this attitude in my students. "I don't read fiction," they declare with a self-righteous ring. "I only have time for fact."

When people make a statement like this, what they are saying is that fiction contains nothing important, that the only things that matter are exterior, verifiable facts. Insights into the human experience, examinations of the conscience, the reality behind closed doors—these sorts of matters count for nought.

Underlying the current distrust of fiction, and the mistaken attitude that important truths are not to be found in it, however, is something more than the fall of the author or the worship of fact: It is fear of imagination. I see this most strikingly among my reporter friends and students, the people whose business it is to write nonfiction; after all, the journalistic creed is never to make things up. They have been trained to think of books as little fact missiles, packed with Useful Information that, like vitamin pills, will make them better people. So when I explain to my fellow reporters that my understanding of my teenage mother came not from research but from what I know of human nature, they blanch.

"But you must have based it on someone you met," they say. No, I didn't. "Then on interviews you did—is she a composite character?" No, she isn't. Sometimes I have even been asked, "Well, were you a teenage mother then?" No, I have to say again, I made it all up. They don't want to believe that an author may be able to imagine what it's like to be a teenage mother (or a nymphet-lover) better than such a person can explain it herself. A current ad for a nonfiction writing program reveals this same fear in its proclamation, "Truth is stronger than fiction"—as if fiction contains no truth at all.

I witnessed how much imagination is feared, and misunderstood, when I read from my novel to an audience that included a number of anthropologists. After I had finished, one raised his hand. "But aren't you exploiting this girl?" he asked.

"This is fiction," I replied. "She doesn't exist. There is no real girl to exploit. I made her up."

The anthropologist didn't get it. I was using this girl for my own means, he insisted; had I at least offered her my advance? Didn't I feel guilty for invading her privacy?

"You can't exploit a fictional character," I replied again. "Fictional characters have no privacy."

The anthropologist could not believe that my character was a figment of imagination because he did not understand how fiction originates. And because he didn't understand how fiction originates, he did not want to believe me. Either I was lying and the girl did exist, or I was telling the truth and the girl was invented, in which case why should he believe anything I wrote at all?

But fiction is not, as many nonwriters seem to think, a random grab bag of made-up whimsies, as undisciplined and unreasoned as a dream. Nor is it simply reporting with the names changed. It is an amalgam of experience, education, reading, insight, analysis, conversations, observation, and conscious research. Tom Wolfe could not be more wrong when he accuses novelists of failing to use the reporter's pen. Novelists never stop reporting. They spend their lives observing, watching, analyzing. And most of them conduct purposeful research as well. Many of George Eliot's novels are historical, packed with accurate details about times way before she was born, likewise for Dickens and Tolstoy. Zola, Theodore Dreiser, and Stephen Crane all lived and researched the harsh worlds they wrote about. Today's novelists are no different. Andrea Barrett, John Updike, Robert Stone, Toni Morrison, Annie Proulx—all these writers and most of their comrades research constantly for their fiction, mining not only concrete facts but truths about the soul. Even if, as a Freudian might say, fictional characters are nothing but extensions of the author, they still contain all the knowledge, insight, wisdom, and experience that author has collected throughout his or her life. In fact, I would wager that the novelists who do not haunt libraries, but rely solely upon their imaginations and memories, are a minority—and they, too, are drawing from a lifetime of meticulous observation. And it is exactly because of this lifetime of work that fiction writers—at least the best of them—can and ought to be believed.

All this is not to say that nonfiction has no value. The very knowledge that an extraordinary story actually happened makes that story especially fascinating. Nonfiction writers have an essential role as recorders of events, exposers of wrongdoing, explorers of mysteries, and explainers of history. They can affect politics and laws in a way fiction rarely does. Nevertheless, even though they can make arguments and challenge injustice, the interior is still hidden. Nonfiction is always dependent on what can be found out and verified, and it is always limited by the private, the secret, the unrealized, and the unarticulated. Nonfiction always keeps the reader on the outside.

Perhaps this is why some readers prefer nonfiction—perhaps they are, in a sense, hiding. The distance between reader and subject in nonfiction is so much greater than in fiction that perhaps it feels safer. After all, it is easier to read about the suffering of the Other than to be pulled into feeling it oneself. Perhaps people resist fiction because, even in this era of voyeurism and confession, there is still a fear of putting oneself in another's shoes.

If that is so, what a loss. In this time of ethnic and religious factionalism, racial division, and gender hostility, when people seem so stubbornly myopic, fiction offers a service that readers—and publishers—would do well to heed: It gives us the chance to escape the cages of our bodies and lives and fly over impossible boundaries to become somebody else. It gives us the ability to break out of myopia and its ensuing prejudices and narrow-mindedness. Above all, fiction gives us the chance to understand the world from the Other's point of view—not from the distant outside, but from deep within.

Paths and Pearls:
A Poet Ponders Memoir and Lyric

by Gregory Orr

Gregory Orr, the author of eight books of poetry, teaches at the University of Virginia.

The lyric achieves its orderings and meanings partly through dramatic focus. A lyric poem tends to center itself and its perceptions on a single incident, image, situation, or scene. The lyric shapes itself by excluding things that it considers irrelevant, not of the essence. It concentrates and constellates in order to create coherence. Its model could be the pearl that grows by wrapping its nacreous layers around an instigating grit of dirt (or hurt). Prose, on the other hand, opens up to the world of incident and lets itself take part in the flow of time—how one event follows another, may even cause another, as characters move through their lives.

When I was a young poet, I had a vision of my life's work. This was way back in 1971, and my vision was as much wishful thinking as supernatural apparition. Nevertheless, I saw my life's project as a series of three concentric circles. The first, innermost circle stood for my first book of poems (not yet finished, let alone published). That inner circle was also the self, my own self. What it meant was that the poems in my first book would occupy that inner circle of the self—their landscapes would be interior landscapes of imagination and dream (and nightmare). These landscapes identify those poems as versions of the surrealism then in vogue in American poetry. The second circle, surrounding the first circle at a little distance, was to be my second book. It would have a wider radius. The self would still be at the center (I was a lyric poet and the self was the central and centralizing power of my imagination), but the poems would extend beyond to a wider range of material that would include accurate renderings of the natural world and also the presence of family and friends. The poems in this second book would find their meanings by dramatizing intimate social relationships and encounters with nature. The third book, the third circle, would include the other two circles and their concerns, but would reach even wider to encompass historical and political issues. Envisioning this third circle strained my young imagination to its limits. It wasn't as if I hadn't already been engaged by social and political subjects, but I was very aware that I lacked the linguistic and conceptual skills to assimilate them into literary form. My belief was that the necessary understandings and skills would come later. I never for a moment doubted that poetry would be the form of expression for this third, culminating subject matter, as it would be for the preceding ones.

Five books and fifteen years later, I wrote some prose poems about my youthful experiences working for the civil rights movement in Mississippi and Alabama. I hoped that the larger and looser sentences and the paragraph structure of prose poems could incorporate the information and context needed to include history and social turmoil in my lyric testimony. But I felt disappointed with the results. There's no question in my mind that prose poems and other lyric forms can engage large social and political themes—there are so many poets I admire whose work did. But mine didn't. Even though the form stretched to include material, too much of the complexity was left out. It was a difficult lesson for me because I thought my poetry could encompass all the worlds of my experience.

It took me thirty years and a memoir to find out that there are things a prose narrative can do that are beyond the capabilities of poetry. Mind you, I am still a lyric poet at heart, but what I've come to believe is that the memoir is an especially congenial prose form for lyric poets, because it so generously accepts the subjectivity of speculation and imagination that poets thrive on. In finally writing a memoir, I feel I found a form of expression that approximated that largest circle I saw so many years before as a fledgling poet.

My whole adult life has been spent as a lyric poet—that is, as someone committed to the ethos and efficacy of the personal lyric, which I define as an "I" poem about experience. What's striking about the personal lyric is its power to handle crisis in the individual. This power has earned the personal lyric an omnipresence in human cultures. It exists as a possibility in all cultures on the planet now and as far back in time as we can reasonably go. My favorite stopping places in antiquity are four love-poem anthologies from New Kingdom Egypt, 3,300 years old, and certain poems from the Chinese *Book of Odes*, also written down over 3,000 years ago.

The personal lyric is one of three essential survival tools culture has invented to assist the self with existential crises, the other two being religion and philosophy. Existential crises are those situations in which the individual self has been overwhelmed by disorder, especially extreme emotions. In effect, the personal lyric says to the self: Translate your crisis into language—bring your disorder over to poetry's primal ordering powers (especially story, symbol, and incantation) and we will make a poem. This poem will dramatize your situation as an unfolding interplay of disorder and order—a model of your crisis, but with this crucial difference: The power relationship between disorder and order is reversed. Instead of your self being overwhelmed by disorder, we will have in the poem the opposite situation—your self as poet mastering what threatened to master you, ordering the disorder of love or loss or fear or joy into the drama of a poem. The same self that was destabilized by the disorderings of experience is here, in the poem, restabilized by taking charge through imagination and making a coherent model of its crisis. The poet thus creates what Frost calls "a momentary stay against confusion." This existential crisis might not necessarily be in the immediate life-moment of the poet. It could be in the more distant past—say, a memory of a trauma or suffering—in which case we might identify with Wordsworth's statement that poetry is "emotion recollected in tranquility." I would substitute the term *safety* for *tranquility* and note that in Wordsworth's definition the poet's self is circling back from a safer future moment to engage some earlier, emotion-based disordering experience. Whether we favor Frost's or Wordsworth's formulation, we have a similar project: using language and shaping imagination to master a confusing situation or emotion and order it into the dense and complex pattern of meaning we call a poem.

The lyric project can be seen as a cultural tool to assist individual survival. When I say *survival*, I mean something basic and down-to-earth about the way emotions and relationships affect our life prospects—the sort of thing highlighted by the insurance industry statistic that informs us that when a spouse dies, the surviving mate has a

50 percent higher chance of dying within the next calendar year than in any other year of his or her life.

Among other things, the lyric project of survival is crisis-oriented. It favors and dramatizes the acute situation, the peak moment of encounter between self and disorder. Such an encounter could concern something as destructive as the unspecified, recurring trauma dramatized in Emily Dickinson's lines:

> It struck me—every Day—
> The Lightning was as new
> As if the Cloud that instant slit
> And let the Fire through—
>
> It burned me—in the Night—
> It Blistered to my Dream—
> It sickened fresh upon my sight—
> With every Morn that came—
>
> I thought that Storm—was brief—
> The Maddest—quickest by—
> But Nature lost the Date of This—
> And left it in the Sky—
>
> (# 362)

or it could be something in an entirely different mode, such as the situation in these lines from Walt Whitman, where the self is threatened (presumably in a pleasurable way) by the sensuous chaos of erotic contact:

> Is this then a touch? quivering me to a new identity,
> Flames and ether making a rush for my veins,
> Treacherous tip of me reaching and crowding to help them,
> My flesh and blood playing out lightning to strike what is hardly
>   different from myself,
> On all sides prurient provokers stiffening my limbs,
> Straining the udder of my heart for its withheld drip,
> Behaving licentious toward me, taking no denial,
> Depriving me of my best as for a purpose,
> Unbuttoning my clothes, holding me by the bare waist,

Deluding my confusion with the calm of the sunlight and pasture-
    fields,
Immodestly sliding the fellow-senses away. . . .

                                (from *Song of Myself*, section 28)

But whether the emotional disordering that engenders it is positive or negative, the lyric's parameters are those of dramatic focus. A personal lyric by its very nature concentrates around a single scene, image, event, moment. This centripetal concentration is the source of its power, but also a mark of its limits.

I have written poems centered in crises and felt their power to help me live by engaging and ordering experiences that were destructively inchoate in my mind and my memory. Perhaps the best example would be a poem that concerned the pivotal crisis in my life, my younger brother's death in a hunting accident when I was twelve years old. What needs to be added to the story is that I was the one holding the gun that killed him.

Here is a lyric about that experience:

A LITANY

I remember him falling beside me,
the dark stain already seeping across his parka hood.
I remember screaming and running the half mile to our house.
I remember hiding in my room.
I remember that it was hard to breathe
and that I kept the door shut in terror that someone would enter.
I remember pressing my knuckles into my eyes.
I remember looking out the window once
at where an ambulance had backed up
over the lawn to the front door.
I remember someone hung from a tree near the barn
the deer we'd killed just before I shot my brother.
I remember toward evening someone came with soup.
I slurped it down, unable to look up.
In the bowl, among the vegetable chunks,
pale shapes of the alphabet bobbed at random
or lay in the shallow spoon.

Here is another poem, centered on another crucial calamity, my mother's death in a hospital in Haiti, where we lived at the time. She had gone in for a "routine procedure," but never came out. This poem is set during a visit my brother and I made to her bedside the day she died.

EVERYTHING
(*for my mother*)

Is this all life is then—
only the shallow breaths
I watch you struggle for?
That gasp right now—
if it was water
it would be such a small glass.
And I could lift your head
from the hospital pillow
and help you sip it
to comfort your parched
throat
into the ease of sleep.

Your agony makes no
sense when air
is everywhere, filling
this room where you lie
dying, where we move
as if in a trance, as if
everything were under water.

So, why did I decide to try memoir? Well, though these two crucial events are so close in time—less than two years apart—no lyric structure I knew of could connect them effectively or convincingly. And there were odder events around that same time that were also part of my experience and part of what I had to integrate into my sense of identity. On the day I killed my brother, my mother came to where I was hiding in my room and said, "Something almost exactly like this happened to your father when he was your age. He killed his best friend with a rifle." After that disturbing statement, silence—she told me no more. My father never discussed this earlier death, or his responses to it, with me. (Enforced silence, by the way, is one source of lyric poetry, which can become an expression of last resort for a silenced self.) It was only seven years ago that I learned anything at all about this mysterious death. From my father's estranged sister, I learned that, twenty-six years before my brother's death, my eleven-year-old father and his best friend had snuck a rifle and some paper plates out of a house and gone to a field to pretend to shoot skeet. My father shot and killed his friend.

There was yet another sudden, violent death hidden in my family's history. I had a brother Christopher, who at the age of four (I was three) climbed out of bed, swallowed a fistful of sugar-coated pills, went back to sleep, and never woke up. Do I remember him? Do I remember his death? It's hard to say, but I certainly saw photos of him sitting next to my infant self in our family album (though most pictures of him were removed; there remained only the smear of dried glue on the gray page and his name and a date in my mother's precise handwriting). Christopher's death was another abrupt, intimate death not spoken of, unspeakable in our family.

At the age of eighteen, four years after my mother's death, I was a civil rights volunteer in Mississippi in the summer of 1965 and endured various violent misadventures, police beatings, and a weeklong stretch of solitary confinement following a gunpoint kidnapping by vigilantes in rural Alabama. Terrifying in their own right, these events seemed to be echoes in the larger world of the violence that haunted my family. Finally, there was a further secret coursing like a turbulent, underground river beneath my childhood: my country doctor father's chronic addiction to amphetamine and the effect that had on our lives.

To engage this life material, I needed to open myself up to the looser and more inclusive structures of prose. This may sound obvious and even easy, but to a lyric poet it isn't such a simple task. It meant giving up the gratifications of powerfully cohesive forms. Abandoning my aspiration to make poems beautiful as pearls. Or, to shift away from the seduction of that metaphor, it meant engaging more realistically the randomness and unpredictability of being a self in the world.

When I wrote lyrics, I was safe on the peaks of being: moments of intensity that rose up out of the surrounding wilderness. But to write the narrative of memoir, one has to connect up the peaks with a path. It may be that the peaks are moments in which the mystery of being can reveal itself to the poet, but the valleys between the peaks, the rough wilderness you must cross to get from one peak to the next—these reveal the mysteries of becoming, of how a self is transformed into a person. Because the path to individual selfhood, to coherent identity, is not necessarily well worn by previous feet and blazed with trail markers on every third tree. The path of becoming is, in memoir, often the story of how a self makes his or her own path—reacting to the terrain, making difficult choices about which way to go, getting lost in thickets, or being forced to find a way to cross a raging stream that wasn't even visible from the peaks and doesn't appear on any maps. Maybe memoir is the story of the journey to selfhood, to a sense of the meaning and purpose of one's life.

It's not only the complicated and vivid terrain between peaks that a narrative engages. There is the necessity to open yourself to the impact and influence that other people have on your life. Again, this may seem obvious. We are, Aristotle tells us, political animals—animals of the polis, the social world. We don't just act and react, we also interact with others. And yet how does one write about other people? It's a gift fiction writers have, just as lyric poets have the gift of being able to dramatize the inchoate forces and feelings inside them. But I was very aware of how difficult it is to create convincing characters, even though they were parents, siblings, and intimate friends. Eudora Welty says, "Imagining yourself inside the skin, body, heart, and mind of any other person is the primary feat, but also the absolute necessity." There's an enormous moral triumph in such an empathetic project, and Welty is right that it is essential to the writing of interesting fiction. But such an admirable "primary feat" is terribly difficult. Chekhov says, "The soul of another is wrapped in darkness." How to unwrap that darkness and make the characters in one's life stand before your reader as autonomous and engaging people?

There's a related issue. Critics sometimes speak of someone's having committed a "poetic novel," and we know it isn't an entirely complimentary remark. We know the critic may be implying that the writer mixed too much personal sensibility and subjectivity into the narrative stew. But in this respect the memoir seems a more forgiving form of narrative than the novel, almost a poet's form, because it lets the self loom large and makes room for a generous amount of subjectivity and speculation on the part of the first-person speaker. A person reading a memoir is in search of what it feels like to be another person dealing with events that really happened. In their search for authenticity, memoir readers are willing, I think, to settle for a smaller and less realized cast of characters in exchange for a sense of the depth and authenticity of the speaker's testimony.

In order to write a memoir, I had to break open the neat concentric circles of my youthful "vision" and substitute the larger, looser meaning-making powers of narrative. And yet to do so was to remain true to the essential lyric project of the self's survival and to the use of language and imagination to ensure that survival. Memoir is an ideal form in which to tell the story of how an "I" persists, resists, chooses, survives, recognizes patterns of experience, grows and grumbles, becomes a complex and sentient being among other complex and sentient beings inhabiting a shared world.

On Essays,

Literature's Most Misunderstood Form

by Michael Depp

Michael Depp is a journalist and freelance writer. He teaches at Tulane University.

This is not an essay. Though maybe, in a way, it is. Because it's a strange thing about essays: Even talking about them, trying to get at what they are, it's hard not to cleave to the spirit of the essay, that inconclusive, most outwardly formless of forms, which spills and seeps into so many other kinds of writing—memoir, feature, commentary, review—and punctuates every assertion with a qualification, a measure of doubt, an alternate possibility.

So, this might be an essay.

It's this very problem, the want of a strict, inarguable definition of the essay, knowing where it stops and where other forms begin, that has perhaps made the essay one of literature's most misunderstood forms, a "second-class citizen" in the world of letters, according to one of its best-known practitioners, E.B. White. And yet to many who write them, essays are some of literature's most rigorous undertakings—both intellectually taxing and more revelatory than fiction, as they lack the soft membrane of fiction's artifice to buffer the impact of the writer's thoughts on the reader.

Long before postmodernism drew the reader's attention to the naked machinations of literature, there was the essay, laying itself bare, the curtain between the writer and reader already pulled back. The writer, caught in a kind of intellectual flagrante delicto, struggles, tests, sounds things out, finds ideas and discards others. For the reader, the very thrill and energy of the essay comes from this intimate exposure, the art of a writer intensely in dialogue with him- or herself, the "dialectic of self-questioning," as essayist Phillip Lopate calls it. O.B. Hardison Jr. sees this self-realization extending even further, to an almost metaphysical level: "The essay is the enactment of the process by which the soul realizes itself even as it is passing from day to day and from moment to moment."

That acting out, that attempt, is the essay's vital center. And so it was coined in the sixteenth century by Michel de Montaigne, whose own prose works on matters philosophical, literary, and moral seemed to find no place among prescribed forms or genres of writing because of their self-effacing, antiauthoritative posture. He called his effort *essai*. (The modern translation from the French corresponds simply to *attempt*.) And thus was a name given to the form and the process, though it was not necessarily born with Montaigne, as certain rhetorical works dating back to the likes of Seneca and Plutarch can be retrofitted with the designation.

If Montaigne didn't, strictly speaking, invent the form, he certainly gave it its tincture, laying out some of its broad parameters, setting the stage for the later identifiable informalities it would accrue. He rejected systemic thinking and hefty, authoritative rhetoric. He showed readers the colliding intersections of his own thoughts. He didn't begin with conclusions, and often he never found them.

Which is why it's so ironic that for many readers, the introduction to the form begins with a high school homework assignment to write a five-paragraph essay, with its standard introduction, three body paragraphs, and conclusion. Robert Atwan, founding editor of the annual *Best American Essays* (Houghton Mifflin), points out that this is a perverse inversion of the form. In his foreword to the 1998 edition of the series, which began in 1986, he writes, "It not only paraded relentlessly to its conclusion; it began with its conclusion. Its structure permitted no change of direction, no reconsideration, no wrestling with ideas."

A real essay, Atwan says, never begins with its end.

So what occasions the essay? If a writer has no surefire argument to make, no point to sway the reader toward, why flaunt personal vacillations in print? Why not leave the questions and doubts to the rough draft rather than give them life?

For Richard Rodriguez, the attraction is the essay's public rehearsal of ideas. "I've always thought of the essay as a way of responding to public life," he says. "For me, the drama of the essay is the way the public life intersects with my personal and private life. It's in that intersection that I find the energy of the essay."

Scott Russell Sanders employs the form for self-revelation. "I write essays as a way of making discoveries about my own life, about the world, about my past," he says. "The essay is a seeking of a pattern, meaning, or understanding in an area where I'm bewildered, puzzled, or confused."

Both writers have worked extensively in other forms. And they keep finding themselves returning to the essay for the allowances it makes for them.

Another compelling feature of the essay is that it opens wide the doors of structural possibility. Essays inherently lend themselves to meandering, anecdote, and disclosure. "They're amorphous; they're protean," says Cynthia Ozick. "They have a million forms, and that's part of the wonder and the freedom of the essay."

And therein also lies the essay's struggle for identity, the point at which it threatens to dissolve into so many other things or into nothing at all. Any form, after all, must have shape, no matter how pale its lines or fluid its borders.

Lopate, editor of *The Art of the Personal Essay* (Anchor Books, 1994), believes that the true essay is never formless. "It follows a track of someone's thoughts," he says. "So it may not have the same form as a short story, and it may not release its epiphanies in the same way as short fiction, but it generally has a rise and fall, and it appears to dig up something, to reach deeper understandings than it began with, and all that's a kind of form."

Atwan sees the essay as having a kind of "intellectual plot." He says, "There's something going on, some dilemma, something at issue."

And the essay is not averse to employing the devices of other forms, says Ozick, who has published novels, short stories, criticism, and essays. "The nonfiction form can give you some of the enchantments of the fiction form, including revelations, moments of suspense, moments of climax, moments of crescendo," she says.

Joyce Carol Oates, editor of *The Best American Essays of the Century* (Houghton Mifflin, 2000), agrees that many contemporary essayists are verging on fiction's domain. "The essayist may be embroidering a little, using some of the devices of the fiction writer," she says. "There's a heightening of suspense, a recollection of dialogue and detail."

This, she says, breaks from nineteenth-century excursions into the form, most notably in the works of Ralph Waldo Emerson and Henry David Thoreau. "The older form is much more rhetorical," Oates says, "and the newer form is much more cinematic."

Yet whatever it might borrow from fiction—or film, for that matter—Lopate says, the essay reverses one fundamental rule of good fiction writing: Show, don't tell. When writing an essay, Lopate says, "It's not enough to render the experience. You also have to put it in perspective. It's not enough to show. You also have to tell."

And regardless of the structural decisions the essayist arrives at, there is another caution: The essay cannot simply become an exercise in narcissism. "It's not fundamentally about the essayist," says Sanders. "The essay speaks about how the mind and the heart of the essayist intersect with something much larger than the essayist."

Rodriguez agrees. "For me, there's a rigor to the essay," he says. "I require that the essay I write in some sense be about experiences or ideas that other people are proposing or arguing about. It cannot simply be about my experience."

Still, the essay's beating heart is the writer him- or herself, the story (or stories) subordinate to what the individual is making of it (or them). "I find that the reliance the reader puts upon an essay is a reliance that I seem to bear rather directly," says Pulitzer Prize–winning novelist Richard Ford. "They want an inquiring intelligence seen to be at work, leading to some distillation or expression of intelligence derived from real-life experience."

But ironically, this desire for intelligence and insight from the essay, with its critical and analytical tendencies, may have put it in lower standing than other literary forms. "In the early twentieth century, the essay was used to explain works of modernism, and it became a great critical tool," Atwan says. "It was used to explain poetry, drama, and fiction, and as a result of that it wasn't considered a literary form itself."

By the 1960s, he says, it had become a kind of endangered literary species, relegated to the lesser tier of journalism and commentary. Putting the essay in critical service to other forms had diminished its own standing, making for a largely absent body of critical theory and vocabulary on the form itself.

And then, a strange twist. As the essay dwindled away in print, exiled to a few literary publications, it began to emerge from unexpected sources. National Public Radio began broadcasting essays on its daily news programs, a practice that can be seen as having led to present-day weekly shows like Public Radio International's *This American Life*. Television introduced its own forays, from Andy Rooney's pieces on CBS's *60 Minutes* to essays by Rodriguez on PBS's *The NewsHour with Jim Lehrer*. Essays began to abound on the Internet in online magazines like *Slate* and *Salon*, introducing hypertextuality to the form and vastly broadening readership.

This revitalization was coupled in the 1990s with the public's growing interest in memoir, the essay's closest literary cousin. Readers' hunger for self-disclosure became nearly insatiable, and readers made genuine stars out of writers like David Sedaris, a humorist-essayist who first gained popularity on NPR, went on to publish collections of his personal musings, and now routinely sells out large theaters for his readings, evoking a widespread popularity of the form not seen since the days of Mark Twain. Suddenly, it was not inconceivable for the essayist to become a rock star.

Rodriguez says his own work, as presented in his appearances on television, introduced a counterpoint to the news that has struck a chord with viewers. "There was some desire to end the official discussion of the day's news with a human voice that was simply mulling it over," he says. "It was a reminder that all this news will play against a consciousness."

But what radio, television, and the Internet lent the form in popularity, even poignancy, they threatened in the essay's potency. Ford, who has written numerous essays for radio, says the medium's limitations are considerable. "The thoroughness that the mind is capable of is foreshortened," he says. "References and second thoughts are foreshortened. Pithiness is rewarded about a subject for which pithiness is not usually a virtue."

Sanders says the Internet's hypertextual nature, too, can have an adverse effect on essay writing. "It will tempt writers to write in more fractured, more fragmented ways, because that's the way most information comes to us now," he says.

Oates agrees. "The qualities that we see on the Internet are brevity and succinctness, and maybe a little bit of flippancy and shallowness," she says. "So you don't quite come away with as much depth on the Internet."

Still, however mutable other media may have made it, the essay has heartily rebounded from the endangered-species list. Anthologies, including the *Best American Essays* series, are flourishing, and essays continue to find a regular home in periodicals ranging from *The New Yorker* and *Harper's* to *Boulevard*, the *Yale Review*, the *Gettysburg Review*, and the *Georgia Review*.

But if the essay has found itself on more solid footing than it was fifty years ago, if the word itself enjoys greater literary standing ("The term no longer has the negative resonance that it did when I started the series," Atwan says), there is still the matter of its shimmering, protoplasmic borders. When does the mere "essayistic" begin to walk securely on the terra firma of the essay? Where does the essay begin to strain under the devices of other forms—the lengthy, unmediated divulgence of the memoir, the multiple points of authority of journalism, the evaluative checklist of the review? When will it offer us the structural assurances of the poem, the short story, the novel?

Perhaps it is the essay's very nature to deny us such certainty. For there just might not be an actual territory of the essay, but only the trying to find it.

The Lingerie Theory of Narration

by Julie Checkoway

Julie Checkoway, a former director of the
Association of Writers and Writing Programs
and the creative writing department at the
University of Houston, is the author
of two works of nonfiction.

There are many excellent ways to learn about narration—reading
John Gardner's *The Art of Fiction* and Gerard Genette's *Narrative
Discourse*, for example—but perhaps the most accessible lessons about
such writerly matters as description, overwriting, and opening and
closing stories can be found by reading (well, *reading* is probably im-
precise) the Victoria's Secret catalogue, that ubiquitous ninety-page
glossy circular that most women (and some men) find in their mail-
boxes about once a month.

Over the years, I've tried not to pay too much attention to these catalogues. Mostly, I've just pulled them out of my mailbox, eyes averted
like a Puritan's, and deposited them straight into the recycling bin. Just
flipping through those pages can make the average gal crave Prozac—
how those women manage to look that glamorous in just their under-
wear can be downright depressing. (For many men, I imagine, it's
another matter. . . .) But not too long ago I started noticing the simi-
larities between the VSC and writing fiction, how both rely on a certain
level of artful seduction.

In his book *Story and Situation: Narrative Seduction and the Power of
Literature* (University of Minnesota, 1984), the literary critic Ross
Chambers reminds us that the storyteller's primary job in narration is
to "exercise power" over the reader, to make him want to listen. In order to succeed at controlling the "other," Chambers says, a story's
speaker must both "achieve authority" and "produce involvement." But

how does the speaker provide enough information but not so much that the reader feels alienated or overwhelmed?

All writers struggle at some time with the problem of balance between authority and involvement, seduction and revelation. Beginning writers commonly struggle with how much description to employ, and more advanced writers commonly struggle with how much plot is too much or too little. And there is no better place to find answers to such problems than in the Victoria's Secret catalogue, where the arts of seduction and revelation are so commonly and successfully practiced. After all, the secret of the effective lingerie ad is the same secret at the heart of effective storytelling: to provide, moment by moment, the illusion of imminent exposure, to give the viewer (read: reader) the uncanny sense that something fundamentally compelling is always *about to be* revealed. In short, it is the art of the tease, the craft of selective "coverage," that works to enthrall.

The Problem of Overexposure

Clear description—of setting, of character—is fundamental to good fiction, and becoming as concrete as possible in description should be a writer's first goal. Some writers know intuitively how much description is enough and how much is too much, but for others it's an acquired skill. There are several useful things to remember in order to master it.

The first is the old saw that fiction is, at its heart, economical (stories more than novels, of course), and that one must choose material with a conservative, even sometimes miserly, touch. Description should therefore not be wasteful or redundant (unless you're trying to make some thematic point by being repetitive or maximal). One needs only to describe a house once, for example, as long as nothing has changed the second time we visit it. One needs to say only once that the paint is flaking and that the tree is dying. And, as my former teacher John Barth, himself a maximalist, used to say, description needs to be "illustrative" rather than "exhaustive," meaning that you need to give the reader information that is useful and thematically important rather than information that is merely compulsively comprehensive or too intently microscopic.

One secret to deciding if a particular passage of description is necessary to the story as a whole is to think of the story as an arrow point-ing toward what Edgar Allan Poe called "the unified effect," that mo-ment when all the story's elements come together. Does the particular passage of description point toward the unified effect or away from it? Whenever you encounter a passage of your own description about which you are unsure, ask yourself: What function does this passage have in this piece? What am I trying to achieve by putting this in, and what of any essential nature would be lost if I were to leave it out?

It wouldn't do, for example, in a lingerie ad for hosiery, to have a model wearing an elaborately sequined and very showy full-length slip. If the unified effect is "buy these panty hose," then the camera should focus on the panty hose and its closely related accoutrements. It's a mat-ter of remembering the overall goal of the work of art. It's as simple as that.

Overcoming Overwriting

Sometimes writers become so enthralled with specificity and descrip-tion that they begin to confuse them with mere wordiness. Overwrit-ing, as this tendency is called, is a form of excessive love of language and as such is important and even necessary for writers to indulge in occa-sionally. The solution to overcoming overwriting is simply to remem-ber the notion of economy and to learn to exercise restraint.

In an effort to conquer her overwriting, an acquaintance of mine used to cut her dearest overwritten sentences (the ones that Annie Dil-lard says in *The Writing Life* come with "price tags" attached) out of her manuscript with scissors and deposit them in a manila folder she called her Goddess file. Anytime she was blue or just wanted to see what a brilliant writer she was, all she had to do was open up the Goddess file and admire snippets of her handiwork. If cutting back on adjectives and adverbs and fancy, unnecessary verbs or keeping a Goddess (or God) file doesn't work for you, you might just have to wait it out. In time, it will pass. But bring supplies along—canned goods and a pup tent—and gather firewood. Sometimes it takes a while.

The important thing to remember is that overwriting occurs when a writer is interested in seducing only herself, when she has become drunk on her own language, inebriated by her own ideas. In the end, overwriting is a date with only yourself, the ultimate lonely hearts endeavor. It's a lingerie ad posed so elaborately and intricately and with so many signals and cues that no viewer will ever be able to, or want to, fully take it in.

Opening and Closing the Curtain

The lingerie ad, like the short story, is neither the beginning of a striptease nor its end, but more of what occurs in the middle. The subject of the lingerie ad was once dressed and will, presumably, not be dressed at all very soon, but right now, in the picture before us, we see the subject frozen in time—in the act of disrobing.

Fiction is also a frozen moment in time. It generally catches characters in the middle of their lives, just when their habitual way of being in the world is about to give way. The playwright Edward Albee once said that the beginning of a piece of fiction is like the opening of a curtain on a scene that was already in progress before the curtain parted, and that the closing of the curtain doesn't mean the action of the story ceases, but merely that we are prevented from watching it any longer.

The challenge facing the story writer—and the model in the lingerie ad—is to imply a great deal about what happened before ("I was once dressed") through exposition or implication ("There are my pants on the floor") and to imply, as well, what may happen once the curtain closes again ("I will soon be undressed. See how my bra strap is slipping off my shoulder?"), but—and this is important—to always keep the reader's attention totally and completely focused on what is happening *right now.*

Beginnings

How do you decide when to open the curtain on a story? How can you know where to begin?

The answer is largely dependent upon the particular story you wish to tell and on the unified effect you wish to reach by its end. Sometimes the beginning of a story is the polar opposite of its ending, as in John Cheever's "The Enormous Radio," a tale that reveals by its end that the main characters, Jim and Irene Wescott, are not all that they seem. Cheever opens the story with a comprehensive description of how the husband and wife appear to others, but makes clear by the last paragraph that they are, in fact, liars and cheaters, far from the middle-class ideal of respectability that they seem at first to embody.

Other beginnings are meant to serve as the planted seed of a story's ending, the original kernel. Shirley Jackson's "The Lottery," which ends with a human sacrifice, begins: "The morning of June 27th was clear and sunny, with the fresh warmth of a full-summer day; the flowers were blossoming profusely and the grass was richly green." Jackson's ending may seem, like Cheever's, to be a reversal of the original picturesque view, but it is also true that the annual human sacrifice (like sacrifices of old) seems to ensure or reinforce the fertility and physical beauty that is so carefully described at the beginning. So, it's important to ask yourself what sort of relationship you'd like your opening and ending to have.

A related question is where *in time* to begin a story. Should you begin far back in a character's past and move forward, or should you begin in the present and make use of flashbacks only where necessary? The answer relates back to issues of description and overwriting. *If* you want to open the story with material about the character's deep past, then there *has* to be an important relationship between that past and what is about to happen in the action of the story. In other words, does the opening material point toward the unified effect?

Most stories open, though, not at the very beginning of events but in the middle of the action, in what is commonly known as *in medias res*. Stories start this way because that is where the energy is, where the *oomph* or the push is to get the story going, to get it in motion on the page. Some examples: "I know what is being said about me and you can take my side or theirs, that's your own business. It's my word against Eunice's and Olivia-Ann's, and it should be plain enough to anyone with two good eyes which one of us has their wits about them. I just want the citizens of the U.S.A. to know the facts, that's all" (Truman Capote, "My Side of the Matter"). "When Blake stepped out of the elevator, he saw her" (Cheever, "The Five-Forty-Eight"). "Powerhouse is playing!" (Eudora Welty, "Powerhouse").

A tip: Because you may be a writer who does character sketches or background first when you're writing a story, you may find your most powerful beginning not in the material you wrote initially but in the material you wrote once you really found the story's voice. Character sketches or background material can be used as exposition later in the story rather than up front, where it can look and feel heavy and not pull the reader immediately into a story. Look for places in your drafts where the voice is especially strong and seductive, where it seems to be speaking with urgency and energy to a listener, where it has power. That, in many cases, will be the best place for you to begin.

Avoiding the Apocalypse

The problems of seduction and revelation arise again when a writer comes to composing the ending of his story. "Great is the art of the beginning," said Thomas Fuller, "but greater the art of the ending." Endings present a complex challenge. Should the ending be the absolute and final-word summation of all that has gone before, or should it be clever, coy, full of riddles and trickery? How much revelation is too much? How little is too little?

Writers today are deeply influenced by film and television, and inevitably, this can show up in our stories in the ways our endings are constructed. If we're not careful, we can fall into the trap of creating big bangs or killing off our characters, not to mention manufacturing cheap trick endings.

The problem with apocalyptic writing (the story in which the car actually crashes, the house burns to the ground before your eyes, the relationship completely falls apart) is that it is filmic rather than literary and, therefore, moves away from the primary purpose of fiction—to let us see into the hidden life of things. Filmic endings are generally simplistic and momentarily satisfying, like the completed striptease. Literary endings are often ambiguous; they let the story rest not in perfection but in the startling beauty of irresolution.

One story that avoids the apocalypse beautifully is Raymond Carver's "Little Things," originally published under the title "Popular Mechanics." Only a page or so long, the story is about a nameless couple who are breaking up and fighting over their baby. As the story progresses, each makes claim to the baby, literally—grabbing an arm and pulling for dear life. Carver's story is obviously a brilliant contemporary rewrite of the famous biblical King Solomon tale, but he is smart enough to end "Little Things" before the baby is actually hurt. The baby is slipping out of the mother's grasp. The father is also losing his grip. Surely the baby is about to fall and be injured, or perhaps even killed, but Carver doesn't show that. Instead, his last line is the biblically resonant "In this manner, the issue was decided."

Avoiding the trap of writing the big summation does not mean that writers should aim for anticlimactic stories. Instead, they should go for a more complex climax, one in which external action does not overshadow the fundamental human story but complements it.

Trick Endings

A related problem for writers is the temptation to use trickery at the end of stories. Trick endings may be startling and interesting wake-up calls for the reader but, like apocalyptic endings, they ultimately draw the reader's attention only to the writer's ability to manipulate data.

Fiction writer Gordon Lish once said that the last line of a story should be like the little piece of string that one pulls when one is trying to build a ship in the bottle. You pull the little string and the whole structure, already fit snugly inside the vessel of the glass, goes up, masts and all, entirely constructed—voilà! Lish's point isn't that the last line should be a big bang or a trick but that it ought to reveal the thematic and structural connections between all that has come before.

In most good literary fiction, you're likely to find such last lines. In Frank Conroy's story "Midair," the main character, Sean, has been haunted and frightened his entire life by the memory of an occasion in his childhood when his father dangled him from the window of an apartment building. In the final scene, Sean, in middle age, finds himself trapped in an elevator with a young man who is as frightened of heights as he was when he was a boy. But instead of panicking—as he always has—Sean reassures the young man until the doors finally open. When the story ends, Sean emerges from the elevator, amazed at his sudden calm. "Here in the darkness, he can see the cracks in the sidewalk from more than forty years ago. He feels no fear—only a sense of astonishment." Similarly, there is the powerful moment at the end of John Updike's "A and P": "His face was dark gray and his back stiff, as if he'd just had an injection of iron, and my stomach kind of fell as I felt how hard the world was going to be to me hereafter."

What separates literary fiction, like Conroy's and Updike's, from popular fiction or film is that, generally speaking, its writers exercise a degree of healthy repression and restraint in their endings. No big car chases, no conflagrations, but rather a moment of highly charged and enigmatic linguistic beauty that suggests cataclysm rather than practicing it. Usually, this is a moment before change is about to occur, before resolution is enacted. At the end of another brilliant Raymond Carver story, called "Fat," a waitress stuck in a miserable and unsatisfying relationship with a cook in a diner says, "My life is going to change. I can feel it." Carver has resisted the impulse to actually change the waitress's life. Instead, he suggests the pathos in her desire to change and in her inability to do so. He resists taking the story to its natural conclusion and ends it instead with a breathtaking look out over the horizon, the suggestion of possible things to come. "It isn't fair, it isn't right," cries the human sacrifice, Mrs. Hutchinson, to the encroaching mob in "The Lottery." "And then they were upon her," reads the last line.

One final piece of advice about endings: Look for them a few paragraphs or pages above where you think they should be, a few moments before the character jumps off the cliff of possibility. Often, surprisingly enough, embedded somewhere in the body of the manuscript is the perfect and subtle ending, waiting for you to find it.

The fundamental secret, then, to the effective ending in fiction is to practice the same sort of restraint one sees in Victoria's Secret lingerie ads: enough coyness to tantalize, enough enigma to tease, but never, ever too much naked abandon. Resist, at all costs, the impulse to perform a fictional striptease for the reader. Practice instead a kind of sexy modesty, which is, perhaps, in the end, the most seductive narrative style of all.

Stuff:

The Power of the Tangible

by David Long

David Long, a novelist and short story
writer, lives in Tacoma, Washington.

I'm reading along and realize I've lost the thread of the sentences—
maybe I'm drowsy, maybe the writing has become bogged down in
abstraction. I skip ahead, wanting something solid to light on. And
there they are, the nouns: *He ran his hand over the velvet and smelled the
fragrance of the chrysanthemums in the glass vase on the table behind him,
and listened to the slow music from the phonograph. . . .* With relief, I dive
in again, into what John Gardner famously called the "vivid, continu-
ous dream."

I want to look at this preference for things, and the weird shivers I
get from passages like this in Philip Roth's *American Pastoral*:

> From over the door of the house, the pediment was gone, ripped out;
> the cornices had been ripped out too, carefully stolen and taken away
> to be sold in some New York antiques store. All over Newark, the old-
> est buildings were missing ornamental stone cornices—cornices from
> as high up as four stories plucked off in broad daylight with a cherry
> picker, with a hundred-thousand-dollar piece of equipment; but the
> cop is asleep or paid off and nobody stops whoever it is, from what-
> ever agency that has a cherry picker, who is making a little cash on the
> side. The turkey frieze that ran around the old Essex produce market
> on Washington and Linden, the frieze with the terra-cotta turkeys
> and the huge cornucopias overflowing with fruit—stolen. . . . Alu-
> minum drainpipes even from occupied buildings, from standing
> buildings—stolen. Gutters, leaders, drainpipes—stolen.

"A book should consist of *examples*," Wittgenstein once wrote. Like a paragraph with its topic sentence, a book is mostly supporting evidence, mostly middle. Argument, expressed as argument, can be kept to a minimum. The mind needs its generalizations, needs to "make sense of things," but abstraction is, by definition, nonparticular, noncorporeal. How alert we become at the sound of: *for instance* . . . Fiction writers know that abstraction is a cul-de-sac. After you've said, "Susanna experienced a great sadness," where do you go? Most fiction writers happily return to the raw data, knowing it's the detail that staggers us, that hangs in memory.

A passage from Toni Morrison's *Beloved*:

> That lady I worked for in Kentucky gave [a pair of crystal earrings] to me when I got married. What they called married back there and back then. I guess she saw how bad I felt when I found out there wasn't going to be no ceremony, no preacher. Nothing. I thought there should be something—something to say it was right and true. I didn't want it to be just me moving over a bit of pallet full of corn husks. Or just me bringing my night bucket into his cabin. I thought there should be some ceremony. Dancing maybe. A little sweet william in my hair. . . . I never saw a wedding, but I saw Mrs. Garner's wedding gown in the press, and heard her go on about what it was like. Two pounds of currants in the cake, she said, and four whole sheep.

Everything depends on the details, and the words chosen to represent them. I want to examine why a homely phrase like "in the press" makes its sentence resonate, why "two pounds of currants" and "four whole sheep" matter, why we need "sweet william" and "night bucket."

Five Good Reasons Writers Write About Stuff

1. We are stuff. Words invoking the physical world tweak the mind's eye, the mind's ear. Reading may be vicarious but it's not just "cerebral." Certain kinds of words set off more complex chemical events in the brain. Compare these passages from Julio Cortázar's *Hopscotch*:

. . . and Oliveira, a little drunk too, felt that the truth now lay in that Bessie and Hawkins were illusions, because only illusions were capable of moving their adherents, illusions and not truths. And there was more than this, there was intercession, the arrival through allusions to a plane, a zone impossible to imagine, useless to attempt conception of because all thought destroyed it as soon as it attempted to isolate it.

. . . the old woman behind the rickety desk greeted them with an understanding air and what else was there to do in this rotten weather. She dragged one foot and it was painful to see her climb the stairs, stopping at each step to drag up her sick leg, which was thicker than the other. There was a smell of toilet soap, of soup, on the rug in the hallway someone had spilled a blue liquid which had taken the shape of a pair of wings.

I sympathize with Cortázar's desire to talk about how jazz affects his characters, but, I'm sorry, my concentration shrivels. Then he puts Oliveira and his lady friend on the stairs of a cheap hotel and I smell the smells and take in the carnality of the moment, feeling how Oliveira must be considering the older woman's damaged body even as he's itching for his lover's nakedness. A simple patch of description, yet it triggers a rich response.

What if we were without physical bodies? I think of the two angels in Wim Wenders's film *Wings of Desire*—they stroll the gray streets of Berlin, unable to touch things, naming what they miss. "Down with the world behind the world," one says, and elects to renounce angeldom. His first act on returning to mortality is to buy a coffee from a street vendor and wrap his hands around the hot cup.

2. Specificity pleases. I don't mind rereading a page I've slid by too fast, but I don't like feeling lost (unless "feeling lost" is the point). Is it still the same day? Who's talking now? Where in God's name *are* we? So: Concrete words are exact words; writing saturated with them orients us in space and time. Strangely, even when the specifics are opaque, they seem to help. Cortázar again:

They came into the Rue Vaneau from the Rue de Varennes. It was drizzling and La Maga clutched Oliveira's arm even tighter, pressing herself against his raincoat. . . .

I don't know these streets, but I like having them named. Isn't it much better than: *They came around a corner . . .* ?

Specificity clarifies, fine-tunes, adds pixels, creating not simply a brighter image but an image that compels our attention, subtly directs it. Philip Levine's poem "And That Night Clifford Died" begins:

> We broke for lunch at 8 P.M.,
> in my case two sandwiches
> of fresh lettuce and Genoa
> salami cut so thin the light
> shone through the slices when Faso,
> the Sicilian butcher, held
> them up to boast of his art.

I'm powerless to resist such an opening, mundane as it is. No, *because* it's mundane—that is, "of the world," fixed in a moment of the world's unrepeatable history.

3. Names count. People have long believed that speaking a thing's name gives one power over it. In science, "separating out by name" is a necessary step in coming to understand a phenomenon; likewise, in daily life, "getting a handle on things" can begin in pinpointing, by name, what's been dogging us below the level of conscious awareness. Ah, it's *jealous* we're feeling, or *beset-by-too-many-obligations*. But for our purposes, let's say that names (especially nicknames) are routinely used by people who have "inside" knowledge. Insider information is often expressed in specialized language, jargon. Writers are usually warned to shun it—readers may not know what you're talking about, and jargon can intentionally exclude outsiders, or obscure the truth. That said, used sparingly and without disdain for the reader's ignorance, these words can establish a writer's authority. *I was there*, they say, *I know how this works. You're in good hands.*

If you tell me you saw "a bird," you haven't said much; I may even have reason to distrust you. *Bird* is an idea, a category. Maybe you were lazy, maybe you didn't think I was worthy of the details, maybe, in fact, you *weren't* there. But say "Late morning a pair of juncos landed on the feeder by the north window," and you've let me see something. Even if I can't remember precisely what a junco looks like, it already sounds sort of finchlike, and, here's the thing, I can place you at the window observing it. I grant you the right to tell me what's what; I'm easy, unless you hold back. I want to feel I'm in the presence of someone who knows more than I do, who has an agile and interesting mind, or life experience different from my own.

4. Concrete words and names often have more punch as words. No matter the style, a body of prose is a thing, an artifact. Beyond its physical presence on the page (blocky, airy, fragmented), it feels a certain way to the reading mind. It has texture, weight, speed, duration, a way of moving. You can describe it with the same adjectives that describe any object (*stolid, fizzy, lush*), or in terms of the vibes it gives off (*forbidding, inviting, dull*).

What do concrete, naming words do for a prose artifact? They roughen up its surface, making it less easy to skim; they give more complex information; they offer pleasure over and above the conveying of information. Such words are also a way to avoid the dull cast of the overfamiliar. *Junco* is not only more specific than *bird*, it's drawn from a pool of less-common words. I'm not talking about showing off, brandishing the three-dollar word. Picture concentric circles of words, the few hundred most frequently chosen ones puddling in the middle. Like everyone, skilled writers rely on this core of shared language, but they stray from it as needed. Out of an array of near-synonyms they sometimes select the scrappy, slangy word; the natty word; the word with a whiff of antiquity; the most squeakily accurate word; the word that gives a little shock; the one drawn from an area of expertise—botany or chess or plumbing; the word that sounds better to the ear (*silky, stately, biting*); or the word that seems right for an unfathomable personal reason.

But what happens when the reader doesn't *know* a word? It's like coming on a dollop of untranslated Polish in a story. Sure, knowing what it means would help, but the *writer* knows, and unless this practice becomes an irritating stylistic tic, the not-knowing doesn't much interfere with the fun of reading. I think of the arcane words in Cormac McCarthy's writing—*pettysingles, hagstrack*—and I don't wish to relinquish them, or McCarthy's penchant for odd coinings—*wormscored, spindle-shanked, mooncobbled.* Furthermore, I don't want to forfeit the pleasure of knowing that other sabbaticals from the ordinary may be around the next bend. This is *exactly* how I want to feel: that anything might occur in the next sentence. Most often this "anything" is plot information, but it may well be "word" information, too.

5. Finally: In real life we have complex psychological relationships to things. We own, we treasure, we wonder at, we're protected by, known by. Or we no longer own, we covet, we're suffocated by, allergic to, get the willies from. Between people and things lie infinite gradations of relationship. Our histories ready us as readers—our histories are, in fact, histories of our tenancy in the universe of stuff. Thus, moving through the pages of a story, we're seldom neutral or indifferent. Hardwired into us, or acquired, are preferences, repulsions, curiosities, affinities. The sight of words representing things sets off chain reactions no one could have predicted; they deepen our involvement in the "dream" immeasurably.

Kinds of Stuff

1. Where you and the world meet. This is your kit, your effects, your props—extensions of body and psyche. Your second skin, your toys and tools, your insignias, the molecules of the world-at-large that penetrate you. This is *catcher's glove, thimble, ball-peen hammer, trifocals, chopsticks, saxophone.* This is *mascara, patchouli, insulin, tongue stud. Feather tick, straitjacket, fanny pack. Spaghetti straps, chemise, panty hose, boutonniere. Tap shoes, flip-flops, cleats.* This is *pesto, gin, Tabasco, nougat, chalk dust, smog.* Your driver's license, your favorite pen, the stuff in your pocket, your wedding ring. The inner circle of things, indispensable; the same for no two characters.

2. Special things. Think of the monolith in Stanley Kubrick's *2001: A Space Odyssey,* its looming physical presence—profoundly black, other. Think of Yorick's skull in Hamlet's naked hand. The Bobby Thomson home-run ball that reappears throughout Don Delillo's *Underworld.* It's Excalibur. It's splinters of the true Cross, the bones of the saints. It's talisman, totem, amulet. It's the lost map, the ribbon-tied sheaf of letters, the dead father's suit hanging mutely in the closet. It's the button accordion passing from hand to hand in Annie Proulx's *Accordion Crimes;* the blue-green suburban pools John Cheever's swimmer traverses in his quest for home; the pinewood casket the Bundrens try with heroic ineptitude to haul across a flood-swollen river in *As I Lay Dying.* It's the birthday cake of a young boy struck by a car in Raymond Carver's "A Small, Good Thing."

Remember a work of fiction and certain objects seem embedded in it. Sometimes they're ordinary, even unlikely things the narrative has burnished with meaning. In Nevil Shute's postapocalyptic *On the Beach*, a submarine crew races from Melbourne to San Francisco desperate to see if the cryptic message they've picked up could be human; they find a Coke bottle jittering on the transmitting key of a radio.

3. *Symbols*—things standing for concepts, nonphysical realities. Innocence. Evil. Impermanence. To be honest, I'm not wild about symbolism. I don't like the notion that behind what floats on the page there's a "true meaning" to be extracted, that the writer has fashioned not an art object but a puzzle, a code. The soldier falls in the posture of a crucified man, so he's "Christlike." Get it? For another, I don't like the implication that story alone is insufficient. It reeks of Middle Ages theology, that what we do on earth is mere shadow. I happen to like the here and now (or, for that matter, the there and then). Ezra Pound once wrote, "The natural object is always the adequate symbol." My own poetry teacher, Richard Hugo, would tell students, "A thing must be itself before it can be something else." (Hugo was trying to fend off lines like "the endless eternity of my soul"—all whipped cream and no fruit.)

But images do resonate; human feelings do cluster about them. When tulips blossom along Puget Sound I feel somehow rejuvenated, and when, later, their petals dry and drop off, and, at the same time, I notice a pair of high school kids sashaying by, it's hard not to reflect on "the sweetness of youth" and all that. But are tulips *symbols?* I'd rather believe that they and high school kids embody the same immutable fact of the natural world. One doesn't "stand for" the other. A skilled writer offering up these supercharged images calls forth their resonances, but in a way that honors the mysterious interrelation between image and mind. A passage from Mark Helprin's "Martin Bayer":

He had left the door open, and before they knew it a swarm of flashing insects circled the lights. In the middle of September, there was always a renaissance of summer insects. They came in waves from the brown grasses and the silent, still forests, their movements urgent and overheated, as if they knew that soon nights as clear as spirit would fell them and they would quickly become only crackling shells among the frail leaves.

The dying insects aren't so much symbolic as rich in association. We feel the brutal wisdom of passing time, but they are never less than fully themselves.

4. A noisy feast. Sometimes, as in Saul Bellow, we get a cornucopia. Bellow's message: Life is fraught with objects (delightfully, this is Bellow, widely regarded to be a novelist of ideas). How many sentences are there in Bellow like these from *Herzog*:

> The whole family took the street car to the Grand Trunk Station with a basket (frail, splintering wood) of pears, overripe, a bargain bought by Jonah Herzog at the Rachel Street Market, the fruit spotty, ready for wasps, just about to decay, but marvelously fragrant. And inside the train on the worn green bristle of the seats, Father Herzog sat peeling the fruit with his Russian pearl-handled knife. He peeled and twirled and cut with European efficiency. Meanwhile, the locomotive cried and the iron-studded cars began to move. . . . By the factory walls the grimy weeds grew. A smell of malt came from the breweries.

That things make his characters think, generate theories, rationales, schemes, is secondary. Bellow is first a writer in love with the world's teeming physicality.

Sometimes we find this abundance expressed as a list—the mind can't (or won't) stop reeling off its examples. Entire stories have been constructed of lists—William's Gass's "In the Heart of the Heart of the Country" or Tim O'Brien's searing account of an infantry unit during the Vietnam War, "The Things They Carried." More commonly, a passage will suddenly bloom into a list. Sometimes it's simply a case of writerly exuberance, but often there's a psychological underpinning, as when Frank Bascombe in Richard Ford's *The Sportswriter*, benumbed by his son's death, sends for catalogue after catalogue, "Catalogs for canvas luggage that would stand up to Africa. Catalogs for expeditions to foreign lands with single women. . . . rare-book catalogs, record catalogs, exotic hand-tool catalogs, lawn-ornament catalogs from Italy. . . ." Or the opening of Stuart Dybek's short story "We Didn't":

> We didn't in the light; we didn't in darkness. We didn't in the fresh-cut summer grass or in the mounds of autumn leaves or on the snow where the moonlight threw down our shadows. We didn't in your room on the canopy bed you slept in, the bed you'd slept in as a child, or in the backseat of my father's rusted Rambler which smelled of the smoked chubs and kielbasa that he delivered on weekends from my Uncle Vincent's meat market. . . . At the dead end of our lovers' lane—a side street of abandoned factories—where I perfected the pinch that springs open a bra; behind the lilac bushes in Marquette Park where you first touched me through my jeans and your nipples, swollen against transparent cotton, seemed the shade of lilacs; in the balcony of the now-defunct Clark Theater where I wiped popcorn salt from my palms and slid them up your thighs and you whispered, "I feel like Doris Day is watching us," we didn't.

5. The thing by itself. Sometimes, by contrast, an object exists in an austere, solitary state. Edward Harkness's poem "Watercolor Painting of a Bamboo Rake" starts:

> Nothing can be this plain:
> a bamboo rake leaning
> against a tree.
> Rice paper, Chinese ink—
> took ten minutes tops—
> a lifetime of observing.

You know this rake. It has *quiddity*, "the quality that makes a thing what it is; the essential nature of a thing" (*Random House Dictionary*). Within a piece of writing, objects may appear in this isolated, thing-by-itself state. But what I'm really talking about is a writer's overall attitude toward things. Sometimes—the opposite end of the spectrum from Bellow—you find a staunch frugality, be it due to modesty or tightwadishness or puritanism. Sometimes it seems chosen on aesthetic grounds, or from a psychic need to take things one at a time. Ford Madox Ford once said that Hemingway's words were like "pebbles fetched fresh from a brook." The simplicity of Hemingway's prose was a conscious purging of all he considered fussy and overblown about the Victorian sensibility. Open his books anywhere and you find classic Hemingway sentences:

> The water from the spring was cold and fresh in the tin pail and the chocolate was not quite bitter but was hard and crunched as they chewed it.

Isn't it essential, if we're to understand a writer, to know how he or she feels about the physical world?

6. The reality of a place. Let's include one other kind of thing: purlieu, environment, physical circumstance. In film, it's the job of the production design team not only to give the characters a place to be but to influence how we view it. Is the film full of windows or long dark hallways or glinting chrome? Is it cluttered? Is there rain? Is the light wan or saturated with primary colors? It's a made-up world, down to its finest particulars. This is what William Gass means when he writes, "In fiction there is no such thing as description, there is only construction."

We might ask which came first, character or place? The only answer can be: They are simultaneous; they exist for each other's sake. A different place has different characters. It *must*—the characters in a particular fictive moment live in that moment and no other. Joyce Carol Oates opens her novel *Because It Is Bitter, and Because It Is My Heart* by showing us the treacherous terrain of the fictional Hammond, New York, "saw-notched ridges, hills steep as attic steps," saturating us in its mood, finally homing in on the moment of the story: "This morning, April 3, 1956, 8 A.M., the mist above the river is chill and clammy as the interior of another's mouth." In *Bleak House* it's the mud and soot of mid-nineteenth-century London; in *Rabbit Is Rich* it's the dusty front window of Springer Motors on Route 111, Brewer, Pennsylvania.

What about the parts of things (*flywheel, tuning peg*) or surfaces underfoot (*terrazzo, blacktop, shag carpet*) or faux things—mock-ups, miniatures, forgeries? What about human structures from bungalow to ballpark or the inner space of buildings, the bedrooms and stairwells and kitchens where so much private drama plays out? What of disgusting things, illicit things? Or things that have lost their luster? Junk, garbage—the lexicon of decay and abandonment is irresistible: *sludge, gunk, muck, scum, rubbish, rubble, riffraff, swill, slops, slag, offal, night soil* . . . nasty material but a wicked joy to say aloud.

Of course, this taxonomy could go on forever. The world is stuffed with stuff. And, as Annie Dillard says:

> Fiction keeps its audience by retaining the world as its subject matter. People like the world. Many people actually prefer it to art and spend their day by choice in the thick of it. The world's abounding objects, its rampant variety of people, its exuberant, destructive, and unguessable changes, and the splendid interest of its multiple conjunctions, appeal, attract, and engage more than ideas do. . . .

Physicists, linguists, psychologists, and philosophers give their life's labor to the conundrum of how we know what we know—truth versus appearance, fact versus figure of speech—and how these distinctions can vanish on closer inspection. Fiction writers are hardly immune to such theorizing, to a craving for answers, but, finally, their mandate is different: Their deepest allegiance is to the evidence itself, to what is, and who we are because of it.

Push Hands:

Balancing Resistance and Revision

by Jeffrey Skinner

Jeffrey Skinner is the author of four books of poetry.

There is a tai chi exercise known as "Push Hands," in which two students face each other and lightly touch palms. Without losing contact, they move their hands and arms in a circular motion while simultaneously leaning into and away from each other. Part of the exercise's purpose is to find that thin mirroring borderline between yin and yang, between giving and receiving. Another purpose is to become aware of any imbalance in your partner, and if you sense that imbalance, to let your body gently give way to it. Often the result is a tiny but crucial shift in pressure that sends your partner (or you) careening to the mat. It is good to catch or at least break her fall if you can. It is not the object of the exercise to cause harm.

I've been writing and teaching in one form or another for some twenty-five years, as well as interacting with other poets as both reader and as writer being read. That's a lot of time on the mat. I should know by now: Writing *is* revision. And yet each time I suggest revisions to a student or friend, each time I face what remains to be done in my own writing, I feel the specter of resistance rising anew.

Is it a deeper, more necessary part of writing than we'd suspected, our struggle with change?

Most of us are familiar with the writer who objects that to change anything in his poem would be a betrayal of his spontaneity, the holy purity of his creative impulse. Ragged expression, unintentional grammar, generalizations, clichés, arbitrary line breaks, and so on—all are part of the realness of his voice, which stands opposed, on a deep philosophical level, to the "academic approach." If this stance takes shape in one of my students, I am generally cast as a tired-out, unhip, card-carrying practitioner of the academic approach. Often this student has read every word Charles Bukowski ever wrote. And nothing else. Often this student is male. Often this is the same student who challenges me in class, in the first week or so of the semester, by suddenly blurting out something on the order of "What gives you the right to say what's poetry and what's not?" Often this student disappears after the third week of class. Sometimes this is a student I become close to—later, after we have been through some necessary changes.

But in a larger sense this issue, which might be reduced to the old "cooked" versus "raw" question, keeps playing itself out in a variety of guises and venues: at writing schools, in literary politics, and inside of every writer. It cuts to the heart of American notions of egalitarianism— who gets to say what good is, and why—as well as to a deep-seated American uneasiness with slickness and polish, and to our belief in the avatars of the *outsider* and the *natural*.

Another type of resistance comes from insecurity, which proceeds from that barbed hook of a question lodged deep in every beginning, and many a seasoned, writer's heart: *Do I have what it takes?* These days an alarming number of writers actually ask this question, *out loud*. But another, larger group keeps it to themselves. Bless them, I say. They are sincere and tortured. They try and they try. But in the end they do not revise, because their first drafts are always called "promising," and if all they produce are "promising" first drafts then they can never be failed writers. Who can blame them? The mystique of the talented beginner has surprising staying power, and its romance often proves irresistible. And it is painful, having to pull that horrible question, that hook, out of yourself, by yourself, which is always in the end the necessary and only way.

Another type of resistance is plain, old-fashioned laziness. This manifestation signals to me one of two things. The first possibility is that this is a writer who will obviously not continue, for whom writing is a momentary whim. This same person might also take workshops in feng shui or Chinese cooking, or leave the gash of a half-finished fish pond in his backyard. A class in creative writing is great because, well, what could be hard about writing poems? Which is fine. We certainly don't need any more poets. And perhaps this restless soul will become a future reader. Of my friend's poetry. Of my poetry.

The second kind of laziness is one with which I myself am all too familiar. It is a kind of weariness before the immensity of language, and before all that previous writers have managed to make out of language. It is the reason so many young poets still favor black clothes, and it is most aptly embodied by a long, deep, bibliophilic, unconsciously Beckettian *What's the use?* sigh. This festering dread, more spiritual paralysis than laziness, keeps the writer from going back to her cluttered, scrawled-over, intense pages. But I have hope there may be a literary future for this kind of student, knowing as I do her inertia, from the inside. I was such a writer. And I can go back there again, with alarming ease. . . .

Lastly I might mention a resistance to revision that is caused primarily by mentor's error. Whether we are friend, spouse, or teacher to the writer, we must guard against trying to make a plum into an apricot. If I encourage a writer to revise in a certain way that pushes against his temperament, then of course he will resist, and properly so. If some teacher long ago had demanded, for example, that I abandon narrative and instead insert classical or mythological allusions into my poems, or structure my poems around such sources, I would have resisted. Such concoctions, produced by a slew of contemporary poets, are very postmodern, very trendy. Some are even good. But if *I* had taken that advice and tried to write those poems, I might not have gone on to write the poems that were truly mine. We write what we can, as Raymond Carver said. A well-meaning reader can hasten a writer on the way toward all she can write. But a reader/teacher/critic can also lengthen the journey by sending her in the wrong direction. Sometimes resistance to revision is resistance to what the writer recognizes, even if perhaps only intuitively, as bad advice.

After Diane Wakoski read my poems one summer at Naropa, she suggested that I try writing prose. Arthur Gregor bummed a cigarette from me, then spent the rest of the conference talking about how great he thought another student's work was. These two encounters pissed me off royally, and as a result I determined to write and publish poems in good places, if for no other reason than revenge. Howard Moss was fantastic at line editing and at the art of inventive cutting. For a while we took the same subway after class. He always wore a bow tie, and was modest and sweet and dryly funny, like Woody Allen's older brother. Phil Levine never said much about the microlevel of my poems. At our sessions he preferred to put the poems I produced for my thesis into three piles: good, okay, and crap. When we got that part out of the way we could shoot the breeze, trading stories about the strange or funny things that had happened in our lives. My first teacher, Dick Allen, was bursting with advice on everything from line breaks to how to make money as a poet. When he signed a copy of his book to me he wrote, "I'm *utterly* confident of your success . . . ," underlining the word *utterly*. I lived for years on that word: *utterly*. And for the past twenty years my wife, the poet Sarah Gorham, has been my first reader. Like Yeats's horseman, she casts a cold eye on my ego, my words.

All these teachers taught me revision. Sometimes it was about revising my poems; other times, my life. I resisted every one of them, in one way or another. It was how I learned.

The two things most necessary to a writer if he is to overcome resistance to revision are passion and an open mind. As for passion: You can lead a horse to water, etcetera. The qualities most necessary to a teacher, if she is to help a student overcome resistance, are passion and an open mind. But in addition the teacher must be inventive, sensitive, experienced, compassionate, interested, willing, flexible, and, perhaps most important of all, intimately involved with her own struggle to make verbal objects.

Every writer is different, and even the same writer needs different kinds of attention at different moments of his development. So when I am with a writer and his work I play a kind of "Push Hands." I try to sense where the resistance is, and why, and then I try to correct the writer's balance. Or, I let his own momentum carry him to the mat.

It is important, I think, to combine in one's attitude a seriousness about the work and a lightness about the self: the writer's self, my self. After all, what is the worst that can happen to us? The writer will not find a way back into the poem. I will fail at helping him. He will either try again or go on to a paying career in some other field. But in either case I am convinced that on some level he will remember the struggle with language, which may come to serve as a useful figure for the difficult mystery of his own life. This is not a bad thing. "If you're willing," the tai chi master said, "and if you're open, then it's okay, it will happen. If it doesn't happen it's okay, too."

Sometimes praise for what is working in the piece is called for. Encouragement is a deep part of teaching, and the efficacy of a strategically applied "attaboy" should never be underestimated. But in another instance it may be better to skip all that and simply put the piece of work aside and move on to the next poem. Sometimes it's appropriate to have a general discussion about theme, barely addressing what is actually on the page. In other cases it's best to stick to the "technical" details of the poem. I have no problem giving specific suggestions for lines, diction, plot points, image, metaphor, and so on. I make clear from the beginning that my ideas for revision can be accepted or rejected, that every artist steals from somewhere—from everywhere—and that in the end the aim of revision is to improve the poem, not to spare or enhance anyone's feelings.

I am always trying to move the writer's attention from the anxiety that centers in the self to a focus on the poem as made object, with a logic and life independent of its maker.

Here are some of the specific techniques I have used and offered other writers as a means to move back into the work: Revisit the scene of the poem in the imagination, and simply take notes. Make a list of sensual images appropriate to the poem's occasion, which may or may not later find their way into the poem. Imagine addressing the poem to a friend you haven't seen in years. Consider that the poem may be part of a series, that what is there is resistant to revision because there are more poems beneath it, asking to be written on their own terms. Change the point of view. Write the poem out in prose. If the writer has another language, suggest he translate his poem into that language. Write the poem out backward. Double or halve the line length. Attempt to fit the poem into a received form, a sonnet or sestina. Or, if the poem started out as a sonnet or sestina, abandon that form. Find the most troublesome sections of the work and freewrite, without looking at the original draft. Put the poem away and write an essay on the same subject. Or a one-act play. Or a letter. Work on the poem while watching a dumb TV show.

Slow down. Wait.

I tell writers to try one or more of these or other methods, without any sure expectation that it will solve the problem. And I encourage them to do the work in the same spirit; I've found that the abandonment or at least lowering of expectation can sometimes create a near-magical entrance into freedom. And even if the writer tries these methods and still cannot make the writing work, he has spent valuable time playing with words, and breaking up his set ideas of what poetry *should* be, what writing *should* be.

The student came to the old monk and asked, "I don't seem to be getting anywhere in my practice—I seem to be stuck. What should I do?" The monk said, "Hardness passes away; only what is supple endures." The student was silent for a moment, and then said, "I'm sorry, but I don't get it. What should I *do*?" By way of reply the old monk asked, "How are my teeth?" and opened his mouth wide for the student to inspect. "Well," the student said cautiously, "you don't *have* any teeth. . . ." Then the old monk said, "What about the tongue?" and, leaning his face close to the student's, stuck out his tongue and wiggled it back and forth.

This was the occasion of the student's first awakening.

The Trouble with Titles

by Nicholas Weinstock

Nicholas Weinstock is a novelist.

Writing a book that lacks a title feels a bit like owning a car with no license plates. Sturdy and stylish as the vehicle might be, as smoothly as the narrative may be running, the thing will not be allowed in public without some assortment of letters riveted squarely to the front.

For many months I attempted to gift-wrap my first novel with a delicate scrap of verse, to encase it in a brassy slogan. I pined for a title as audacious as those of F. Scott Fitzgerald. What grander territory could possibly be staked than that claimed by a book called *This Side of Paradise*? What customer could resist the fiery urge to read of *The Beautiful and Damned*? Take *Tender Is the Night*: the gentlest of sentences, deftly emboldened by its inverted syntax to a nearly biblical proclamation. *The Last Tycoon* and *The Great Gatsby* fairly command you, as tycoons and great men do, into awe. Fitzgerald's blend of swooning self-importance and piano-scale prose made him one of America's finest namers of books. I, on the other hand, spent nearly two years trying unsuccessfully to name mine.

It's not that I neglected to come up with a decent title; in fact, I've gone through several. *The Wedding Planner* was the first name of the first draft stored on my computer for a year, and it worked, albeit straightforwardly. (The novel is a comedy about a downtrodden editorial assistant at a publishing house who is forced to plan his boss's wedding.) But then came the urgent phone call from a reader of *People* magazine with the news that pop star Jennifer Lopez was filming a big-budget movie by that name. After weeks of reconsideration and several legal pads of free association, I retyped my title page to read: *The Rules of Engagement.* The novel was done. I sent it proudly to my agent. It was a month later that I saw the commercial for that big-budget movie starring Tommy Lee Jones.

As a result I was left flailing, rushing to fill in the blank that threatened to void the entire book. No object or accomplishment can be said to exist if it can't be called something—hell, anything—and so I frantically groped for a couple of words. Eventually a friend suggested *The Assistant*: bold and simple, easily marketable, and strangely familiar in a way that I considered a virtue. I e-mailed my agent the new title. She sent out the manuscript to publishers. Weeks after signing a contract, I realized why the title rang so true: There it was on my bookshelf, emblazoned on the spine of Bernard Malamud's 1957 novel. Maybe no one will notice, I thought feverishly. It's not as famous as *The Natural.* It didn't win Malamud a Pulitzer like *The Fixer.* A few months later I was invited to read an excerpt at the annual meeting of the Authors Guild. I finished and stepped down from the podium amid a swell of laughter and polite applause. "And what's the title of the novel?" inquired the Guild president into the microphone. As I took my seat, I murmured: "*The Assistant.*" A sudden chill came over the musty room. "With *apologies,*" she intoned over the sound system, "to *Malamud.*" To which I nodded apologetically, wordless once again.

I was back to square one in a literary game whose stakes have become, in these heady days of high hype and low attention spans, rather daunting. A winning title, after all, can be the start of an out-of-the-gates success story, gaining a book the sort of marketing momentum that has prelaunched such catchy packages as *The Horse Whisperer* and *The Girls' Guide to Hunting and Fishing.* *The Wedding Whisperer,* I pronounced aloud to myself. *The Assistants' Guide to Tying the Knot.* The subject of weddings ought to be a treasure trove of handy double entendres—*The Veil of Secrecy, The Ring of Truth*—but they were all either frilly and vapid or, even worse, taken. I quickly reached that stage of titler's block that makes every passing collection of words glitter like fool's gold. *The Crest,* I thought—climactic, mysterious—in the morning while squeezing out toothpaste. *Harry Potter and the Story That Has Nothing to Do with Him,* I considered while wandering the best-seller section of the bookstore in despair. *A Scintillating Work of Occasional Hilarity. The Perfect Sturm und Drang.* All the good titles had been thought of already. All the bad titles, mine in particular, had rotted my ability to come up with more. How had the canny and poetical Fitzgerald done it?

He had scrambled to title his books, it turns out, nearly as gracelessly as I. He called his first novel *The Romantic Egoist* and nervously switched it to *The Education of a Personage* before publishing it as *This Side of Paradise* in the spring of 1920. *The Beautiful and Damned* was, for a time, *The Flight of the Rocket*. *Tender Is the Night* took turns as *Doctor Diver's Holiday, Our Type, The Drunkard's Holiday, The World's Fair, The Melarky Case*, and, at the suggestion of the author's wife, Zelda, *The Boy Who Killed His Mother*. Still, no eleventh-hour fumbling could compare with his contortions upon finishing his third novel at the end of 1924.

Fitzgerald had completed the work when he announced its new title, *Gold-hatted Gatsby*, to his editor, Maxwell Perkins. But a few weeks later he'd changed his mind: While working to revise the final proofs, he was vacillating between *Trimalchio* and *Trimalchio in West Egg*, in ambitious reference to the banquet-thrower from the ancient text of Petronius's *Satyricon*. He considered the rather literal *Among the Ash Heaps and Millionaires*. In November he experimented, more jauntily, with *On the Road to West Egg*. He confidently proposed, and subsequently rejected as "too light," *The High-bouncing Lover*. As the date of publication approached, the choices were whittled down to two—neither of which, Fitzgerald informed Perkins by letter, was quite right. "*Gatsby* is too much like Babbit [*sic*]," he wrote in January, alluding to the Sinclair Lewis novel, *Babbitt*, published three years before, "and *The Great Gatsby* is weak because there's no emphasis even ironically on his greatness or lack of it." As late as March he sent an emergency cable in an attempt to halt the presses, his spelling blurred by panic: "CRAZY ABOUT TITLE 'UNDER THE RED WHITE AND BLUE' STOP WHART WOULD DELAY BE."

But there could be no more delays. *The Great Gatsby* was published, to the continued second-guessing of its creator, in April of 1925. "If the book fails commercially," he griped upon its release, it would be primarily because "the title is only fair, rather bad than good."

My book was released in April 2001, precisely seventy-six years later, and the e-mails and faxes between author and publisher—I would have cabled if I could—continued until the presses ran. At one point the novel was retitled *The Aisle of White*; a few months later, *As Long as*

She Needs Me; and then, with time running out, the hunt was called off. I don't mind *As Long as She Needs Me*: It comes from an old Sammy Davis Jr. song, closely resembles a campy *Oliver!* show tune, and is unlikely to be an upcoming multiplex movie starring Harrison Ford. That means, for anyone interested, *The Boy Who Killed His Mother* remains up for grabs, as does a batch of unused titles discovered in Fitzgerald's notebooks after his death. *Journal of a Pointless Life* tops the list. *The District Eternity* and *Jack a Dull Boy* are also among his ideas. He had scrawled enthusiastic stars beside *Mr. Ridinghood* and *God's Convict (Title for a Bad Novel)*. Me, I prefer *Result—Happiness*, jotted toward the bottom; for that's the goal, as impossible as any dream under the red, white, and blue, that keeps us writing and titling as if we could ever get it right.

SECTION 2

Initial Contact:

Getting Your Work off Your Desk

and onto Someone Else's

Loose Bottoms:
On Becoming Ready to Send
Your Work Out

by David Hamilton

David Hamilton is the editor of the
Iowa Review.

How do we know that it's done? I don't suppose we ever do, and so we turn to the more practical question of when to let go—of a story, let us say—and allow the world a shot at it while we begin afresh. And while no formula will suffice, it may help to propose one anyway, as a position to consider.

When I accept a story for the *Iowa Review*, which I have edited since 1978, the interval between acceptance and publication tends to be about a year. Before our acceptance of it, a submission will have been read more than once and usually by more than one reader. Then the manuscript will sit for several months in one of three files filled for the year ahead before we pull it out again and begin production. Now we will give it another reading; some light copyediting may occur, and it will get yet another quick once-over as electronic downloading channels it into our design for pages. Galleys go next to the author, who we hope will reread with care. We ourselves read each work again, aloud this time, two persons reading to each other. We collate the author's findings with ours and enter all corrections.

Quite regularly our proofreading sessions lead to questions for the writer—occasional awkwardness and redundancies uncovered, inaccuracies and illogicalities revealed. And so we pose our questions and negotiate changes as needed. Ideally, we should have seen these problems at an earlier copyediting stage. Ideally, I should have seen them. Ideally, given all the work that comes to us, we should have selected work that is done, finished, clean, and requires no late correction. Ideally . . . that region out in some yonder elsewhere.

Recently Chris Offutt returned his galleys of a fine story with the request "please delete my last sentence." He was right, and we did. Absolutely the most frequent change—aside from correcting some single blunder of grammar or spelling, or a word left after a cut-and-paste that didn't quite cut all that it should have—is to delete the first or last sentence, or more. The story doesn't really begin for another one or two paragraphs; the story ended a sentence or a paragraph before you made yourself stop. Poems beg often for the same judicious cutting, at least of a line or two. Our eyes don't see all at once, nor do our minds register all that they should. It takes time, repeated effort, and patient familiarization with one's work, and still, if we seek perfection, we can only seek it.

Nor do we ever really know the effort the author has put in. I'm sure I have accepted work from time to time that was hot off the desk but read (at least to me) as if it had matured like sipping whiskey. And I'm sure I've rejected work as unfinished that was poked and probed until it just rolled over and died.

At last, in any case, I get fresh page proofs of the whole issue and read it once more, silently, before we go to press. Quite regularly, at this late point of production, I will notice a problem I have not seen before—a minor grammatical error, a clumsiness, an inaccuracy or improbability too obvious, suddenly, for me to fail to note—and we scramble for a correction. It always amazes me why I have not seen the problem before and why now it suddenly glares. Having noted the problem, I would be remiss not to attempt a correction, however minor. Occasionally I'll improvise if our schedule is tight and I cannot locate the author. Quite regularly, a late e-mail or phone call will prompt a thankful writer's remark that he or she is amazed that we have taken that much care. And still, of course, errors are bound up in our pages.

My all-time favorite, which I did correct, read—you will see why I half wish I had let it stand—"loose bottoms on her blouse were seldom preludes of seduction."

The whole process takes about a year. So let me suggest, as a rule of thumb, that anything worthy of the attention we give to work that we accept deserves equal time for finish and maturation before you send it off. Let most of what it takes us time and rereading to discover reveal itself to you during an interval at least equal to that which you then hope we will devote to your work. Take a year to read it aloud once each month. Doesn't your ear always find wordings it would change? Keep that up until you find that, as Raymond Carver once put it (I paraphrase from memory), "I am changing periods to commas that I had once changed from commas to periods." Then, perhaps, it's as ready as you will get it.

Spontaneity often seems a virtue, and there are, and have been, respectable aesthetic programs founded on just that. Who now would not be proud to have lavished a year of care on "The Red Wheelbarrow" even if it was dashed off in a minute on the back of a prescription pad? And don't you share my quiet admiration for the errant fingers, and brain (we were typesetting everything then, letter for letter) that saw "buttons" as "bottoms"? "Let all surrealism stand," the subversive in us smiles.

Nevertheless, I confess, it is difficult to care strongly about work that seems to have required less labor than I will give it myself, in my secondary fashion. And it baffles me that a writer would admit in a cover note that his story is the work of last week—it is his very latest, as if that pseudo-urgency will sell it. Nor am I much taken by poems that are dated, sometimes to the hour, as if each were a journal entry, even though I keep a poetic journal myself.

Carver's wariness, after all, was based on classical advice, which is rarely bad—Horace's in this case, from his *Art of Poetry*—to put your work in your closet, or drawer, "for nine years." Nine years! That's twice a college education, or a BA, the Peace Corps, and an MFA as well. Talk about caution. His warning turned on the possibility of being shamed later by one's work. Once you send your poem out, he went on to say, "it is no longer yours to destroy," which is to suggest that most of what you write does not deserve publication, much less require it. Alexander Pope, I believe, reduced the term to five years. Regularly, now, we receive the effort of someone's last workshop, or last summer.

I'm enough of a classicist at heart that I respect the older view. And I have work in my drawers (or electronic files) that has met that test and more. On the whole, though, those pieces find acceptance more rarely than work that is much fresher—that is, I have a certain amount of practical experience that leads me to doubt Horace's old advice. Still, I cannot bring myself to admire freshness in and of itself. And boasting of it is not likely to win me over. Nor am I much taken by a related and equally unearned sense of urgency, that all one writes deserves publication somewhere. The cover letter that is even less persuasive than the one announcing one's work of last week is that which says "I have a collection coming out next year and these stories (or poems) are still available." My first thought, always, is well, good for you, but not everything in your collection needs to be published twice. My second, why should I be interested in the leavings of what has already been picked over? And my third, I'd rather give our space to a writer less fortunate.

Akin to the virtues of spontaneity, however, is another understanding of revision, that as we set work aside, or send it out, we simultaneously, somehow, assimilate the lessons of our past and get on with things best by starting over: that a writer does better to take a fresh cut through what is much the same material, however different-seeming on the surface, than to insist on correcting work that has already gone awry. Such must be the assumption of many of our poets, famously led by William Stafford, who compose afresh each day and leave evaluation up to readers. Disarming themselves of their "standards," they let history be their judge and far-flung editors their revisers by rejection. Only they don't really let editors revise and prune them all that much; instead, they keep everything in circulation until it finds its slot, or so it seems anyway.

Once I listened to a famous French critic lecture in Iowa City. I forget who, by which I mean no disrespect; it has been a few years. I was struck though by the frequency with which he paused to correct his text, putting ballpoint to his page right there at the lectern. I assumed I was learning something about his writing methods, his copious bibliography, and its satisfactions. We in the heartland were not a meager audience, and he seemed untroubled by readying his next publication before us. It's a small step from that behavior to each semester's lectures flowing directly into a book and the point of it all being less to study something through and then explain the understanding reached than to display one's journey toward it. But then we have been celebrating process over product since the '60s anyway.

So there you have the boundaries of possibility: at one extreme, not completed but "abandoned," as a poet put it, or "finally unfinished," as

Duchamp said of one of his constructions; and at the other, no attempt to finish but instead to be lifted by the moment and pass on, and to be found out by time.

From an editor's point of view, I'll repeat my lack of passion for spontaneity. Why should I make much of what someone else has made so little? Why should I read and reread work that may have been reread by the writer less often than it will be by me? I'll acknowledge a kind of perverse joke in all that, an "upsodounness" of expectation, as Chaucer could have said. And perversion is a mainstay of our pleasures, in the arts as elsewhere. It works though only when it wins us over. I am in no position to be sure of how often that happens, since a writer has no reason to confess. I do suppose that it is infrequent. Or perhaps I only hope as much.

Submission Strategy and Protocol

by Amy Holman

Amy Holman is a poet and the former director of Publishing Seminars for Poets & Writers, Inc.

You're ready. The poems choking your dusty filing cabinet have finally been revised and your polished short story is waiting on your desktop. You want to send out your work, but what else is there beyond the ever-growing slush pile at *Harper's*? A lot, actually. The literary market is teeming with publishing opportunities in periodicals—journals, glossies, e-zines—and the key to getting your work read is knowing the protocol and strategy for submissions.

Resources

Sending your work out blindly is like attaching your poem to a balloon and hoping the right person finds it. Familiarize yourself with the literary magazine market by *reading* what's out there. If you're going to submit to a given journal, take the time to read its latest issue. Get a sense of what its editors are looking for from its contributors and learn to recognize if your work might fit. Editors of literary journals are often writers themselves, so do a little research and send to editors whose writing you like. If you're fond of Hilda Raz, send to *Prairie Schooner*. If you like Rebecca Wolff, consider *Fence*. This is also true for magazine competitions—submit work to judges whose writing you respond to. The 2003 annual *Boston Review* poetry competition was judged by Richard Howard; the 2003 *MARGIE* poetry contest was judged by Robert Pinsky. Chances are, if you're fond of a judge's work, you probably have similar literary values and you're one step ahead of those who didn't take the time to do their homework.

Some journals print an editorial statement that describes the type of work its editors are seeking. The editors of the annual *Quarter After Eight, A Journal of Prose & Commentary*, for example, consider that "much of what is most interesting in contemporary letters is a prose that defines, redefines, and erodes genre distinctions," and the table of contents doesn't specify which titles are prose poetry, short fiction, or essays. *Seneca Review* is not at all interested in fiction as a genre or a technique; it publishes innovative poetry and "lyric essays," or what associate editor John D'Agata calls "something that would make me nervous if I was wearing it at a convention of nonfiction writers."

Pay attention, no matter the genre, to subject matter and tone of the work published in the journal you are considering. Don't send a traditional villanelle to an editor who wants eroded genres, and don't look to the name of a journal to clue you in: *Night Train* and *Drunken Boat* are not looking for work about transportation and cheap wine.

Some magazines focus specifically on one genre, such as the journals *Poetry, Fiction*, and *Creative Nonfiction*. Not all are interested in writers at all levels of experience. Some give preference to beginning writers and others to established ones. Some represent a particular population or point of view. Though the literary magazine market offers a wide spectrum of writers, familiar large-circulation magazines such as the *Atlantic, The New Yorker*, and *Harper's* generally publish the more well known.

Peruse the *Guide to Literary Magazines and Presses*, published by the Council of Literary Magazine and Presses (CLMP), or *The International Directory of Little Magazines and Small Presses* from Dustbooks for magazine addresses, submission guidelines, payment, circulation, issue price, and subscription costs. Creative nonfiction writers may also want to study *Writer's Market* from Writer's Digest Books for information on larger magazines that regularly publish essays. The resource guides will alert you to which magazines are well established by the names of writers they have published, but be sure to read from actual issues of the magazines to see if your work would fit and if they are interested in unknown writers. Publishing is a series of stepping-stones, but you want your path to wind around into many neighborhoods to cultivate the widest possible audience. Browsing magazine selections is a better strategy than buying magazines whose description in a book makes them seem apt. Bookstores and libraries in cities or university towns ,may stock some literary magazines, but you can also access a broad spectrum of magazines online (both print journals with a Web presence and electronic-only venues). Four sites that offer links are: litline.org, webdelsol.com, newpages.com, and pw.org/pages_links.

Submission Guidelines

In order for your work to be considered it must first be read, and ignoring submission guidelines is the best way to get your manuscript thrown in the trash. A few basic rules: Most magazines want one short story or essay per submission, or three to six poems. The type size should not be smaller than 12-point, the typeface preferably Times Roman, and by all means double-space. Simultaneous submissions—the submission of the same piece of writing to more than one magazine—is becoming more acceptable, but you must inform the editor in your cover letter that you are doing so, and you must notify him or her immediately should your piece be accepted elsewhere.

Since you are asking the magazine to consider publishing your work, you must pay the postage for its reply by sending a self-addressed stamped envelope (SASE), or a self-addressed stamped postcard if you want them to recycle your submission. Some magazines accepting online submissions, such as *Glimmer Train*, will send an e-mail receipt of your story with a tracking number. Print and place this in a file, or save it to a special folder in your e-mail program, and track your submission's progress electronically.

Accept early on the fact that you will receive rejections more often than acceptances, but do not reject common sense by sending poems in July to a magazine that closes for the summer, or by sending a 10,000-word story to a journal with a limit of 5,000 words. Check your resources. The *Hudson Review*, for instance, reads nonfiction from January 1 through March 31, poetry from April 1 through June 30, and fiction from September 1 through November 30. If you were to ignore this reading schedule, your manuscript would be returned unread.

Cover Letters

Once you've carefully selected your magazine choices, don't ruin your chances by writing a flip, messy cover letter. If you are not a good speller, keep it a secret. Philip Fried, editor of the *Manhattan Review*, says, "Think of yourself as writing a letter to someone who is distracted and may be in a bad mood." Ninety-nine percent of the editors of literary magazines read manuscripts on their own time, without pay, so he is right to warn writers away from chatty letters to strangers. You should not presume the editor's sense of humor is the same as yours, or just waiting to be tempted by those most common baits, sarcasm and self-deprecation.

Stick to a basic business letter addressed to the right editor. List the title(s) of the work(s) enclosed. Write a brief bio with publication credits if you have them, where you've studied, where you work. You can mention that your poems are part of a series, but do not summarize your story. If an essay from one issue of the journal you are sending to inspired you to submit yours, mention it. Particularly with the glossies, let the editor know why you think your piece is a good fit for her magazine. Say that you look forward to her reply in your enclosed SASE.

E-mail submissions require much less in the way of a cover letter—a few lines inside a submission form is all you need. Attaching your work is best, but you can also copy and paste into an e-mail message and add a sentence or two of bio. It isn't so much that editors at online journals are less interested in your credits, but rather that long e-mail messages are harder to read than letters of equal length. Learn to be concise. The clearer your cover letter, the farther down the page an editor will read.

Mailing and Record Keeping

Once you've decided on a handful of magazines and written your cover letters, give yourself an afternoon to assemble clean, organized submission packs. Prepare fresh copies of your work and your SASEs. Prose writers should remember that photocopies weigh less than pages from a printer, so postage on their submissions will be less if photocopies are sent. Poets should get a box of No. 10–sized business envelopes and prose writers should get a packet of 9-by-11-inch manila envelopes, preferably with a sticky seal strip, but not with metal clasps, which can jam a postage machine. One first-class stamp (37 cents at this writing) and one "second-ounce" stamp (23 cents currently) should be enough postage to send six poems and an SASE to a magazine. Weigh a few envelopes containing stories or essays and folded SASEs on a postage machine or scale, and jot down the costs. Stamp and address five SASEs and stamp five blank envelopes and put them away in a drawer with clean copies of your work for future submissions. Keep track of where you've sent your writing by putting a copy of each cover letter in a special file, or by keeping a list of the work you've sent, where you sent it, and when.

Make the process of reading your submission effortless. An organized package and a concise cover letter will keep your submission in an editor's hands just long enough to get past the preliminaries. Then your work can speak for itself.

Little and Literary

by Natalie Danford

Natalie Danford is the series coeditor for
Best New American Voices.

You dream of being published in *The New Yorker*. Just admit it. Don't be ashamed. If you're a writer in North America, dreaming of being published in *The New Yorker* is as natural as breathing, as inevitable as aging. Virtually all the fiction writers and poets you know dream the dream, whether they admit it or not. And this is the dream: You will one day be plucked from obscurity by a fiction editor at *The New Yorker* who recognizes how brilliant your prose is. From there, it will be only a short hop to the *New York Times* best-seller list. You will, finally, be a writer.

It's a nice fantasy, but you're just starting out: Pace yourself. Go where you're wanted. And if you're a good writer with a solid command of craft, there are magazines that want you. These aren't *The New Yorker* and its ilk, but literary and "little" magazines, which comprise a whopper of a category, encompassing everything from the truly tiny (i.e., pages of work stapled together) to the long established, some of which look like paperback books with artful covers.

In fact, the category is so wide-ranging that it's hard to pin down the exact number of literary magazines in North America. The Council of Literary Magazines and Presses (CLMP) estimates that there are approximately 600 such magazines that publish regularly (mainly on a quarterly or semiannual basis) and another 700 that either don't adhere to a regular schedule or publish in such small numbers that it is difficult, if not impossible, to keep track of them. Most of these magazines publish poetry and short fiction. Some include essays, artwork, or other material.

"The magazines we represent run the gamut," says Jeffrey Lependorf, executive director of the nonprofit CLMP. "We have well-known magazines like the *Paris Review*, new magazines like *Tin House* that function almost on the level of a commercial magazine, as well as small magazines like *Fence*, or *One Story*, which publishes a single story in each issue, or *Gumball Poetry*, which publishes one poem in each issue, wrapped around a gumball, and comes out of a vending machine."

They are a varied group, but there are identifiable subsets. First, there's the Old Guard, with magazines like the *Paris Review*, founded in 1953 by Peter Mathiessen and Harold L. Humes, both writers themselves. But the *Paris Review* is a teenager compared with others: the *Sewanee Review* has published regularly since 1892, and the oldest magazine still publishing is the *North American Review*, which debuted in 1815.

Another large subset, which intersects with the Old Guard, consists of literary magazines affiliated with universities. This doesn't mean that the work comes from students, but that the universities provide funding and house the offices on campus. These include the *Iowa Review* and the *Yale Review*. The *Iowa Review*, now in its thirty-second consecutive year of publication, publishes essays, stories, and poems. *Prairie Schooner* at the University of Nebraska–Lincoln was founded in 1926.

Recent years have seen a rejuvenation in literary magazines, with several notable start-ups, including *Tin House* in 1999 and *McSweeney's* (founded by author Dave Eggers of *A Heartbreaking Work of Staggering Genius* fame) in 1998. New magazines have proliferated on the Internet as well. Online journals such as John Tranter's *Jacket* (jacketmagazine.com) and Katherine Swiggart and D.A. Powell's *Electronic Poetry Review* (www.poetry.org) have proven that the Internet is a legitimate medium for literary publishing. These newcomers have a more swinging image than the Old Guard and the academic crowd, but ultimately they're all looking for the same thing: high-quality writing.

With such a large number of magazines out there, how do you decide which publication to submit to? The straight answer is to send your work to magazines that publish the kind of work you write, but to read all 600 would take years.

One useful strategy is to purchase an annual anthology such as *The O. Henry Awards* or *The Best American Short Stories*, which cull their work from magazines. Read through a few of these and note which stories seem similar to yours and where they were published. Another tactic is to select likely looking titles from a directory such as *The CLMP Directory of Literary Magazines and Presses* or *The International Directory of Little Magazines and Small Presses* from Dustbooks. Still, and I cannot stress this enough, do not simply submit to magazines according to the instructions in these guides.

Instead, use the directories, or the addresses in the back of such anthologies, or the Internet (almost every magazine has a Web site these days) to order sample copies or subscribe. Before sending away for copies, you might check a local bookstore as well. A good one will have a nice selection of literary magazines, and any magazine that can find its way onto a bookshelf in a store, particularly a store not located in the town where it's edited, is at least serious about distribution, and probably serious about publishing on a regular schedule as well.

So, read. You must read at least one issue, and preferably two or three. First, if you are submitting poetry, be sure the magazine publishes poetry, and likewise for fiction. This advice is so basic that I considered deleting it, but then I remembered the college professor who, several years ago, submitted a batch of poems to *Best New American Voices*, the short story anthology I edit. "Since you publish fiction, I'm assuming you'll take poetry as well," he wrote authoritatively, but he was wrong. The one firm way to make sure that your work doesn't get published is not to send it out, but another strategy that will work equally well is to send it to an inappropriate publication.

Once you've determined that a magazine does publish short fiction or poetry or whatever it is you write, read an issue carefully and discern whether your own work is a good fit. This is tricky. Read the magazine's contents once for enjoyment. Then, assuming you did enjoy what you read, go back and read the work a second time, with a more critical eye. Who is the audience for this work? Is it the same audience you address with your own? If your work is experimental, you're wasting your time sending it to a magazine that publishes only narrative stories with a beginning, middle, and end.

Don't just read the stories or poems, either. Learn to evaluate your chances by studying the biographical notes on contributors in the back. If every author mentioned has published six or more books, it's likely that the magazine is looking for work only by well-established writers. But if several of the contributors mention that this is their first publication, and the magazine still looks fairly professional and has a piece or two from a writer whose name you recognize, it's a good candidate.

In addition to literary journals, grant competitions and writing contests are great destinations for your burgeoning work. (Deadlines and submission requirements are listed in each issue of *Poets & Writers Magazine* and on some useful Web sites; see also the back of this book.) Some of these offer cash prizes, some offer publication, and some offer both—but even a place as a runner-up is useful to you when submitting to literary magazines. Such recognition is a great tidbit to include in a cover letter with your next round of submissions.

Literary magazines themselves often run contests. Sometimes those contests include monetary prizes that are slightly larger than payment would normally be. Fairly typical are the yearly poetry and fiction contests sponsored by *Nimrod*. Entrants pay a fee, which entitles them to a one-year subscription to the magazine. A well-known guest editor does the judging. In 2002 the magazine received 590 poetry manuscripts and 485 fiction manuscripts. Other magazines award an editors' prize, which means that the editors simply select the best story, poem, or essay published by the magazine that year.

So, you've got a great story or poem, and you've done your homework and have identified five magazines you think would be perfect for your work. What next?

Be sure to read any submission guidelines (whether in the magazine or on a Web site) carefully. Then read them again, just to be sure. Some magazines, particularly university-affiliated ones, take submissions only during a certain period of the year.

The usual rules apply, whether you're submitting to *The New Yorker* or a tiny magazine: Make sure your manuscript is neat. Include a brief cover letter that introduces you but does not explain your story or poem. Mention in the cover letter if you have earned an MFA in creative writing and if your work has been published elsewhere, and touch on any awards, grants, or prizes that you have won. If you have never published anything, don't be afraid to say so—editors love to discover writers. Also appealing is an indication that you've read the magazine, so if you can, make a comment on a piece from a recent issue. (Note: This is not an invitation to critique the magazine.) Send a self-addressed stamped envelope (SASE). Never include your only copy of a story or poem. Then, once you have dropped that manila envelope in the mail, put it out of your mind.

Small magazines have small staffs. The average annual budget for a CLMP magazine is $10,000, and most have volunteer staffs. Count on a long response time, and keep a log of your submissions. If you have not received a reply after six months or the response time given on the magazine's Web site or in its writers' guidelines, write a note asking whether your work is still under consideration. Include a SASE with that note as well. It is not unusual for a magazine to hold on to work for a year before publishing it, and sometimes before accepting it.

Given these protracted waits, what about simultaneous submissions? I know editors say not to do it—it's an inconvenience for them, after all—but most writers I know submit a story to two or three places at once. With odds so slim, it seems only fair, but you should submit simultaneously only to magazines in which you are equally interested. Don't, for instance, send work to a magazine you'd consider your top choice and another that's halfway down the list—you can't ask one magazine to wait until you've heard from another.

The statistics about the number of submissions such magazines receive are discouraging. Joanna Yas, editor of *Open City*, estimates that the magazine, which has a circulation of about 5,000, publishes one percent of the stories submitted. That number sounds dire, but keep in mind that many, many people submit stories and poems to magazines, but few do it well. If you are well organized about your submissions, if you follow the rules a publication has provided, heck, if you format your manuscript in an acceptable way, rather than single-spacing it and printing it out with magenta ink, you are in the minority. Because when it comes down to it, many people write, but few are capable of following the submission methods laid out plain as day in writers' guidelines.

It's also useful when weighing your chances to remind yourself that many people send out their work too soon, or simply don't write seriously. *Prairie Schooner* (circulation 2,500) receives about 500 submissions every month. Managing editor Kelly Grey says, "The odds aren't great, but if you're looking at it in terms of quality of work, the odds increase." In other words, they receive a lot of work, but they don't receive a lot of good work. Make yours the exception.

With long waits, heavy competition, and general difficulty in this area, you might expect to hear that literary magazines pay well enough to make your effort worthwhile. Sadly, that's not the case. Payment may not even be monetary at all, but in the form of contributors' copies.

So why bother? For one thing, it's important to get your work off your desk and out into the air where it can breathe. Even if only 1,000 or so people read the magazine that's publishing your story or poem, that's 1,000 more pairs of eyes than would have seen it sitting on your desk. And the eyes that read those magazines can be important. Beth Bosworth, author of *A Burden of Earth* (Hanging Loose Press, 1995) and *Tunneling* (Shaye Areheart/Crown, 2003) and editor of the *St. Ann's Review,* was first contacted by agent Andrew Blauner after he read a story of hers in the *Kenyon Review.* He now represents her. "The difference between having your work moldering at home and having it out there is enormous," says Bosworth. "The simple fact of putting it in the mail changes your relationship to the work itself."

Agents aren't the only ones paging through literary magazines looking for fresh talent—editors at larger magazines read them too, and sometimes solicit work from contributors. Even more important, when you're ready to submit to those larger magazines, you'll have a list of publications to include in your cover letter that will make you look professional, and smart, and dedicated—someone who is clearly and patiently working his or her way toward *The New Yorker.*

The Glossies

by Joanna Smith Rakoff

Joanna Smith Rakoff is a contributing editor for Poets & Writers Magazine.

For many fiction writers, access to the glossies, those high-circulation, high-profile, high-paying magazines, can seem like gaining membership to an exclusive club—only writers with established reputations or superpowered agents or serious connections allowed. But ironically, when you talk to fiction editors at such magazines, most say their biggest thrill is uncovering previously unpublished or not yet well known writers. Of course, the big question is: How do you become one of those writers whose stories get pulled out of the slush? The answer seems absurdly simple: Don't give up.

"I probably sent Adrienne Brodeur half a dozen stories before she took one," says Boston short story writer Steve Almond. Brodeur is one of the founders of and, at the time of this interview, an editor for *Zoetrope*. She subsequently left to pursue her own publishing career. (*Zoetrope*'s publisher, Francis Ford Coppola, gives the award-winning quarterly major gloss factor.) "She was kind and generous enough to respond to the stories I sent, and eventually she said, 'I really like this story, but I think it needs some work.'" Instead of balking at Brodeur's proposed changes, Almond eagerly implemented her suggestions for his story "Among the Ik." Almond explains, "Because I come from a journalism background, revision is no big deal to me." Brodeur bought the revised story.

Almond perceived Brodeur's encouragement as an act of spectacular kindness, but the editor insists it was nothing of the sort. "That's what we do. Putting the magazine together is an organic process. We get *very* involved with our writers." While *Zoetrope* may mentor its writers more than other magazines—putting agents and book editors in touch with them, getting involved with parties for the book deals that result from those partnerships—Brodeur's attitude reflects those of the fiction editors at the eight mainstream magazines that still find room for fiction between celebrity profiles and fashion spreads, political coverage and serious journalism. And the editors all seem to approach the selection of fiction with one criterion in mind: quality.

If that emphasis on quality—rather than, say, marketability—sounds surprisingly similar to the editorial values of literary magazines, well, it is. As is the handling of unsolicited stories. All submissions (both agented and unagented) are read, whether by the fiction editor, assistants, or freelance "readers," both paid and unpaid. In some cases, the deeper pockets of the glossies—such as *Esquire, Playboy, Harper's,* and the *Atlantic Monthly*—allow fiction editors more time to work with writers on extensive revisions than those at smaller magazines usually find. In others, the relatively low status of fiction and the editors' many other responsibilities do not allow for this kind of collaboration.

Novelist Thisbe Nissen (*The Good People of New York*), who published one of her first stories in *Seventeen,* says that editors at glossies tend, on the whole, to be more involved in the revision process. "I've never done edits on something that's been in a university literary magazine. I think because the editors are often MFA students who are working on the magazine as part of their financial aid or for credit, they just don't have time." Nissen's *Seventeen* story went through a year's worth of revisions with the magazine's fiction editor, who ended up leaving before the story was published. A year or so later, the new fiction editor found Nissen's story and asked her to do another revision. Three years after she'd originally submitted it, the story finally saw print. Did all that revision make for a better story? "Well, it made it a more *Seventeen* story," says Nissen.

Darcy Jacobs, who was *Seventeen's* fiction editor until recently moving to *Lifetime* magazine, says she tried to buy pieces that were as polished as possible—like novel excerpts, which comprised about half of her acquisitions—simply because her time was quite limited. If she loved a story, though, she found the time to work with the writer on revision. Along with editing other sections of the monthly magazine, Jacobs, who *was* the fiction department, received about 100 to 150 stories a month.

Seventeen may not immediately spring to mind as one of the heavy hitters when it comes to publishing distinguished fiction. But the list of writers who published early work in the pages of America's oldest teen magazine reads like the table of contents for an anthology of contemporary fiction: Lorrie Moore, Annie Proulx, Anna Quindlen, Ann Patchett, Alice McDermott, Anne Tyler, Meg Wolitzer, Jill McCorkle, Edwidge Danticat, Joyce Maynard. During Jacobs's tenure she published such comers as David Schickler (*Kissing in Manhattan*), Stacey Richter (*My Date with Satan*), and Nissen (Jacobs published an excerpt of Nissen's novel)—writers who list *Seventeen* on their CVs along with *The New Yorker, Zoetrope,* and the *Atlantic.*

Fairly regularly, Jacobs came across a story that she loved but couldn't accept because it missed the mark for *Seventeen*'s audience. In such cases, she usually called the writer to say that it was "a great story." Otherwise, she sent form rejections, even for stories with a little glimmer of something in them. Unlike Brodeur, she didn't have the time to draft encouraging notes to potential contributors. Moreover, the magazine has so little space for fiction—it runs only six to eight stories a year, each no more than 3,000 words—that only the tiniest fraction of submissions can pass muster.

The recent ad recession hasn't tremendously affected *Seventeen,* which caters to one of the advertising industry's most beloved demographics, but it has threatened the number of pages allotted to fiction in some magazines, not to mention the number of magazine pages period. According to the Magazine Publishers of America, most commercial periodicals follow an advertising/editorial ratio of 55/45. The more ads a magazine sells, the more pages it has for content. Thus, when ad sales slow, editorial pages get cut.

"If you look at everybody's January and February [2002] issues," says Jeff Johnson, fiction editor of *Jane,* "they're so terribly thin." *Jane,* a relatively new magazine but one that carries the substantial weight of editor Jane Pratt's reputation for creativity and ingenuity (in the 1980s Pratt founded the late, lamented *Sassy,* a smart glossy for teens), is bracing itself for cutbacks from advertisers, though it hasn't had any problems yet. "One of the first things to go is fiction," explains Johnson, who also edits the magazine's music pages. "We have more of a commitment to other things, like music and fashion. If we send a reporter out to write about an event that is meaningful to everybody going out to buy a magazine, well, we've got to run that reported piece rather than a piece of fiction." The magazine publishes ten issues per year; it runs stories in about seven.

Although *Jane* is ostensibly aimed at eighteen-to-thirty-four-year-old women, the magazine's insider, hip style appeals to a somewhat broad range of readers. "It seems like a lot of guys read our magazine," says Johnson, "especially compared to other women's magazines." Johnson chooses most of *Jane*'s fiction from somewhat less mainstream writers with "dark but hilarious sensibilities," like Sam Lipsyte (*The Subject Steve*) and Diane Vedino (former managing editor, or as Dave Eggers calls it, "helping person," of *McSweeney's*).

A fiction writer himself, Johnson loves working with writers, but like Jacobs he finds himself baffled and annoyed by the many writers who send him inappropriate material—writers who appear to have not even glanced at *Jane* before tossing their stories into the mailbox. "Sometimes you get somebody who's figured out this formula—like a sitcom—that works for five or six pages and that's it. That's what they think a women's magazine is going to publish—this formulaic stuff."

Johnson has amassed a small group of agents who understand his aesthetic and thus consistently send him stories appropriate for *Jane* (which doesn't mean, of course, that he runs them all). But more often than not, Johnson deals directly with the writers themselves (sometimes forming relationships with those who frequently submit interesting but unpublishable material). "My agent sends out my stories to the big slicks where she knows somebody, but I don't think that matters," Almond explains. "All an agent can do is get you to the top of a pile." *Zoetrope*'s Brodeur agrees. Here's how she explains the first step of the magazine's selection process:

"Depending on the day, we can get anywhere from fifty to a hundred stories. First, they're opened and put into three piles. There's the slush pile; *slush* basically means 'no one we know.' Then there's a pile for solicited or impressive material. That's for people who have written to one of us, or know one of our writers, or have an impressive bio—it means there's one step of familiarity. Then, finally, there's the agented pile. The basic difference between the three piles is that the agented pile and the priority pile are read more quickly. That's it."

Well, sort of. While the agented and solicited-impressive piles land directly on the desks of the editors and editorial assistants, to whom the manuscripts are addressed, the slush goes first to the magazine's readers—a group of volunteers and unpaid interns, many of whom are MFA students—who slowly sift through it. "The readers divide the slush into four categories: (1) Buy immediately; (2) Consider with revision; (3) Reject with encouragement; (4) Reject. They are told to give something a total no only if they are absolutely *convinced* it's a no," says Brodeur. "If it's not a no, it goes to assistants and editors." How often does a reader dig up a "buy immediately" in the slush? About twice each year. "It's always thrilling to find something in the slush. It's our greatest joy, obviously, when it happens," says Brodeur. "If there's something that separates *Zoetrope*, it's that we pursue finding new writers."

Indeed, in the past few years *Zoetrope* has discovered an impressive cast of writers, from Melissa Bank to Adam Haslett to Almond. But every editor of the eight interviewed shared a similar enthusiasm for and commitment to discovering new talent. It's not surprising to hear that *Harper's* and the *Atlantic Monthly* seek out young writers—these are magazines committed to intellectual culture—but it does come as a small shock when Barbara Nellis, *Playboy's* fiction editor, declares that she's "trying to find a whole carload of young writers, both men and women, who are writing about the contemporary human condition. I want to be with the people who are getting discovered by the small, solid literary mags, who have a reason to get a greater audience."

Playboy's history with fiction, Nellis explains, is long and somewhat schizophrenic. "Hefner was buying stories right from the very beginning. The magazine has had a series of fiction moments that have changed over time. There was a period of time when it was more literary, a period when it was more commercial, periods when we mostly did genre fiction." Nellis experienced these moments firsthand: She's been with *Playboy* for over thirty years, though she took over the fiction editorship less than a year ago (replacing the legendary Alice Turner). And so, a few months back, when Hefner asked why the magazine wasn't winning the kind of fiction awards it used to, Nellis was able to point to his recent edict asking for fiction that falls on the more commercial side of the fence. The silk-pajamaed mogul took Nellis's point to heart and reversed his decree, allowing her to do whatever she felt was necessary to raise the caliber of fiction in his high-end skin magazine. "I'm trying to attract the younger men in my audience [with these literary stories by young writers]," she explains. "But we still publish commercial fiction. We like to mix it up."

Just as *Seventeen* and *Jane* don't exclusively publish stories by and about young women, neither does *Playboy* limit itself to stories by and about men. Nellis cites the magazine's long relationship with Joyce Carol Oates, and recalls that her predecessor published stories by younger luminaries like Mary Gaitskill.

The fiction published by *Playboy*'s more reserved compatriots—*Esquire* and *GQ*—isn't fueled only by testosterone either. Although Adrienne Miller, *Esquire*'s fiction editor, admits, "It's not as if we're going to publish stories whose focus is exclusively female—female-relationship stories. The stories are, frankly, about men, but that doesn't mean they're all written by men or of interest only to men." Walter Kirn, *GQ*'s fiction editor (and also a writer for the magazine), has a slightly less scientific approach. "I definitely have the readership in mind when I'm looking at stories. But what that means, I've never analyzed. I mean, male protagonists show up pretty frequently. Yet my calculation about what's going to appeal to the reader is not really based on sex itself or gender itself, but rather on an intuitive sense of what will work."

In recent years competition from other men's titles like the successful, and decidedly lowbrow, *Maxim* has led *Esquire* and *GQ* to play more to their readership's lowest common denominator. But both magazines have a long history of excellence—in both reporting (*Esquire*, in the 1950s and 1960s, published some of the best of the New Journalism) and fiction—that overshadows their fin de siècle forays into the world of, *ahem*, T&A. *Esquire*'s Miller is constantly aware of her place in the magazine's fiction dynasty—and chooses stories that she hopes will have as important a place in history as those the magazine ran fifty years earlier, stories by Hemingway, Fitzgerald, Cheever, Steinbeck, Nabokov, Barth, Richard Yates, Truman Capote, and Flannery O'Connor, and later, Don DeLillo, Denis Johnson, Joy Williams, and Richard Ford. During her five-year tenure, she's published Russell Banks, Joanna Scott, David Foster Wallace, Heidi Julavits, Aleksandar Hemon, David Means, Nicole Krauss, Richard Russo, and Tim O'Brien, among others.

"We get, as you can imagine, an enormous amount of submissions—about ten thousand a year. It's totally crazy," says Miller. "I have freelance readers who come in and help me slog through the stuff. Most is crap, but we need to take it seriously. We dive in with hope." Slush-pile discoveries include Arthur Bradford (*Dogwalker*) and, in years past,

Raymond Carver and Richard Ford. Like *Zoetrope*'s Brodeur, Miller prizes her relationships with writers, especially young writers. "While working on a story, I'll talk to a writer a dozen times." And she, too, insists that stories submitted by agents get no special preference. "Honestly, the stuff that agents send isn't better than the stuff in the slush pile." *GQ*'s Kirn agrees: "I get a lot from agents, but it doesn't matter to me who sends it. I don't discern any higher quality in the stories that are submitted by agents."

While Miller works out of *Esquire*'s New York offices and is involved in the day-to-day rituals of the magazine's publication—she's concerned, for example, with ad cutbacks and page allotments for fiction, like *Jane*'s Johnson—*GQ*'s Kirn selects stories in a slightly less hectic environment: his home in Montana. "I am pretty divorced from the publishing side of the magazine. Those concerns are other people's jobs. Being in an office—in the hurly-burly of everyday decision making—can be distracting from the real mission. A little detachment from everyday concerns helps to carry that mission out." And publishing fiction, he says, really *is* a mission. "It's not something that magazines do for the money. It's an opportunity to show the world stuff they otherwise might not see."

Kirn attempts to read submissions with "as few preconceptions as possible." While some writers and agents submit stories directly to him, others send them to *GQ*'s Times Square offices, where they are read by staffers who pass on to Kirn anything promising. *GQ* doesn't receive as high a volume of submissions as some of the other magazines, and what Kirn does receive generally comes from "people with whom I'm familiar. Or, a lot of it is from people I don't know personally but whose work I may know. Many of the stories we get, and publish, are from writers who are somewhat well known," says Kirn, citing writers like David Gates, Elwood Reid, and James Ellroy. Although Kirn, like the other editors interviewed, insists that "quality is my only standard," his "mission" doesn't really include seeking out new writers. "Writers who have established themselves have often established themselves for a reason: because they're good. It so happens that a lot of the highest-quality stories are from people who have practiced the art."

Harper's, on the other hand, views its mission in terms of diversity of style, according to Ben Metcalf, one of the team of senior editors who oversees the magazine's fiction. "Everyone is free to bring in what they like, even the younger editors, but it tends to be the four of us: Charis Conn, John Sullivan, Ellen Rosenbush, and me. We all have very different tastes, so there's no one mind defining what fiction is at *Harper's*. And that's the way [editor in chief] Lewis Lapham wants it."

If that sounds like a recipe for disagreements, it is. But it's also "fun," says Metcalf. "We have arguments, and we get our minds changed." The committee style of selection also allows the magazine to do some strategic planning. "Basically, we have twelve slots a year and we're simply trying to publish the best twelve stories we can get our hands on during that year. So sometimes that means a really good example of a well-known writer's work and sometimes it's a writer's first published work." Publishing debuts give Metcalf and his colleagues "a special thrill." Though more nonfiction than fiction has come out of the slush recently, Metcalf says he plucks stuff "more often than you would think." He grows excited recalling the moment he found the story "Half-Mammals of Dixie" by then-unknown South Carolina writer George Singleton in a pile of unsolicited work—"It was just wonderful!"

More so than many of the other editors, Metcalf and his *Harper's* colleagues maintain a somewhat old-fashioned relationship with their pool of writers. "I have a few writers who know I take a special interest in their work. They send me every story they write." Those whom he's interested in, he brings to his colleagues for a consensus (Lapham has final approval). This is not to say, however, that the *Harper's* team doesn't value the slush pile. "*Harper's* is all about the original voice. Even though the amount of mail we get is an undeniable burden, we would never want to discourage any writers from sending their work our way."

While every story sent to *Harper's* gets read, it may not happen quite as quickly as at the *Atlantic Monthly*, where C. Michael Curtis has presided over the fiction pages for twenty-five years (he's been at the magazine for forty). Curtis, who's known as Mike, regularly astounds junior staffers by zipping through a huge pile of manuscripts in a few hours. "One writer I know got a rejection from him less than a week after he sent the story," says a Curtis fan. "He thought Mike hadn't even read it. But he had! He's just amazingly quick." Curtis explains that while he reads all submissions addressed specifically to him, a team of five or six interns, "chosen for what appears to be their skill and intelligence in evaluating fiction," screens all stories addressed merely to "fiction editor" or sent to the magazine's general box.

In total, the magazine receives about 1,000 stories each month, and in previous years the *Atlantic* published a larger percentage of them. But according to Curtis, "For several years now, we've run only one story in each issue. We used to have three or four in each issue—that continued up until the 1970s." Why the cutback? "Well," he says, sighing, "it's partly the cost of paper, which has increased exponentially since that time, but also because we began to publish smaller issues. Part of the thinking came from our discovery that only a tenth of our readership cared about our fiction and poetry. In my view, since we're talking about a total readership of five hundred thousand, that's *fifty thousand* people who are readers of fiction. But we aren't a magazine that has made its way on fiction or poetry or criticism, but on the package of things—reportage, politics, cultural affairs." Indeed, in the 1970s the *Atlantic* published entire novels by Saul Bellow and long sections of Updike novels, only to find that those issues didn't sell well on the newsstands.

So many submissions, so little space—is it any wonder Curtis rarely solicits work from writers? "Every time I see a writer whose work I respect, I say, 'Gosh, I want to see your next story,' but we only publish twelve stories a year, so it seems foolish to strongly encourage people to send me work when there's a good chance I'll have to reject it." He also has no particular interest in publishing big-name writers. "They need us less than the relatively unpublished writers. We'd rather invest in discovering talent that no one has come across, though we see a lot of work by very good and professional writers, and quite often the work is so attractive to us that we feel we must publish it. We print usually three or four stories that have come from the slush pile or from writers who somehow got my name; often these are people in MFA programs. Some of the writers we first publish go on to fame and fortune, others are still not well known. Rebecca Lee is one of those. Her work is brilliant. In due course, she'll receive the recognition she deserves."

And when she does, she'll undoubtedly thank Curtis, as did Erika Krouse, a young Colorado writer whom Curtis discovered. Last year her wry first collection, *Come Up and See Me Sometime*, received glowing reviews in many major papers. (Curtis appears in the acknowledgments.) "Every story that comes to me gets either a rejection slip or a letter," says Curtis. "I spend a good deal of my time writing letters to people whose stories are too good to simply deflect without a nod, writers who I hope will keep submitting to me."

But what is it that makes a story too good to deflect without a nod? While the editors of magazines like *Seventeen* and *Jane* and *Esquire* and *GQ* must constantly keep their specific readership in mind, editors of general-interest magazines like *Harper's* and the *Atlantic* have no such constraints. Like the editors of small quarterlies, they're looking at stories purely on their literary merit, no matter the gender or sensibility of the protagonist, no matter the subject or tone of the story.

Writers often grumble about the difficulty of landing stories in the glossies. In fact, they often grumble about merely getting their stories read by the editors of glossies. In Steve Almond's words, "I know it's easy to be envious and cynical and believe that there's some sort of secret trap door that gets you into *The New Yorker* or one of the other big slicks, but the simple truth is that if you write really good stories you'll get into the best magazines. I do believe that the fiction editors of these magazines are looking for the best stories out there. Our job is to write them." As for *The New Yorker*, Bill Buford, until recently the magazine's fiction editor, declined to be interviewed for this article.

But in a way, it doesn't really matter whether Buford revealed his slush-reading secrets, because if the editors profiled here make one thing clear, it's that their selections, while guided by principles and goals, are ultimately based on taste. In the end, selection comes down to an editor, alone, laughing or crying or merely admiring a particular story. Just as in the end, a good story comes down to a writer, alone, writing.

How to Read Rejection

by C. Michael Curtis

C. Michael Curtis is a senior editor at the Atlantic Monthly, *where he has edited fiction and nonfiction for more than thirty years.*

Though publishing isn't—and shouldn't be—the primary measure of artistic worth, it goes a long way toward affirming one's status as a writer. It certainly provides a lubricant in the complicated business of bringing together the writer and his or her audience.

Ultimately, of course, the "validity" or excellence of a piece of writing is subjective, and no writer should be intimidated by critical standards that seem unduly rigid or limiting, or which rest on arguable assumptions. On the other hand, the people who decide what gets published will necessarily have decisive ideas about where value lies in arrangements of the written word. Within reason, the more writers can do to engage the interest and sympathy of these editors, the more their manuscript submissions will get fair readings and eventually make their way into print.

Some writers unintentionally reduce their chances of getting this sympathetic and attentive reading, often for reasons that, in a perfect world, would seem only marginally relevant to the serious business of editorial assessment. Manuscripts that are single-spaced or printed on both sides of the page, for example, place a burden that gets in the way of friendly consideration. Similarly, narrow margins, which result in lines of type too wide for the eye to grasp without moving from side to side, can interfere with attentive reading. Other potential obstacles are misspelled words, faulty punctuation or grammar, needless adjectives and adverbs, repeated use of ellipses, sentence fragments, non sequiturs—in short, any writing lapse or quirk that seems certain to be followed by others will disappoint even the most willing reader.

What most editors look for, in addition to a respect for the conventional strengths of orderly composition, is a sentence or two suf- ciently complex in structure and idea to signify a serious mind at work. Editors look for an engaging sensibility, a writer with wit, imagination, and an appreciation for the benefits of a well-constructed sentence.

Eventually, of course, a fiction editor will look for fully developed characters, for plausible and distinctive dialogue, for themes (or at least variations of familiar themes) that seem fresh and perhaps even (though not necessarily) redemptive. Editors will normally want something to happen, unless the story is static by design and offers shrewdness or an eye for unexpected detail in place of narrative momentum and resolution.

Careful writers will not lose sleep over these matters, which tend to sort themselves out automatically. Even so, they need to be on the alert for awkward repetitions or for sentences that sprawl out of control.

With a well-honed manuscript, a helpfully phrased cover letter (of which more later), and a stamped return envelope, a writer can reasonably expect sympathetic attention and a timely response. If all goes well, the manuscript may win acceptance, and even a check.

The road to publication is long and bumpy, however, and a few of the rough spots are worth examining.

A friend told me recently that she was struggling to recover from a letter of rejection she'd received from an editor at *The New Yorker.* Knowing that magazine's reputation for gentleness in such matters, I asked for details. "He did say my story was 'nicely done,'" she told me, "but he explained that *The New Yorker* wasn't taking that kind of story for the time being."

As someone who has been writing letters of rejection thirty or forty times a day for more than thirty-five years, I have considerable sympathy for my friend the writer—and an appreciation for the dilemma of "the editor," someone compelled to reject far more often than accept and to manage relationships with writers that are wildly lopsided. The editor has almost obscenely exaggerated power, since the ratio of candidates to published stories is so enormous (at least 1,000 to 1 at the *Atlantic Monthly*) and the writer's emotional stake in acceptance or rejection is so huge.

I tried to soothe my writer friend by pointing out some obvious mitigating factors: The letter was, after all, more complimentary than assaultive; most stories, inevitably, have to be returned, in spite of their virtues; editors vary widely in their tastes and tolerances; rejection at one venue doesn't mean that it won't be embraced at others; some work is too demanding for general readers, and is better suited to the quarterlies and other periodicals whose readership, though small, is also well educated, in literary terms, and is more receptive to experimentation, testing of boundaries, deliberate challenge of the conventions of mainstream narrative.

The truth, however, is that publication in large commercial magazines offers far more material reward—in fee, potential audience size, and stature among literary high rollers—than does an appearance in a quarterly, no matter how honored by academic or literary professionals. The pain a writer experiences in rejection, therefore, is more than a gauge of authorial tenderness. It has also to do with the wish for fame and fortune, a conviction that the smiles of certain gods are measurably sunnier than the kindly benevolence of certain others. And to some extent, of course, this perception is accurate. Publication in Magazine A rather than Magazine B may well multiply the chances of being noticed by literary agents looking for promising new clients or book editors scouting for undiscovered talent. In an important sense, however, authentic gifts have a way, even if a slow and meandering one, of making themselves known to respectful and discerning audiences. Every magazine, no matter how rigorous in its screening and selection of candidates for publication, has a history of writers misjudged, talent unappreciated, opportunities for discovery overlooked.

Some writers are spotted early and spend years struggling to justify substantial but premature reputations. Others labor fruitfully in the vineyards, publishing their work in obscure magazines and small or antiestablishment publishing houses, and then emerge suddenly and spectacularly, most often because a careful reader has written the sort of detailed and appreciative review that encourages a long second look at writing not widely circulated or taken seriously.

An overriding truth about the business of publishing is that the "good" is permanently locked in a struggle for attention with the "bad." Much of the writing that pours onto the desks of literary editors at both the serious-minded but commercial general magazines and the smallest, most fiercely independent quarterlies is inept, undeveloped, amateurish, crazed, obscene, unintelligible, or some combination of the above. Sometimes the problem is developmental: The author may well have talent, but has little sense of form or is lazy about detail, mechanical or otherwise. Such writers may develop the discipline and controlled imagination necessary to engage the attention of serious readers. Others won't: They are like untrained athletes who haven't learned fundamentals, good practice habits, or how to position themselves in relation to the competition. Or they are handicapped by temperament or other cognitive shortcomings. Whatever the problem, their work must be assessed by readers who bring to every manuscript the hope that it will prove artful or publishable. Being this open is time-consuming, and can often break down into impatience, irritation, and eventually a resignation that gets in the way of attentiveness to the off-beat, slow-paced, loosely stitched, or otherwise idiosyncratic fiction offering. Fiction editors may read as many as forty or fifty stories a day, and the chances are that the ratio of good to bad will be roughly one to ten. Writers can do nothing about this, of course, but realism about the process may make living with it more comfortable.

How to Read a Rejection Slip

Virtually all magazines use printed rejection slips. Some make their points succinctly, with little attempt to soften the blow. The basic message is straightforward: "We've decided not to publish your story." Some rejection forms make a halfhearted effort to explain away the obvious: "We're not reading fiction for the time being" or "Another editor may think differently" (i.e., the problem may be ours, and not yours). A few try diplomacy: "We're grateful for the chance to read your work." And others are mildly apologetic: "We're sorry that the quantity of manuscripts we consider makes it impossible to reply to each one personally." At bottom, however, the message is no more and likely no less than, simply, "No."

Some stories returned with form rejections may have intrigued an editor or two, or even been seriously considered for publication. The vast majority, however, have simply failed to make the cut, though they may have inspired reactions ranging from instantaneous and wholly justified disenchantment to deep admiration. Either way, a writer ought to fight back the impulse to read the rejection as a repudiation, a sign of hostility, or proof of ineptitude.

Magazines that have a reputation for thoughtfulness in their selection of fiction—particularly magazines that, like the *Atlantic Monthly*, read all work submitted, whether sent by an agent, a writer, or some other friend of the court—receive many more manuscripts each day than the fiction editors can respond to individually. In a typical day, roughly 100 fiction manuscripts arrive at the *Atlantic*. Of those, no more than a dozen or two are likely to be returned with a personal reply. Apart from the most pressing reason for this impersonal response—the shortage of staff members to write personal notes—most editors would rather not explain how unimpressed they are by a story that wildly misses the mark. Nor do they want to take the time to think through and then articulate their reasons for deciding against a story whose first few sentences or paragraphs are grammatically unsound, visibly inept, or essentially incoherent. Why make explanations that can only wound? And why misrepresent your judgment by pretending admiration that isn't felt?

In short, little can safely be read into a form rejection, and the safest course, it seems to me, is to accept the verdict as gracefully as possible and to try other markets—very quickly, so as to transfer emotional energy from the depleting slough of despond to the hopefulness that arises while a manuscript is "under consideration elsewhere." One writer I know took the further step of using his rejection forms as a style of interior decoration. He covered his bathroom door with them, and thus greeted each new one as an artistic challenge: He sought the most pleasing assemblage of typefaces, paper qualities, and manner of editorial apologetics.

Some magazines confuse the issue by using more than one rejection form. The *Atlantic Monthly*, for many years, sent a rejection slip printed in italics, conveying measured admiration for the work being returned and apologizing for the necessity of the printed form. Many writers who received this form (some of whom had long experience with the more cursory basic rejection) believed they were finally on the verge of an important breakthrough and would remind us with every submission that they were now among the chosen. Little could they have imagined that those italicized forms were intended, by a now-departed editor, to be sent to the population groups who seemed most likely to expect special handling: the very old, the very young, prison inmates, mental patients, and others with an exaggerated sense of professional importance. Editors or others at *The New Yorker* have for years diluted the damaging potency of form rejection by adding, in pencil, the simple word *sorry*. I'm certain that thousands of would-be *New Yorker* contributors have been heartened by that small note of personal regret, and have felt, rightly or wrongly, that an actual person had read their story submission and had felt right at home in it.

A significant step up from the rejection form is the personal letter, no matter how brief or general in its response. Fiction editors rarely write such letters unless they've seen writing of real quality, even in stories they don't want to publish. The exceptions: manuscripts from writers who seem to warrant a personal response by virtue of professional reputation, personal acquaintance, or documented volatility. Editors know, however, that once a writer hears personally from an editor that writer will expect personal communiqués from then on. As a consequence, the temptation to use form rejections is all but irresistible.

The personal letter may or may not offer detailed criticism or suggestions for the repair of "flawed" stories. One reason they don't: Some writers are fiercely protective of the quirkiness in their work and resist the idea that editorial resistance equates with authorial flaw. Editors are entitled to their opinions, such writers reason, but the "problem" may be less in the writing than in the limitations of the readers. From time to time this position is surely justified, and writers ought not to blithely accept criticisms of their stories that don't seem sensible or sensitive to their intentions. On the other hand, the editors are speaking for the sensibilities that determine what is chosen for *publication* and what is not, and their letters should be read with that practical object in mind—and not taken as definitive judgments of a story's worth, tactical logic, promise, or objective coherence. A balance is useful, however, between writers' wholly understandable and necessary obligation to defend their work and the possibility that an editor's trained eye has spotted genuine flaws or has at least made intelligible the reason(s) for rejection.

In most cases, the editor will have responded favorably to aspects of the work and is hoping that a revision, or another story by the same author, will lead to publication. The desirability of this stance cannot be overstated, and wise writers will do all that is possible to nurture it—all that is possible, once again, without abandoning their creative vision and purpose.

Cover Letters

Most short story submissions arrive accompanied by a cover letter, introducing the story and its author and effecting a sort of breaking of the ice, rather like a handshake greeting with a complete stranger. This introduction is a good idea, for the same reason that a brief, general greeting helps set the stage for other, more complicated social occasions. The absence of a cover letter signifies if not a disdain for interpersonal protocol, at least an indifference to it. I doubt that a publishable story has ever been turned away simply because its author failed to send a cover letter, but editors are as susceptible as anyone to the small gestures that convey friendliness. Just as an overly aggressive or inappropriately personal greeting can undermine a social transaction before it has a chance to develop, so too a poorly conceived cover letter can discourage an editor from proceeding on to read the story to which it is attached.

Some mistakes are fundamental. Few editors like to have a story submission explained to them, and few experienced writers feel they can "explain" in a few short sentences what required the length of their narrative to express. Indeed, stories that can easily be summarized in a sentence or two may be little more than exercises extending or dramatizing the proposition embedded in those sentences. In general, the more sophisticated and successful writers resist the impulse to encapsulate stories that, to borrow from Archibald MacLeish, "must not mean, but be."

To make matters worse, writers, particularly beginning writers, are not always clear about the purposes or effects of their stories, and their cheerfully sculpted explanations may differ markedly from the conclusions likely to be drawn by a careful reader. Better by far to let the story speak for itself.

Another occasional error, usually made by beginners (and thus inadvertently damning—why advertise your relative lack of experience when what you hope to do is convince an editor of your wisdom and mastery of craft?), is a reference to the response of other magazines to the story now being submitted, or, in extreme cases, a copy of another magazine's rejection letter.

While intended, no doubt, to suggest long and complicated involvement with the inner world of literary publishing, this recounting of one's history of rejection has several unintended consequences, none of them fortuitous. In addition to announcing yourself as a beginner, your shared confidence permits magazine editors to surmise at least the following: (1) Their magazines are well below the top of your list of preferred markets; (2) Their magazines may even be the sort of "what's to lose" fallback options, to be exercised only once you've exhausted the markets you think may be appropriate for your story.

The truth, of course, may be quite different. A writer's order of submission may have to do with which editors he knows personally, for example, or a willingness to honor a specific request for material from one editor or another. These aren't matters to be discussed in a cover letter, however, and the best solution is to keep a dignified silence about them.

In keeping with the above, a battered, coffee-stained, oft-folded-and-unfolded manuscript suggests that a story has been making the rounds for years without success. Prickly editors may well come up with, and be displeased by, the notion that their magazines are courts of last resort.

These matters aside, some writers believe their cover letters provide an opportunity to catch the eye of an editor with witticisms, evidence of substantial ego strength, or thinly disguised declarations of artistic independence. These messages do catch the eye of editors, but historically they have been coupled with inept or artless manuscripts so frequently that their unhappy effect is often to discourage further reading.

One writer, for example, sent me a cover letter with the following candid note:

> I have taken writing courses at [schools A, B, and C] but none of them have done me much good. Currently I teach at [school D], where they have been unable to nullify my contract. My publication list is unimpressive, and I am ugly.

This is hardly an in-your-face cover letter, and it conveys, at the least, a disarming humility. It does not, however, inspire an editor to read further.

Another, noticeably less self-effacing writer accompanied a story submission with a letter that included the following:

> This [story one of a series] is enclosed for your reading satisfaction. You won't understand it, so don't even try. All you need to do is assess its value.
>
> You must naturally assume that the less you understand of it, the better it is. All you need to determine is whether or not you can market this talent. That you are inept at judging its merit I already know from experience. That you will probably waste a lot of time and continue in your blindness, I already know.
>
> I think very little of your profession. People like you have been wasting my time for almost half my life now. Since I already know that the likelihood that you are qualified is extremely low, would you please do me the favor of responding in a timely fashion so that I may attempt some other method of gaining notoriety?

All this from a writer unknown to us and submitting to the *Atlantic*, so far as we could tell, for the first time. This letter has the virtue of finely honed pugnacity, and it makes mildly interesting reading. But would any thoughtful reader expect the story attached to it to be inspiring or artfully imagined?

What should a good cover letter include? In my judgment it can provide at least two kinds of helpful information—helpful in the sense that it may dispose the editor to whom it is addressed to give the accompanying story the benefit of the doubt, to trust that if the beginning is slow or eccentric, further reading may reward. The information that may fortify an editor's willingness to push on is this: (1) citations of stories published elsewhere, particularly in periodicals of comparable size and reputation; and (2) mention of the fact that the writer is or has been enrolled in a reputable MFA program or has in some other way (residence at Bread Loaf or Sewanee, for example) demonstrated an interest in writing as a long-term endeavor, along with a willingness to be helped toward that end.

Virtually all editors of serious fiction realize that today's Iowa or Stanford or Johns Hopkins MFA student may be tomorrow's Raymond Carver, Flannery O'Connor, or Ethan Canin. These and other graduate writing programs generate a steady flow of talented, still-forming writers of fiction, and work from such programs tends to merit close readings.

Finally, a cover letter ought to be brief and to the point. It should not be an impediment to respectful attention, and it may greatly increase a writer's opportunity to be read with seriousness and conditioned hopefulness.

How to Get a Grant

by Scott Bane

Scott Bane is a manager of the New York City–based JEHT Foundation.

So admit it: Whenever you read about a poet, fiction writer, or creative-nonfiction writer who has been awarded a large grant or a prestigious fellowship, you can't help but fantasize about what that money, and the time it bought, would do for your work and career. A small grant might cover your tuition at a writers workshop for a week, while a large one could cover your living expenses for a year. You know there's money out there for literary artists in the form of fellowships and grants sponsored by private foundations and nonprofit literary organizations, but not much of it has come your way. Sometimes it's easy to assume "it's all a matter of who you know," but that wouldn't be accurate or helpful. Obviously there's no guaranteed formula, but as with many aspects of the writing profession, there are certain steps you can take to better your odds. And as with the process of getting published, though you may receive many rejections along the way, it takes only one "yes."

Grants and fellowships are cash stipends paid to literary artists by foundations, nonprofit literary organizations, and governmental agencies. As tax-exempt institutions, foundations and nonprofits exist for charitable purposes as defined by the Internal Revenue Service. Beyond applicable tax codes, though, they are at liberty to define for themselves how they will support literary artists and the literary community. Foundations are as different from one another as the people who endow them; nonprofits are as diverse as the individuals who found them. This is the first lesson for grant-seekers: No two funders are exactly alike. It is important to remember this, as it will inform each step of the funding process, sometimes overtly, sometimes subtly. Savvy grant-

93

seekers learn to develop strategies that can accommodate these idio-syncrasies.

While research is time-consuming, if done carefully, it will save you time, money, energy, and heartache and increase your chances of get-ting a grant. Several trade journals and magazines list opportunities for writers, including this one, and the writing organization Poets, Essay-ists and Novelists (PEN) publishes *Grants and Awards Available to American Writers*, which is updated every two years. But one of the most comprehensive collections of information for writers looking for fund-ing is the Foundation Center, a nonprofit resource center devoted to promoting public understanding of philanthropy. It has branches in At-lanta, Cleveland, New York City, San Francisco, and Washington, D.C. If you live in one of these areas, a visit would be worth your time.

At any of these branches you can research grant-makers, review trade publications, and consult with Center librarians free of charge. While the Foundation Center publishes a book entitled *Foundation Grants to Individuals*, the database of the same entries on CD-ROM is easier for most users. It includes a tutorial that walks you through the process of creating searches, reviewing funder profiles, and printing out records.

When you create a search, you should choose "Literature" as your field of interest. (The database is not broken down by genre.) However, depending on what type of work you do, you may also want to look un-der "Arts," "Humanities," or another related field in order to find addi-tional potential funders. Once the results of your search are in, you'll be able to review grant-maker profiles, which include contact information, financial data, type of genres supported, application procedures, publi-cations available, and a description of the program. The Foundation Center's database condenses relevant information for grant-seekers to help them decide whether they want to pursue more in-depth research on a particular organization.

If you don't live near one of the Foundation Center's branches or don't have the time to visit, the Foundation Center's Web site (fdncenter. org) offers an abundance of information, including a listing of over 70,000 private, community, corporate, government, and nonprofit U.S. grant-makers in all fields, not just literature, and a search engine de-signed to harvest information from the Internet on philanthropic sup-port and related topics. Information will not be as easily targeted as it is on the Center's *Foundation Grants to Individuals* database, since the Web site's search engine is similar to any other in which a number of solid hits are captured together with superfluous material. A poet or writer will have to spend time combing through the hits to distinguish between useful and extraneous information. Still, the site is easy to navigate and offers the majority of its services free of charge, and carefully constructed searches will yield results.

When entering the Foundation Center's Web site to use the search engine, grant-seekers should click on the button "Finding Funders." From there writers or poets can narrow a search with the help of "Sector Search." Key phrases to input might include: *creative writing, fiction, poetry, fellowships, funding for individuals, grants to individuals.* It is important that you specify *fellowships, grants to individuals,* or some variation of this idea, because many private foundations do not support individual artists directly. You may also want to limit your search by geographic location, gender, race, age, sexual orientation, religious affiliation, or some other characteristic, since many funders target specific populations of writers and poets. Limiting your search will help you connect with the funders that most reflect who you are as an artist. It will also help narrow your search to a manageable number of hits. An advanced search of *grants to individuals* recently yielded 28,449 hits. Using *creative writing* as a restrictive term on the same search reduced that number to 2,719, while specifying the state, in this case Minnesota, turned up 543 hits. Although this is still a considerable number, a short list can be arrived at fairly quickly, and the search process is comparatively convenient and economical. Even if you don't have a computer at home, you can sign up for some free Internet time at your local library.

The main advantage of research based on CD-ROM or the Web is speed. But you shouldn't overlook the value of print resources, especially if you are an emerging writer with only a few publications. Print listings will typically include funders that make smaller gifts, in the $500–$2,500 range, while grant-makers with their own Web sites, those most easily picked up using a search engine, will likely be larger funders that more often support established artists. This is changing to some extent as more and more funders develop a presence on the Internet, but using a combination of electronic and print resources will be the most thorough and efficient approach to your research.

The next step is to begin reviewing guidelines. Guidelines describe what a grant-maker does and does not fund. The preferred method of reading them is on a funder's Web site, because it's fast. If funders don't have Web sites, then you will need to contact them by telephone or in writing to request their guidelines. The receptionist will be able to help you or tell you to whom your request should be addressed. Grant-makers are very familiar with these queries. Whether visiting funders' Web sites or contacting them, you want to get as much information about them as you possibly can. You should request copies of their guidelines, a recent annual report (or grants list), and an application form. You should also ask if the foundation or nonprofit has any other materials that it sends to grant-seekers, such as a list of frequently asked questions or profiles of past grant recipients. Remember that each organization will be a little bit different, different in what it funds and different in what it distributes. Once you begin reading through guidelines and annual reports, you will develop a better sense of any additional materials you might need. But the important strategy for grant-seekers at this initial stage of their search is: information, information, information. The more information you have about a funder, the better positioned you will be to submit a smarter proposal.

Before actually digging into some guidelines, here are some general rules:

Do . . .

- *Follow the funder's guidelines exactly for manuscript submission.* Some funders go so far as to specify the sizes of left, right, top, and bottom margins for a manuscript. The Loft, a nonprofit literary organization in Minneapolis, has a funny and helpful essay on its Web site (www.loft.org/contests.htm) that gives tips on how to prepare manuscripts for contests. Many of these suggestions apply to making submissions to funders as well.
- *Call and ask questions if you don't understand something in the application materials.* Many questions can be cleared up quickly. If a funder has a staff, assistants and secretaries can be very knowledgeable about basic procedures; use them as a resource. However, if the funder states in application materials that it doesn't accept phone calls, don't call.

- *Be brief and concise.* Observe word limits on autobiographical statements and essay questions. Many funders review hundreds of inquiries and proposals each year. You have limited time to get your point across; make the best use of it.
- *List other grants received if asked on the application.* It's a stamp of approval to have been supported by another funder. As in other professional communities, members of the philanthropic and nonprofit communities know and talk to one another.
- *Ask for the right amount.* Many funders will have set amounts for which grant-seekers apply. If a funder typically makes $1,000 grants and you ask for a $10,000 grant, your chances of getting approved fall precipitously. Your request shows that you haven't done your homework, and your application is likely to be weak in other areas.
- *Demonstrate that you have enough money to cover the complete cost of your project.* If you plan a $5,000 trip to India to research your novel and are applying for a $2,500 grant from a funder, you should be able to point to an additional $2,500 from other sources to cover total expenses. Unless you can do so, no funder will want to support your project, because it's inadequately funded right from the start and thus likely to fail.
- *Plan for the funder's taking a generous amount of time to make a decision.* Funders often follow a thorough review process that culminates with a final decision by a board of directors or other governing body that may meet only a few times a year. Many funders take four to six months from receipt of an application to announce results; others may take longer. Funders generally are not set up to respond to emergency requests, nor do they see it as their role.

Don't . . .

- *Apply to foundations that do not accept applications* (for example, the Lannan Foundation and the Mrs. Giles Whiting Foundation). You will receive no support from these funders until the day you get that unexpected telephone call or letter saying that you've been chosen.
- *Exaggerate your publication credentials.* They are easily checked. Having a letter to the editor published in *The New Yorker* is not the same

as having a poem accepted by the magazine. Funders will investigate all applicants' claims.

- *Apply to funders whose guidelines you obviously don't fit.* If a funder supports older women writers, as does the Thanks Be to Grandmother Winifred Foundation, and you're a twenty-something male poet, don't waste your time or theirs.
- *Send videos, audiotapes, or press clippings with your query or application unless specifically requested to do so by the funder.* Even if your videotape captures your stellar performance at last month's poetry slam, don't send it unless the funder asks for it.
- *Blindly approach funders just because they make large grant awards.* Obviously, the temptation is great, because the need is even greater. But it's fairly safe to assume that the larger the grant or fellowship award, the more competitive the process will be.

In short, follow the stated guidelines. Not following them just marks your application for an easy rejection.

Now for the tricky part: figuring out how funders interpret their own guidelines. Stated guidelines are general limitations to funding; not following them will get your application declined, but following them will not necessarily ensure that you'll get a grant, for the simple reason that there are more talented poets, fiction writers, and creative-nonfiction writers out there than there are financial resources to support them all. To determine how grant-makers translate their guidelines into grants, you'll need to look carefully at the autobiographical statements and published work of past grant recipients and to think seriously about each funder's mission.

Broadly stated, a funder's mission is its individual approach to grant-making. Some grant-makers focus on the quality of the art alone. Others believe emerging artists are most important to the field. Still others advocate for greater diversity among poets and writers. This information will often be stated at the beginning of a funder's annual report or guidelines, but may not be labeled as such. It can sometimes be found in the history of the organization or in the biographical sketch of a foundation's donor. While you want to be yourself and truthfully portray your career and work, there are ways to present your grant application so that it aligns your work squarely with a funder's mission. Grant recipients may or may not be better writers or poets than the rest of us, but many of them have learned to craft their applications so they appeal to funders.

Most grant applications will call for the following: a cover sheet of contact information, an artistic and/or autobiographical statement, responses to essay questions, and a manuscript submission. Contact information is in most cases straightforward, but some grant-makers who limit their funding to a state or region will require an applicant to verify residency through income tax returns, voter registration information, or other documentation. You should be prepared to provide copies of these documents if asked to do so.

Artistic and autobiographical statements are more complex. You should keep an autobiographical statement or résumé on your computer to make it easier to tailor for individual funders. It should include publications, education, awards, residencies, scholarships or fellowships, and any relevant work experience. Not every funder will require these materials, but many will, so it is helpful to have them handy. You should also be ready to describe your artistic interests in terms of either form or content (it depends on the funder), your creative process, and anything else that will help convey a context for your work.

The key to autobiographical statements or essay questions is to make them well integrated with the rest of your application and with the funder's mission. The Kentucky Foundation for Women (www.kfw. org), a progressive funder of women artists, for example, asks its applicants how their work will further social change, as well as what their most meaningful artistic accomplishment has been to date. Given these two questions, a strong candidate likely will be one whose most important artistic accomplishment involved social change. You don't want to lie about yourself, your interests, or your work, but a poet whose essay portrays her as socially conscious and explains how her proposal involves social change is going to be advanced in the review process over one who has not established a track record in this area. Funders likely will think that if she were to receive a grant, she would use it successfully for the intended purpose. She's done it before; she'll do it again.

Looking at the published work or autobiographical statements of a funder's current or past grant recipients is a good place to begin thinking about manuscript submission. Amazon.com's search engine or your local library's card catalog are excellent ways to see if a writer has been published. If you can't find any publications for a funded writer, it's probable that the funder supports writers at early stages of their careers or creative development. Autobiographical statements typically appear on the funder's Web site or in its annual report. Looking at poets' or writers' work and reading their autobiographical statements are the best ways to gauge the level of artistic development expected by the funder. But this material will tell you other things as well. Is experimental work supported? Do common themes and subjects emerge? Is there a noticeable absence of other subjects? Does a funder of literary artists in Oregon favor work about life in the state, even though it doesn't say so explicitly in its guidelines, or is the field wide open?

The New York Foundation for the Arts (www.nyfa.org) states on its Web site that it "helps artists turn inspiration into art." The published autobiographical statements of its 2002 grant recipients make these terms a little more concrete to the applicant who takes the time to review the submissions and statements of past recipients: Out of a list of nineteen grant recipients, over half describe making cross-cultural connections in their work. Thus, a Korean American fiction writer who examines dual cultural identity in his work might have a good shot at being supported by this funder, depending on competition in a particular batch of applications. Looking at the work of past or current grant recipients will give you important insights as to how a funder interprets its guidelines.

Another important question to answer is, Who makes decisions? In many cases funders hire artists who are not affiliated with the organization to submit recommendations to the board of directors, which has the final vote on applicants. If a funder lists the writers or poets who make up its nominating or advisory committee, then you are well advised to look at the work of these judges, asking yourself if you share an aesthetic with them. People pick what they like, and much of decision making in the creative world is a matter of taste. If nominators are kept secret, then you should go back and look at the work of past grant recipients to determine their level of artistic development and to see if they share any common themes or styles.

Because nominators and advisers are usually paid for their time, their services are often a luxury only larger funders can afford. At smaller foundations, the board of directors may be actively involved in both the review and the decision-making process. This is particularly true if the board is composed of artists. The difficulty in such a situation is that the grant recipient will need to be someone upon whom everyone, or at least a majority, can agree. One or two negative responses from board members can easily derail an otherwise strong application. One possible tip-off that a board directly reviews applications is the requirement that applicants submit multiple copies of their materials. Unless you feel that you have a pretty strong chance of fitting such a funder's program (i.e., your work measures up to that of past recipients and you meet other guidelines), you may not want to invest too much of your time on this application, because the chance of its being declined based on individual tastes—the imagery in your poems leaves one or two board members cold—increases with each board member who will interpret the funder's mission a little bit differently from his or her colleagues.

Once you've gotten this far in your information-gathering and strategizing, you'll have already done the bulk of the hard work. You'll know which funders you want to apply to, and more important, why. Filling out applications, polishing and formatting your manuscript, and tweaking any other documents in your application will be the easy part. But it will inevitably happen that someone puts all this work into an application and it's still turned down. The rule here is: Don't give up. Some funders will provide feedback on declined applications (the Leeway Foundation in Philadelphia—www.leeway.org—does), and if they do, you'll want to get all the information you can. If a funder's materials don't mention feedback, ask if someone will talk to you on an informal basis. This information could be very useful in preparing your application to the next funder, and in many instances, being declined by a funder does not bar you from reapplying at a later date. A writer should consider reapplying to a funder if she feels that her work and career are comparable with those of past recipients, or if the funder uses outside judges or nominators who change from year to year. You may find a like-minded judge next year. One benefit of applying to foundations and nonprofits is that many of them either have or raise money to cover overhead, so there are usually only minimal fees at worst. Remember, don't give up, because all it takes is one "yes."

And what if your application is accepted and you get a grant? Congratulations! The money will provide crucial support to help you do your work, and will give your résumé an important boost. A grant from a foundation or literary nonprofit will look good to artists colonies and agents, not to mention other funders. Nothing breeds success like success. There will also be award letters and forms to sign, and, later, reports to write on how the grant was spent and, perhaps, meetings to attend to describe your experience to other grant recipients. In terms of your reporting, you should address whether you were able to fulfill the expectations of your application; if you weren't, you should have a good reason why. All these matters are important, but they are pretty straightforward, too. For money and recognition send clear messages, and no doubt you won't have too much trouble figuring out what to do next: write.

Building Your Team:
How to Work Well with
Publishing Professionals

How to Land an Agent:
Strategies for the Search

by Noah Lukeman

Noah Lukeman is a New York–based literary agent and best-selling author.

As a literary agent, I've come into contact with thousands of authors over the years, and many tell me the same story: They spent years completing a manuscript, approached the publishing industry, were rejected, and gave up (if not in general, then at least on a particular manuscript). When I ask them what their "approach" consisted of, they invariably tell me they sent their manuscripts to a handful of agents (usually about six) over the course of several years, and based on those rejections, deemed themselves to have been officially turned down by the publishing industry.

When I inquire further, I discover that in nearly every case the authors made two fatal errors: They approached inappropriate agents for their work, and they approached them improperly, so that even if they had been the right agents, the outcome most likely would have been the same. After years of working on their manuscripts, after laboring over every word, these authors never even gave themselves a chance.

There do exist immensely talented artists who simply do not know how to approach the industry, and as a result, never get discovered. It is depressing, not because they've been rejected by the publishing industry (in reality, they haven't), but because a few tips could have saved them years of needless waiting, of putting their careers on hold—could have even, in many cases, made the difference in their manuscripts being published. These simple, concrete tips are what this article offers.

To begin with, you will need to find an agent. Querying publishers directly is a mistake. If you try, you'll find that the majority of them will simply return your query letter and instruct you to find an agent. And if by some remote chance a publisher does respond to your query letter and eventually accepts your manuscript for publication, you, as an unagented author, will likely be offered a smaller advance, and will be left to negotiate a contract on your own.

In addition, querying publishers directly is potentially detrimental to a future relationship with an agent, because if you actually manage to get the attention of an editor at a major publishing house and your work is rejected (as will likely happen), and you subsequently find an agent, the agent will have a harder time submitting that work to that house. When an editor rejects a manuscript he rejects it on behalf of his publishing company. Because industry etiquette discourages agents from submitting the same work to two different editors at the same house, your agent will not be able to approach any publisher that has already rejected you. Thus, you may narrow a legitimate agent's chances of success, which also means the agent will be less likely to offer you representation. (The only case where it might make sense to query a publisher directly would be if you had written a book you were confident agents would not want to represent—for example, if it were intended for a small, local, regional, specialty, or technical publisher.)

So, for the vast majority of writers, the first step is finding an agent. It's not as difficult as it might seem, but it does take time and effort. After years of working hard on a manuscript, a writer is understandably excited, and the impulse is to immediately get it onto others' desks. However, rushing into the submission process can hurt your chances. Indeed, it never ceases to amaze me that writers will spend years writing their manuscripts yet only a few hours deciding its fate by hastily and randomly creating a list of agents out of a (usually outdated) guide. The reason 99 percent of manuscripts get rejected is, simply, because writers have approached the wrong agents. As writers, we know there is no comparison between a good word and the perfect word. Similarly, there is no comparison between any agent and an appropriate agent.

To compile a list of appropriate agents, thorough research is required—not three hours' worth but three months' worth. Such information used to be difficult to obtain; today, however, there are abundant resources that were unavailable to writers ten years ago. Indeed, because of them, the writer of today stands a much greater chance of being published. Writing is not a business, but getting published is, and when it comes time to approach the publishing industry, it is also time to switch a writer's hat for a private investigator's hat, and to commit to the research and preparation necessary to make sure your work is seen by the right people, in the right way.

Below are thirteen good resources to help you get started. As you do your research, write down not only the name of the agent but also the book titles and authors he handles. This information will be crucial when it comes time to approach the agent (to be explored later). Don't stop until you've gathered the names and contact information of at least fifty appropriate agents.

Free Resources

Deal Lunch

Deal Lunch (www.publisherslunch.com) is a free, weekly e-newsletter that reports the latest publishing deals. It is probably the single best resource for writers for several reasons: It is free; it reports deals regardless of how big the advance; it offers up-to-the-minute information; it lands right in your e-mail inbox; it reports an abundance of deals, sometimes more than fifty every week; and it names the agents involved in the deals, their agency, and a description of the book they sold. If you study this newsletter alone for several weeks, you will likely be able to build a list of appropriate agents for your work. Potential downside: Any agent (or editor) can report a deal, so it is possible that in any given week there might be agents mentioned who are not as consistently effective as other agents, or who charge reading fees (more on this later). In general, look for the names of agents who land deals with major publishers or who represent authors known to you. And of course, all information gathered here (as with any resource) should be triple-checked and cross-referenced with information gathered elsewhere.

Publishers Weekly *on the Web*

Publishers Weekly's Web site (www.publishersweekly.com) posts a "Hot Deals" link that offers reliable, free information on major deals consummated in the previous week or so, listing names of agents. Possible downside: *PW* tends to be more exclusive than other sources when reporting deals. Many listings will likely be substantial (six figures or more), which often means the reported agents are more established, which often means they are less likely to take on new clients. The site, in general, offers a wealth of free industry information, as does the magazine's free weekly e-newsletter, *PW Daily*. These resources might not be as directly relevant to your needs, but it never hurts to absorb industry information—and you might even encounter an article that drops the name of an agent who interests you.

Search Engines

Search engines allow you to look up pertinent information by typing in relevant search terms, such as literary agent. (I just tried it on Google and it yielded 339,000 pages.) It can take you months to sort through all of these pages, and much of the information may be irrelevant, but a casual search might reveal an agency site or listing (or other piece of relevant information) you missed elsewhere.

Literary Agencies

Many literary agencies now have their own Web sites. Typing the name of an agent or agency into a major search engine (like Google or Yahoo) will often yield the exact URL within seconds. Some agency sites are extensive, and you will be able to glean a lot of up-to-the-minute information about the agency you won't find elsewhere. Often you'll find a comprehensive client list, recent deals, current submission requirements and preferences, change of address or contact information, or notification that the agency is no longer accepting queries—all of which can save you time and energy.

Publishersmarketplace.com

Publishersmarketplace.com contains some free information that can be useful to aspiring authors. (Fee-based information on this site is discussed later.) Most relevant will be its listings of the "10 most visited agents" on the site. If you follow these links you can learn more about them, their clients, and the deals they've done. This feature is updated frequently, so it's worth checking back regularly.

Acknowledgments Pages

Acknowledgments pages in published books often contain a reference to an author's agent. Spend some time in large bookstores (and libraries) browsing acknowledgments pages. The information is often minimal, but it is yet one more source to be used for cross-referencing.

Fee-Based Resources

Publishersmarketplace.com

Publishersmarketplace.com (the fee-based portion) offers a membership to the site ($15 a month), which entitles you to many features, including the use of a searchable database. Instead of being able to access only the ten most visited agents on the site, you can access information on *any* agent in the site. You can also enter the name of a particular book or author you feel is similar to your work to find the name of the agent. The database might not be as effective for older deals (three or more years in the past), but for recent deals it is excellent.

Publishers Weekly "Rights Alert"

Publishersweekly.com offers a fee-based e-newsletter, *PW Rights Alert* ($199 a year), which it sends out twice a week. Each issue averages about ten or more recent deals. The newsletter also includes *PW*'s "starred reviews" of soon-to-be-published books, which often list the names of the books' agents. It is a similar service to *Deal Lunch*, except that it appears twice weekly and tends to be more selective in reporting deals.

Writersmarket.com

The online counterpart to the successful *Writer's Market* book offers a service, for approximately $30 a year, that gives you online access to its database of agents. The information is fairly comprehensive and up-to-date, since it's online. Of the fee-based online services, this is certainly one of the least expensive and can be very helpful for cross-referencing information. Incidentally, writersmarket.com also offers a free Q&A with agents, which it archives on its site.

Agent Research & Evaluation

Agentresearch.com is a fee-based service that gives you information on the agents in its private database. It offers a variety of services, from a newsletter ($35) to a "customized fingerprint" matching you to agents ($330). The benefit of the service is that the information it gives about the agent, in multiple-page reports, tends to be extensive, probably offering more in-depth information than other services about the agent, his clients, and the deals done. Downside: It is expensive for many writers. Also, the criteria for including an agent's deals in the database are so strict that AR&E's report on an agent might not include every deal that agent has actually done. (For instance, it reports me as having only 17 identified clients, when in actuality I've represented more than 100.)

Books

Books that list agents and are updated yearly are often relatively inexpensive and yield a tremendous amount of information. The disadvantage is that they can quickly become dated (often there is at least a six-month delay between the time the information was collected and the time the book appears in print), so any information gathered in these books must be verified using other sources.

A few of the good books out there are *Guide to Literary Agents* and *Writer's Market* both from *Writer's Digest*; Jeff Herman's *Writer's Guide to Book Editors, Publishers, and Literary Agents*; and *Literary Marketplace* (known as the *LMP*). The latter is expensive (around $300), so it is probably best used as a reference in your local library. It tends to list little information on agents' particular needs, but it is selective as to which agents it includes (an agent must receive three referrals by industry professionals in order to get listed), so the information is usually reliable. Jeff Herman's guide tends to give a lot of in-depth information on agents' particular needs, although it doesn't list every agent or agency.

Magazines

Magazines are likely to be more current than books, given that the information is usually only a month or two old by the time it hits the newsstands. Also, you are likely to stumble across an in-depth article or interview with an agent that yields a lot more information than you might find elsewhere. *Poets & Writers Magazine*, of course, has always been an excellent resource, and continues to be. The same holds true for *The Writer*, *Writer's Digest*, and *Publishers Weekly*, the hard copy of which yields unique information on agents in its "Hot Deals" section and in the "Forecasts" section at the end of its book reviews. Even some literary magazines occasionally run interviews with agents. And of course, all of these magazines have informative Web sites where you can garner much information for free.

Conferences

There are a plethora of conferences out there, and I wouldn't necessarily recommend all of them. But there are a handful that attract good agents. The key in choosing a conference is finding out in advance which agents are attending, and the ratio of agents to writers. Sometimes it is possible to establish a personal connection with an agent at a conference through a consultation, workshop, talk, or chance meeting. At the very least, you can walk away knowing more about the needs of a few of them. Possible downside: These conferences can be expensive for many writers; thus I would recommend attending only if you have the money to spare.

As you do your research, also take into account other variables: Consider how established the agent is (how many years she has been in the business and how many books she's sold), to which publishers she has sold books (large or small, literary or commercial), how many clients she already represents, and whether she is actively looking to take on new clients. All of this information will be helpful in determining not just the agent's legitimacy (to be explored below) but her appropriateness for you. For instance, the longer the agent has been in the business, the less likely she may be to take on new clients. Or, if an agent has sold a book similar to yours, she might not want to take on your manuscript for fear of competing with her own client.

As a rule of thumb, beginning writers stand a much better chance of landing an agent if they target one who is just starting out, someone who has been an agent for three years or less, someone who has proven himself by securing at least a few deals with major houses but is actively looking for more clients. Just because an agent is starting out doesn't make him any less competent or capable; in fact, it often makes him work harder on your behalf, which can make the difference in getting you your first deal.

Once you've completed your research and compiled a list of fifty agents, you are ready for the next phase of action: the approach. If fifty names seems excessive to you, keep in mind that it could make the difference in getting published or not. No matter how appropriate an agent may seem, landing one (like landing a publisher) is ultimately a numbers game. Nearly every book I've sold as an agent had first been rejected by at least twenty publishers. If I'd given up after ten or even nineteen rejections, these books would never have been published. I don't take it personally when the rejections come; I understand that no matter how appropriate an editor may seem, editors have different needs at different times. If multiple editors end up wanting the book, great; if not, I am prepared. The same should hold true for you.

I recommend your sending a query letter (more on this later) to five or ten agents at a time—for instance, in five rounds of ten agents. I would wait no longer than four weeks to hear back; if you haven't landed an agent by that time, send off the next round. This is important, because many writers wait for months or even years to hear back; this unnecessarily delays the process and can even hold up your career. I can't tell you how many writers I've met who tell me they've been querying agents for many years regarding a particular manuscript and are waiting to "see how it goes" before they think about starting their next book. In actuality, the entire process of querying fifty agents should take no longer than six months.

If one or more of these agents requests sample pages, send them, but also keep querying other agents; if an agent requests exclusivity—that is, that she be given an exclusive time period to consider your manuscript—you need to decide if it's worth it to oblige her, because granting exclusivity will put your querying process on hold for that given time period. You need to decide on the seriousness of the agent's interest, the quality of the agent or agency, and the duration of exclusive reading time requested. In general, I would advise you to indeed give the exclusivity, but to limit it to a certain period of time (for instance, six or eight weeks for a 250-page manuscript), and to advise the agent of this. If you don't hear back in the given time period, resume querying.

Of course, this can get messy: If during that exclusive time period another agent contacts you and requests to see the manuscript, you are in a tough spot. You'll have to simply wait until the exclusive six or eight weeks are over; then, if you haven't heard back positively from the first agent, send it off immediately to the second agent. But what if the first agent you sent it to is a lesser agent, while the second one is your dream agent? Do you risk potentially alienating the dream agent by making him wait eight weeks? And would you even *want* to sign with the lesser agent if the dream agent is potentially interested?

To prevent situations like this, it is best, when sending out your rounds, to try to submit to agents who are on a par with one another at the same time, and to start with the top agents first. Still, publishing is not a science, and awkward situations can easily arise, each of them different. In general, the best thing to do is to be up front with everyone, to honor your word when you give it, and to be very careful when deciding to whom you will make a commitment. No matter how awkward it might potentially become, it is still better than the alternative, which is waiting for several months or years while agents consider your query letter and manuscript one at a time.

In general, don't call, since agents (who are overpressured as it is) will construe this as too much pressure. When in doubt, always err on the least aggressive path: Not calling or not showing up at an agent's door will never hurt you, but calling, faxing, e-mailing, or "dropping by" unannounced might just tip the scales in the wrong direction.

If an agent asks to see a revised version of the work, and her comments are specific as to what she'd like to see revised and you agree with them, then give it a shot. However, don't assume a nice or long rejection letter detailing problems with the work is an invitation to revise and resubmit; only come to that conclusion if the agent specifically requests to see another version. In most cases, if an agent rejects a work and does not ask to see a revision, she will be biased against it if it comes back revised (even dramatically), and your chances of being accepted on the second round will be remote. You don't want to fall into a trap of following false leads and revising a manuscript endlessly.

I don't like advising writers to spend money, but if you can afford it, it is certainly worth spending on guaranteed overnight delivery (such as FedEx or UPS) when querying or sending requested pages. When a package that requires a signature arrives it will stand out from the masses, and it can also signal to the agent that a certain level of time and care has gone into the query, and this might help it get taken more seriously. In addition, it is always best to follow up on a request for additional material as soon as possible so that your query will remain fresh in the agent's mind. There have been many times when I've requested to see thirty or so pages based on a query and eight weeks later pages have arrived with no cover letter and no reference to my original request. Hundreds of queries and manuscripts will have passed through my hands in those eight weeks, and I'll inevitably have no recollection of who sent these thirty pages, what they're about, or why I requested them. Thus, when sending requested pages, always include a photocopy of your original query letter, a copy of the agent's request to see them, and an adequate SASE (self-addressed, stamped envelope). In addition, if the agent requests 10 pages, send 10 pages; if he requests 23, send 23. Many times I'll ask for 50 pages and receive 250, with a note saying, "You just had to see what happened on page 248!" This is the first red flag.

Finally, the query letter itself. It is an art form, and entire books have been devoted to it. Often you'll read conflicting advice, making it even harder to grasp; it is by no means a science. Here, in condensed form, is what I would recommend.

To begin with, limit your query letter to one page. In fact, the shorter the better. As Mark Twain said, "I didn't have time to write a short letter, so I wrote a long one instead." There is truth in this: A short letter is indicative of what all good writers should exhibit—economy of words. And since most query letters tend to be long, tend to cram in as much information as possible, a short letter often stands out.

I recommend three paragraphs in total. The first should consist simply of one sentence, saying something along the lines of: "I am writing to you because you represented [title] by [author], and I feel my book is similar." This is where you get to use your research, where your months of preparation pay off. When an agent sees that a writer really knows his client list and his tastes, the agent knows the writer has carefully selected him and that the work is more likely to be appropriate to his tastes. It also shows that the writer has taken extended care and effort with his approach (unlike the writer who addresses his letter "To Whom It May Concern"), and the agent knows that such care usually carries over to the writing itself.

The second paragraph should offer a brief description of the plot. Limit it to two or three sentences at most, touching on major issues such as the time, the setting, and what occurs. It is hard to describe a novel in one or two or three sentences, but it is crucial, for many reasons: It shows you've achieved enough objectivity toward your own work to be able to say what it's about; it helps the agent summarize and pitch the work; and it immediately lets the agent know if it is the type of work she's looking for. A major mistake most writers make is going on about all the twists and turns of the plot (including character names and subplots) in an initial query letter. Most agents can tell right away if it is the type of work they're looking for and don't want to spend time reading about all the twists and turns (at least not at this stage). There's always time for a one-page synopsis, which you can send if requested, or when you're sending in requested pages. The goal at this stage is merely to get the agent to pay attention to your letter and to request more.

The third paragraph should consist of your professional biography—I stress professional, since many writers elaborate more than they need to, including personal information irrelevant to their writing credentials or career. If you don't have any credentials to include, just keep it short; again, economy is best. Include relevant education or workshops, endorsements, publication credits; don't include credits that are extremely minor, however, since these won't really make a difference and might even make an agent associate you with the amateur publication.

Always include a SASE and your contact information. (I've received queries that contained no contact information, and thus was unable to contact the author.) Don't put the contact information into the precious space of the query letter itself; rather, relegate it to the letterhead. Speaking of which, I wouldn't suggest using anything overly fancy or cute or hard to read (bright pink letters in a script font won't make you stand out—it just makes it harder for the agent). Use good paper (for instance, résumé paper), with a nice, clean font. Keep the tone and content of the letter simple, formal, and direct. Don't be overly personal, cute or sales-ish, all of which can turn an agent off. Remember, you want the agent to perceive you as an artist, not a salesman.

Unfortunately, as you begin approaching this world, you'll find there are agents in the industry who prey on unsuspecting writers; often this comes in the form of a requested reading fee, or "editing" fee, or in the form of a referral to a book doctor or organization as a prerequisite for agency consideration. Be wary of scams, and stay as far away from these companies as possible. Many legitimate agents will ask to be reimbursed for certain office expenses (for example, photocopying or postage) from clients they have agreed to represent, but this will always come in the form of a detailed invoice and will be directly related to the submission of your work.

If you are asked to sign an agency agreement and you are unfamiliar with the agency or cannot easily verify its track record, you might want to first show the agreement to a publishing lawyer or other industry expert. If you do not have the funds or access to do this and are intent on moving ahead with the agent, then at the very least you might request that the agreement be limited to a specific time period (for instance, one year) with a mutually agreeable option to renew, and/or that you have an "out" clause, which allows you to terminate at will, usually with thirty or sixty days' notice. Such concerns should escalate in proportion to your lack of knowledge of the agent or agency and to your level of discomfort with (or lack of understanding of) the agreement you are being requested to sign.

There are many good sources that offer guidance on various scams, and on agency dealings and agreements. On the Internet, www.agentresearch.com offers some good basic tips; www.aar-online.org has some good questions you might ask an agent in advance; www.anothe-realm.com/prededitors lists certain agents or scams to watch out for. And there are many other resources to help you. In general, be careful, and follow your instincts. The only thing worse than not landing an agent is landing an agent who is a scam artist, who is ineffective, or who keeps you bound to an agreement you can't get out of.

If you've followed all these steps carefully and your work is rejected by all fifty agents, you can at least take comfort in knowing that the problem does not lie with your research or your approach, but likely with the writing itself.

There are countless ways to work on and improve your craft as a writer, from workshops, to writing groups, to conferences, to MFAs, to articles and books on the craft of writing—to the process of sitting down and writing itself, which is ultimately most important. How hard you're willing to work, how much time you're willing to devote, how long you're willing to stay with it until you get your break—this will make the difference. Robert Penn Warren's first two novels were rejected, as were Stephen King's first four. The world is a better place because they never gave up.

Neither should you.

Negotiate Your First Book Contract Without Losing Your Deal, Your Future, or Your Mind

by Kay Murray

Kay Murray is general counsel and assistant director of the Authors Guild.

If your first book has been accepted for publication and you are about to receive a contract in the mail, remember that half the battle in successful negotiation is understanding the other side's agenda. Publishers do not offer book contracts to new authors out of the goodness of their little (or better, nonexistent) hearts. To publishyou a book is to make a large investment, and since most publishers are in business to make money, they only offer contracts to publish books they have predicted will earn back their investment and more. The author who knows that an offer for publication has come through because professionals at a publishing company have run a detailed profit-and-loss analysis of the author's book and projected that it will make money is in a better position to negotiate the best deal possible.

When the contract arrives, you'll be tempted to sign the long and complicated document (much of it "boilerplate," convoluted and formulaic sections of one-size-fits-all legalese) without even trying to decipher, much less negotiate, it. To protect your book, your finances, and your career, resist that urge. The publisher drafted the boilerplate contract and it favors the publisher, not you. The terms you ultimately accept are the one and only set of rules that will govern your relationship with this publisher for years to come. If you sign the contract as you received it, chances are you will rue that decision later. If you have an agent, she should understand and be able to negotiate the terms, but agents agree that authors need to understand the negotiation and terms of the contracts they sign.

To simplify what may at first glance seem like a dense, impenetrable document, think of your book contract as having four components: (1) the basic dynamics of the deal: your grant to the publisher of parts of your copyright in your book—and the contract terms that embody that grant; (2) the provisions that comprise the publisher's obligations; (3) the provisions that comprise your obligations; (4) bad ideas—those provisions that are so unfavorable that you must try to eliminate or change them.

First, some negotiating basics: Arm yourself with as much information as you can get about this publisher, the market, and the industry. Do some online research, look at other books by this publisher, talk to your colleagues, and consider joining the Authors Guild, which offers written contract reviews to its members. Keep in mind that the publisher has placed a monetary value on your book, has already invested resources to make you an offer, and doesn't want to lose the deal any more than you do. Your goal, then, is to get the publisher to make its last, best offer for every important term.

You might find yourself pressured to sign quickly. Try to take control of the agenda and timing. Put your comments, questions, and requests for changes to the boilerplate in writing. If the publisher responds in kind, so much the better—the more time the company invests negotiating with you, the more concessions it's likely to make. Don't agree to anything without taking the time to think about it.

Even a first-time author can successfully negotiate many of the "standard" provisions in a typical publishing contract. The boilerplate contains lots of provisions you didn't discuss when the monetary offer came through, and you are under no obligation to accept them as written. Publishers would prefer not to have to negotiate their first-offered terms, but they understand the necessity and won't be surprised if you ask for changes. They will not resent your attempt to protect your interests (as long as you stay professional and cordial). Any publisher that does shouldn't be in the business and is not worthy of your book.

On the other hand, stay realistic. A publisher that is willing to discuss your concerns is not necessarily willing to agree to many of your requests. In the end, you'll have to accept the publisher's last, best offer for all terms, unless you decide to reject the deal. If you negotiate, though, you will surely end up with better terms than were initially offered, and you will gain your publisher's respect as a professional.

Dynamics of the Deal:
The Grant of Rights

Think of all the ways in which a literary work can be exploited commercially. (In this context "exploitation" is good.) It can be sold as a hardcover book, a "trade" or "mass market" paperback, as an "e-book," in different languages and territories; it can be excerpted in periodicals, adapted for stage, screen, radio, or audiobook, turned into merchandise, even inspire a theme park (think *Jurassic Park*). As the creator of your book, you alone own the rights to exploit it in these ways. Together, these rights comprise the copyright, and you may choose to license any combination of them.

The basic transaction involves your grant of these rights to the publisher in exchange for specified fees for each right. Naturally, the publisher wants all the rights for as long as possible, and for as little as it can get away with paying you. The dynamic of the negotiation involves your seeking to limit the scope of your grant of those rights and to get paid fairly for every right you do grant. The boilerplate "Grant of Rights" clause might call for you to grant to the publisher every possible means of exploitation, even those not yet invented, but it's in your best interest to try to limit the grant to those rights the publisher can effectively exploit. Most important, do not agree to grant the copyright in your work, and *never* stipulate that your work is a "work made for hire," which would legally make the publisher the author. Both such grants are harmful to your interests and not standard in the industry.

You'll need to grant the right to print, publish, and sell your work in book formats. With publishing conglomerates increasingly going international, many publishers routinely demand "world" rights—exclusive English-language rights in all nations. It's also appropriate to grant the rights to formats related to print publishing, such as abridgments, book clubs, reprints by another publisher, first and second serial rights (magazine excerpts before and after book publication), and sometimes audiobooks and e-books.

Secondary rights that are not directly exploited by your publisher but are instead licensed to third parties to use are known as subsidiary rights, or "sub rights." Either the primary grant or a separate clause will address these rights and the allocation of income from them. By definition, it costs your publisher very little to allow a third party (called the "sublicensee") to exploit a subsidiary right. For that reason, the publishing contract will promise the author a relatively large share of the publisher's proceeds from sublicenses. Subsidiary rights can include print-related uses, syndication, merchandising, motion picture, television, and multimedia and interactive adaptations. Foreign-territory and translation rights are sometimes treated in the contract as subsidiary rights, sometimes included in the main grant.

If you have an agent, he will reserve as many of these as he can, so that control over and income from these rights remain entirely yours. If not, and you authorize the publisher to license dramatic or multimedia rights, try to retain the right to approve the sublicenses or get other safeguards, such as the right to approve any abridgment or anthologizing; and approval over any illustrations, sound, text, or computerized effects that may be added. For digital uses, obtain assurance that the publisher will protect the work from unauthorized copying.

The Publisher's Obligations

Publication

The publisher usually promises to publish the work within twelve to eighteen months of its acceptance of the manuscript. Any period longer than twenty-four months is too long. Most contracts allow the publisher sole discretion to publish the work "in a style, manner, and price" that it determines unilaterally. You won't be able to change that, but title, design, and artwork are also key elements, so try to get the right to approve or consult over them. Insist on a right to approve any substantive changes to the manuscript, although the publisher might want that approval to be "not unreasonably withheld."

Promotion is the area in which publishers almost universally frustrate authors. Unless your contract contains specific provisions for promotion, expect nothing from the publisher beyond a listing in its catalogue and, perhaps, the mailing of promotional copies. The more money the publisher has advanced you, the more it might be willing to spend on promotion. Plan on creating your own publicity, but it is worth discussing an advertising budget and promotional plans during contract negotiations, although it is difficult to get any such promises written into the contract.

The Advance

The advance is the money paid to the author before publication that is then recouped out of royalty earnings. The advance, which is agreed upon before the issuance of the contract, has traditionally reflected projected royalties on sales of the first printing, but it's unlikely that your publisher's first offer approaches that. When negotiating your advance, try to learn the size of the planned print run and the approximate expected retail price, both of which the publisher calculated before making you an offer. Sometimes the author's share of projected subsidiary rights income can be included. Even asking if the first offer is the best the publisher can do often yields surprisingly good movement. Except for advances higher than $50,000, the publisher normally pays half of the advance when the contract is signed and the balance on acceptance of the manuscript.

Royalties

For adult hardcovers, publishers typically offer 10 percent of the retail price on the first 5,000 copies sold in the U.S., 12½ percent on the next 5,000, and 15 percent on copies sold thereafter. These primary royalty rates are usually based on the book's suggested retail (or "list") price. "Net receipts" means the amount the book retailer or distributor actually pays to the publisher, so net-based royalties usually are 40 to 50 percent lower than list-based royalties computed on the same percentage rate. Either avoid net-based royalties or try to increase your rate accordingly.

First fiction is often published in trade, or "quality" paperback form. The initial royalty rate offered for trade paperback editions is normally 7½ percent but can start at 6 percent. Sometimes a flat rate of 8 percent is offered. Some authors can do even better.

Mass-market paperbacks are the cheaper, smaller books you find for sale at newsstands and checkout lines. Most contracts provide at least 6 to 8 percent royalties on mass-market sales of up to 150,000 copies and 10 percent thereafter.

"Deep Discount" Royalty Rates

Virtually every contract provides that for copies sold at a discount of more than 45 to 48 percent or so, the royalties will be based on the publisher's *net* receipts instead of list price. These "deep discount" terms could sharply decrease your royalties and place far too much control over your royalties in the publisher's hands. An unscrupulous publisher could actually increase its profit, and give retailers a better deal, by selling at just enough of a discount to slash your royalties by up to half.

To protect yourself, try to specify that the net-based royalty will apply only when the triggering discount is given "to a purchaser outside traditional retail channels" (or a "special sale"). Do your best to increase the triggering discount percentage by at least a few percentage points. As a good compromise, agree to reduce your royalty rate by one-half of one percent for each one percent that the publisher increases the discount over the triggering percentage. Many publishers will agree to this kind of "shared loss" royalty provision.

Contracts vary in royalty rates offered for mail-order, book-club, export, and other sales outside normal trade channels. Negotiate for higher royalties for these sales, especially if you think your book might sell many copies through these channels.

Electronic Rights

Many contracts provide that e-book royalties will mirror hardcover royalties (that is, from 10 percent up to 15 percent of retail price); this amount ignores the low retail price of e-books. The costs of production and distribution are dramatically lower than the costs for print editions, so it is better to try for as high as 50 percent of the publisher's net income from sales of e-books (Random House offers that rate), or to agree to negotiate e-book royalties if and when an e-book is marketed.

Subsidiary Rights Royalties

If you grant sub rights to the publisher, don't agree to give the publisher more than 10 to 15 percent of the income for motion picture, merchandising, and similar rights (25 percent for foreign sublicenses). The division of income for print-related sub rights is usually one-half to the author, one-half to the publisher. It is unacceptable for any publisher to take more than 50 percent for *any* subsidiary right.

Accounting and Statements

Most publishers agree to send semiannual statements and payments accounting for your book's sales and royalties and license fees owed to you. Do not accept a less-frequent schedule. Royalty statements are notoriously indecipherable, so be prepared—and don't hesitate to ask for information needed to verify any statement's accuracy. Statements should include the subsidiary rights income received in each rights category and the name of the licensee.

Almost every publisher refunds retailers and distributors in full for books that were ordered, shipped, and then returned. Publishing contracts typically allow the publisher to withhold a reserve against returns—that is, to retain some of the royalties currently due in order to avoid overpaying the author. Try to provide that the reserve will be "reasonable." You could also ask to limit reserves to the first three accounting periods, after which the possibility of significant returns is remote.

Your Right to Audit Sales Records

Most publishers' contracts give the author the right to audit its records regarding the book's financial performance; if yours does not, it is very important to add it. Make sure it allows you or your representative to conduct the examination, and that the publisher will pay your examiner's fee if the audit reveals errors in your favor of more than 5 percent of the total owed. Try not to let the contract limit your time to examine the records.

The Author's Obligations

Delivery of a Satisfactory Manuscript

All contracts oblige the author to deliver a "satisfactory manuscript," which, while understandable, could allow your publisher to reject your manuscript and terminate the contract despite the work's quality. If this happens, you'll be obligated to repay the advance. If the clause requires only that the manuscript be "satisfactory to the publisher," the subjective judgment that the manuscript is not "satisfactory" will not be set aside unless you prove that the publisher acted in bad faith.

If the publisher has made an offer after reading your entire manuscript, try to have the contract state that the publisher "has accepted" the work. If the work still requires editorial input and revisions before publication, the publisher might resist, but try to note that the author "has delivered" a complete manuscript, if possible. If you haven't yet delivered the manuscript, make sure you set a realistic deadline. After signing, if you agree to extend the delivery deadline for any reason, make sure you get that extension in writing and signed by the publisher.

Try to agree that the manuscript must be "satisfactory to the publisher *in form and content*" or "satisfactory in the publisher's *editorial* or *reasonable* discretion," not "sole discretion." Try also to add a "first proceeds" clause (a limit on your advance repayment obligation to the amount you earn from selling the work to a new publisher) and a requirement that the publisher give you written editorial assistance within sixty days of delivery as well as the opportunity to submit revisions before it may reject your book.

Warranties and Indemnities

Your warranties are your guarantee, backed up by your wallet, that your book will not generate a lawsuit against the publisher. You must warrant that you own the work and that its publication will not infringe on anyone's rights or cause anyone harm. Make sure this is the case as much as possible. If you fear any problems with the work, discuss it with your publisher now. Even then, there is always a remote possibility that your work will be the subject of a lawsuit. Most contracts require the author to indemnify the publisher not only against judgments resulting from an actual breach of a warranty but even against any alleged breach.

Most publishers don't enforce their rights to full indemnification unless the author was truly at fault, but it's also unlikely that you can negotiate changes to the boilerplate warranties and indemnities. If possible, limit your financial liability to damages resulting from an *actual* breach of your warranties. A more realistic protection is to get yourself covered by the publisher's insurance. If the publisher has such insurance, it should agree to cover you. Yet even that isn't a panacea; the deductibles tend to run in the high five and six figures. Some publishers will agree to share expenses with you equally until the deductible is reached. Try to limit your share of the deductible to a portion of your total advance.

Bad Ideas:
Clauses to Remove or Revise

Out-of-Print Provision

Most contracts make your grant of rights last "for the term of the copyright"—that is, until seventy years after your death. Any reasonable contract will include an out-of-print or reversion-of-rights clause. It is meant to encourage the publisher to keep the work selling for as long as it is profitable by giving back your rights when the work is no longer available for sale. Today, the literal concept of "in print" is no longer relevant because publishers can (and do) argue that the existence of nonprint versions and "print-on-demand" capability make the work "available for sale" even if no copies are selling. Stipulate in this clause that you must earn a minimum in royalties (say, $300 to $500) in each accounting period or your rights will revert automatically.

Option Clauses

Do not mistake an option for a two-book contract, which could be a fine deal for an author to make, as long as the contract terms are fair. Options give the publisher the privilege, but not the obligation, to publish your next book or books. Under most options, the publisher need not even read your next submission yet still keep you from showing it to others for a long period of time. An option could bind you to the publisher for your subsequent work even if the relationship sours or you can get better terms elsewhere.

Many publishers are willing to delete the option clause on request. If yours refuses to strike it entirely, it is crucial to make changes to it. Do not give an option to publish your next work on the "same terms" as the previous contract, or give the publisher "last refusal rights" (which allow it to acquire your new work by matching the best offer you have received). Change such terms to permit the publisher a limited-time "right of first refusal," on terms "to be negotiated." Provide that you must submit only a summary or proposal of the optioned work, not a complete manuscript. Do not let the publisher's time to consider your new submission start to run upon publication of the current work, make it begin upon acceptance. Try to limit the option to cover only books similar to the current work.

Noncompete Clauses

Most contracts prohibit the author from publishing another book that competes with sales of the current work. You should limit your publisher's room to make such an argument. Don't give the publisher "sole discretion" to decide what competes. Describe the type of work that might "reasonably" or "actually" compete with the current work as specifically as possible, including subject matter, market, and format.

Cross-Accounting

Joint accounting provisions allow the publisher to commingle your accounts for different books. They are unfair and should be stricken from the contract wherever they appear. At the least, specify that unearned advances from other contracts will not constitute indebtedness to be repaid out of earnings from the current contract.

Don't despair if your publisher does not agree to change all the terms that you'd like to negotiate. As your writing succeeds in the marketplace, you'll develop more leverage. For now, select those issues most important to your current needs and concentrate on negotiating the corresponding contract terms in your order of priority. Consider a successful negotiation of the more important terms a significant accomplishment, and know that your next contract negotiation will be easier.

Editor Etiquette

by Betsy Lerner

Betsy Lerner, now an agent and formerly an editor, is the author of several books, including Forest for the Trees: An Editor's Advice to Writers.

Whenever I am asked to weigh in on questions of etiquette, I do not pass go, I do not collect $200, I do not do anything without consulting my bible, the handsome volume I keep beside my dictionary and thesaurus, *The Amy Vanderbilt Complete Book of Etiquette*. Mrs. Vanderbilt offers no advice on author-editor relationships per se, but she does have an entire section devoted to your professional life, and it is worth quoting from here:

> You may associate manners with social events—weddings, dining out, cocktail parties—yet manners are the basis for getting along in all aspects of our lives. Nowhere are they more important than in the business world. . . . Whether business is being conducted over the telephone, on a corporate jet, or in another country, good manners smooth the way and, along with intelligence and hard work, are the key to success in the working world.

Nowhere is this advice better heeded than in the author-editor relationship, a relationship that usually begins much the way a blind date does with both parties having only heard about the other, yet hoping for some kind of magic to transpire. If you have employed an agent to sell your book, you probably haven't had much contact with the editor who acquired your book. Sometimes an agent will set up phone conversations or office meetings in the course of trying to sell the project, but more often than not writers first meet their editors after the deal is done. In this way the relationship between author and editor more closely resembles an arranged marriage. But here's where the analogy breaks down: The writer feels like a bride, whereas the editor, a true polygamist, has simply made another addition to his harem.

When your book is first acquired there is often a great deal of attendant fanfare, especially if the book is bought at auction or if the advance is steep. Now is the time for your editor to call or, if you live nearby, to take you to lunch. For many writers this initial contact is ripe with fantasy and expectation. You assume the person who loved your work will love you and vice versa.

No matter how excited you may be, try, when you first talk with or meet your editor, not to overwhelm him. Don't tell the story of your life, don't ask if he'll read the seven unpublished manuscripts you have at home in a drawer. Don't ask to set up a series of meetings to go over your work line by line. Many editors feel like the old woman who lived in the shoe. Despite their initial enthusiasm for your project, once they've signed you on, you essentially become one more mouth to feed. Your editor needs time to absorb the extra work, both actual and psychic, that a new author generates. If from the get-go you appear to be someone who requires a lot of management, most editors will duck for cover, some permanently. Once when I was an editor I sat across a bistro table from a woman who wept with happiness and relief that her project of many years was going to be published. At first I was touched by her tears; eventually I wondered if she needed a medication adjustment.

Authors want their editors to be their friends, therapists, bankers, mothers, teachers, champions. In the best cases they are, and this usually happens when an author stays with an editor over a long time and many books. Many an author-editor pairing, however, fails to evolve into a happy, long-term marriage. Editors change houses. Authors switch publishers. Sometimes editorial relationships that otherwise should work well start off on the wrong foot and never achieve a good balance, usually because the editor takes more than a few days to call his new author or fails to promptly return calls in general. I don't think this behavior is excusable, but the reason for it is rarely personal—and authors almost always take it personally. A little understanding (and good manners) on the part of both parties can go a long way toward preventing rifts.

Editors today are overworked in the extreme. If you imagine that they sit at their desks all day reading and editing, your image couldn't be more inaccurate. Most editors do all their reading and editing on their own time, in the evenings and on the weekends. During the work-day editors chase new projects, try to meet the varying demands of their stables of writers, and attend meetings about their lists of books already in production. An individual author's sense of urgency about any given need is real, but most editors are bombarded with many tasks on any given day, and they must set priorities according to their own schedules.

Therefore, do not swamp your editor with calls. I cannot stress this enough. Don't leave multiple voice mails. Don't send thousands of e-mails. Don't think that by commiserating with the assistant you're getting anywhere. Don't leave long, whiny messages or terse nasty ones. Don't hit the send button on your computer unless the initial moment of anger has passed and you're still sure you want to risk alien-ating the person most responsible for the success of your book. Re-member, you do have your agent to do the pestering. (Of course, you don't want to make a total pain in the ass of yourself to your agent, ei-ther, but if this is a game of good cop/bad cop, you always want to be the good cop.) I have watched so many authors get branded as Nudgie McNudge after calling their editors just a few times. The problem is, once you get branded as a nudge, there's no recovering.

Most writers fantasize that their editor will be like Maxwell Perkins, devoted entirely to their work, the way Perkins nearly lost himself in thousands of manuscript pages by Thomas Wolfe. Writers are not the only ones in publishing to harbor grand fantasies. Most editors come into the business out of a love of books, after all. Many editors dream of discovering the next writer who changes the way we look at the world or the novelist whose new book sets the chattering classes a-brew. Some editors imagine a nightlife full of carousing with their writers, others see themselves hunched over a manuscript knowing its author will respond to their notes, delivering a draft better than imagined— and in that dance between editor and author something true is realized. Editors, too, are looking for love.

One of the reasons editors and authors can have strained working rela-tionships is that writers are on the outside of the publishing process. The better the writer understands what to expect, the better the chance for a good rapport between the two working parties. Editors are creatures of corporate culture, saddled with all the mind-numbing requirements of budgets and reporting lines and memoranda that businesses require. Their workdays resemble a three-ring circus. In the first ring are the projects they are actively trying to acquire, in the second ring are the books that need editing, and in the third the books about to be published. Thus their lives are a complicated cycle of meetings and preparations to launch the books on their lists, including writing and making sales-and-marketing presentations, writing flap and catalogue copy, collaborating with the art department to create a jacket, and otherwise trying to do everything possible to get their projects read and attended to as their books move toward publication day.

Authors, being on the outside of all this, don't understand how their calls can go unanswered, their pages unread, their ideas seemingly unheard. Every editor knows well the 9 A.M. phone call from the writer who has spent the night gnashing his teeth about some aspect of his publication. Every editor has received a barrage of e-mails from a writer wanting answers to a million different little questions. Being on the outside puts the writer at a terrible disadvantage; it's hard to take on faith that the pages will be read, the editing delivered, the jacket composed when you're living in Missoula or Newark or even the Upper West Side of Manhattan. Writers have no sense of the rhythms of their editors or their companies.

An editor's job is to let the writer in on some of the mysterious goings-on behind the corporate wall of silence. Some are better at it than others. A great many difficulties in the author-editor relationship could be solved if editors provided schedules for their writers. And to those writers whose editors don't offer a working time line: ask for one.

Find out when you can expect your pages to be read and returned with notes. Agree on deadlines beyond those specified in the contract; find out how long your editor needs with your pages; determine whether he wants to see each chapter singly, a few chapters at a time, or the whole thing—in draft or a more polished version.

It's usually a big mistake to give an editor a rough or first draft, or anything that's sloppy. Remember, your editor has only so much energy to give to your project, and if you give him a big mess, then you're defeating him—and yourself—at the starting gate. You want to present your best possible pages and therefore get his best possible response and, hopefully, bring the manuscript into even better shape. Sometimes I used to refer to certain editorial jobs as "correcting papers," because there were so many grammatical and spelling errors on top of fuzzy, unfocused thinking. Once an editor deals with all that, it's hard to see the author's strengths. (To be fair, I have worked with pages that were a mess, but the brilliance came through.)

Other scheduling questions that should be addressed once the manuscript goes into production: When will I receive the copyedited manuscript, how much time will I have with it, and what is the extent of the changes I can make? When will I receive the galley pages and how much time will I have with them? When do we send out pages for blurbs and how can I help? When do I see the jacket and catalogue copy and when is it appropriate to give my feedback? When do I see the jacket art? When do I meet my publicist and when will I know the plans? Should I hire my own publicist?

There are many other questions that authors have, such as: Will I tour? How large is the first printing? Will the publisher throw a party or should I organize one myself? Can we do a postcard mailing announcing the book? How do books get assigned to the *New York Times Book Review*? And so on. It would be crazy to bombard your editor with all these questions at once, but they are relevant and important. Finding a comfortable flow of communication will enable you to better grasp all the big but nuanced aspects of the publishing process.

What a lot of authors don't understand is that in the roulette wheel of getting published, not even the publisher knows whose number is going to come up. Try as you might to push a book, it can sink. And a little title for which the house has no particular expectations can suddenly take off thanks to a surprise NPR booking or rave review.

I don't think publishers willfully keep authors in the dark. The truth is they don't know exactly how a publication will roll out, or how the media will (or won't) break. It can be extremely frustrating for authors in those anxious prepublication months because after all the busyness of preparing the manuscript, there is this lull, this quiet time, and in the silence many writers hear pistols being loaded and cocked, critics taking aim. Others fantasize riding the best-seller charts to new heights of literary celebrity. The best editors will manage expectations, as will the best publicists. But you need to take some of that management into your own hands and figure out how best to work within the structure of the publisher.

There are many famous stories of authors who took matters into their own hands to promote their books. And I think writers should do everything they can to get their books out there. Some authors and editors take the Patton approach and make their demands known. Others believe the old adage that you'll catch more flies with honey. If your editor has become the editor of your dreams, consider yourself very fortunate. If he hasn't materialized as the bespectacled confidant you had secretly prayed for, you will have to work that much harder to get the most out of the relationship. No matter how great your frustration, try not to alienate your editor; he is your conduit to the company. With work this personal, it's often hard to remember that publishing is still business, but remember it you must, and thus, in all dealings, take to heart the words of my beloved Amy Vanderbilt: Good manners smooth the way.

Midlist and Other Fictions

by Sol Stein

Sol Stein, the author of nine novels and Stein on Writing, was publisher and editor in chief of Stein and Day for twenty-seven years.

Imagine a tall apartment building, nine stories high, with a penthouse on the top, a street-level floor, and nothing in between. It's impossible—the penthouse would fall down. The same is true of any publishing list. If at the top it has one or more best-selling authors, and at the bottom of the list are books that are likely to sell to libraries and not do much more, that list is economically insupportable in any publishing enterprise. Adequate publishing functions cannot be maintained only for the benefit of one or more best-sellers. Moreover, if a prospective best-seller flops, the loss can be enormous in unearned advances and remaindered books. There has to be a list of 50 or 100 or 200 or more books each season, depending on the size of the house and the amount of its fixed overhead. Yet the most dreaded, dismissive, punishing word in the publishing lexicon today is *midlist*, despite the fact that the majority of books on every publisher's list falls between the very top of the list and the very bottom. That's the disgraced midlist, which every publisher has.

The term is an outgrowth of the conversion of publishing in the last decades of the twentieth century from firms usually headed by book people to firms usually headed by people to whom books are products that bear no relation to what is passed on from generation to generation as a part of a country's culture. The term *midlist* is used daily to dismiss authors and books from consideration even though every rational dismisser knows that a midlist not only has to exist, but that the majority of books on any list are midlist.

Authors live on hope. Those who live on unrealistic hope often turn their disappointment in on themselves when a book doesn't do well in the marketplace. The self is the wrong target. In the majority of instances the fate of a book has already been determined by the publisher before the appearance of the first review. Let's take a hard look at the process.

The first people that your ally, the editor who chose your book, has to convince about its merits and salability are the editor's colleagues, other editors; marketing, sales, and promotion people; and sometimes the publisher or his deputy. This usually takes place at a meeting termed *editorial* but that frequently focuses on economic considerations. This discussion may take place even before a book is acquired, though some more experienced editors may acquire books on their own say-so within certain prescribed bounds.

After a book is chosen and put on a seasonal list, it is formally presented at a national sales meeting. These meetings take place two or three times a year, depending on whether the publisher divides a year into two or three seasons. The meeting takes place several months before each season starts. A catalogue will have been prepared describing the forthcoming books. Formerly at such meetings the books on a given list were presented to the sales force by the editors. That has undergone a major change. In large firms, the books are now often presented by the publisher or his deputies. The editors, sadly, are urged to stay away. In one major firm, editors were told, "You're welcome to come if you don't move or breathe or speak to anyone," which characterizes the new attitude toward editors, who used to be the heart and mind of a publishing enterprise.

At these sales conferences, the audience consists of "reps," the salespeople who call on bookstores in their respective territories around the country. Like audiences everywhere, the sales force responds to some degree to the skill of the presenter and the enthusiasm with which a forthcoming book is announced, described, or gossiped about in the coffee breaks. The books presented by senior executives sometimes get special attention, but what counts most of all is the ranking of any book on the list, which is decided before the sales meeting.

If a firm has paid a small fortune as an advance for a title, the book automatically moves high up on the list of its publishing season. So will a new book by an established, well-known author whose previous books have been best-sellers. Celebrity writers who have made reputations in fields other than writing, particularly those who have ready access to the media, will also have their book high up on the list. At the sales meeting, each of the books at the top of that season's list is announced with fanfare. The assembled force will hear the quantity of the first printing, important evidence to them and to their bookstore customers of the publisher's commitment to the book and expectation for its early sales. Time will be devoted to the promotion plans. An advertising schedule and sample ads will be provided with sales kits. If the author is to be sent on tour, a list of cities with tentative dates will be distributed. Advance quotes from successful authors may have been collected. The publisher may have prepared bound galleys that look like hardcover-sized paperbacks, a special edition for advance reading that doesn't have to be read; the fact that it has been printed and distributed to the trade is enough to convince booksellers that this book will be pushed by the house. An exceptional novel will sometimes capture the attention of booksellers by means of bound galleys.

Books high up on the list are often discussed in terms of what will be done to make the book sell. This is important to the attending sales-people because their customers, the bookstore buyers, have grown accustomed to asking "What are you doing for the book?" and being guided by the answer in deciding whether or not to stock enough copies for face-out display in the store.

A book can move up the list because people with money to offer like it—that is, if a book club picks it up, or if movie or foreign rights have been sold for large sums prior to the meeting. Once upon a time a major prepublication license to a paperback house could result in a book's being positioned higher up on the list, often because the licensee required a big advertising budget as part of the deal. Paperback editors competed aggressively to buy the titles that were already high on the publisher's list, eager to pay too much money in order to keep a title out of the hands of their competitors. With almost all of the major publishers now owning their own paperback companies, the big paperback sale to another publisher is much less frequent, and therefore less likely to affect the book's position on the publisher's list.

The position of all books on a publisher's list is determined by a group that will usually include the director of marketing, the sales manager, the head of publicity and promotion, perhaps the editor in chief, perhaps the publisher. In most houses, the marketing and sales directors, not the editors, have the greatest influence on the order of the books on the list. An author eavesdropping on this meeting might conclude that these friendly people were actually deciding which books will live and which will die, or at least which will sell a lot of copies, and which, at the bottom of the list, will be sent to market without publicity, promotion, advertising, or anything else that will tell the public that this baby has been born and wishes its unique cry to be heard.

It wasn't always this way. Some decades ago, if an editor truly loved a book and gave his heart to its presentation, it would have some effect on the rest of the publishing team. As publishing became a bottom-line business, love was replaced by money; what counted was the amount guaranteed to the author that had to be earned back from sales of the book. That is now the driving force that garners advertising and promotion money for a book and thrusts it up the list.

At the sales conference, as the presenters (sometimes but not always the books' editors) take turns and move down the list, sales reps learn of each book's title, author, alleged print run, and price, as well as each work's "handle," a short description of the book designed to evoke interest in it. The presenter may mention that the author will give readings in his local area, or do a local newspaper interview; this may play negatively with the audience, because it means there will be no national campaign to attract readers in every salesman's territory, and that therefore the book's chances for a sizable initial sale are probably slim.

Are there exceptions? Of course. When Oprah Winfrey selected a book for her on-air book club, that was, at least initially, a signal to the publisher to print a million copies and go all out in promoting it. In time, the effect of an Oprah selection settled down to half a million copies sold, but still produced more than a million dollars of royalties for the author. Other television-based book clubs sprang up. Their selections sold well. Of special interest to writers is that some of those selections had marked literary quality but might not have succeeded without the promotion on television. The fact is that the oft-despised medium of television has had a profound and quite favorable effect on book-buying. Of course, information on books reaches their audiences by other means as well. An occasional sleeper or a book of particular quality will intrigue an influential reviewer, who will give it undreamed-of coverage. A review in one of the few remaining book media or daily papers that carry book reviews will sometimes be syndicated to numerous other newspapers. Sometimes a book is "hand sold" by independent booksellers who fall in love with it and recommend it to customers. Sometimes a book of dubious literary merit will sell because the author is willing to travel by car to every town in America that has a paucity of local authors but that has a bookstore with an owner—or an influential clerk—who can be charmed. Jacqueline Susann started this practice in the '60s with *Valley of the Dolls* and Robert James Waller continued it in the '90s with *The Bridges of Madison County*.

Flukes will happen. A military book about a World War II campaign advanced more than any other title in Texas but didn't do particularly well elsewhere in the country. On investigation, it turned out that the salesman in Texas had been in that campaign and had a once-in-a-lifetime chance to tell his war stories on the road. Fine novels and deserving nonfiction also sometimes get a lucky break through a single excited salesperson whose enthusiasm is contagious. Literature survives. Also, the sale of topical serious nonfiction has increased, as have books pinpointed to a special-interest market.

The publisher's salespersons take orders from booksellers months before physical copies are available. The sales rep presenting many dozens of new books may have had an opportunity to read only the books deemed by the publisher to be lead books. For the rest, the salesman has to rely for his pitch on the catalogue copy or what was said at a sales conference. A rep has about thirty seconds to convey the title, author, price, size of first printing, and what the book's about. In most circumstances the handle can only be a sentence or two. If the book is by an author with a track record, the buyer is reminded of it.

Obviously the rep presenting 50 or 100 or 200 titles, having discussed the promotion plans for the lead titles, doesn't have time to be fair to all the other authors on the list. Inevitably a bookstore buyer's attention span runs out and he declares, "Enough!" That means sales reps voluntarily skip some titles altogether. In this way the salesman in the field becomes the chief decision maker, pulling the life support off the skipped books. Those unmentioned books, usually from the bottom of the season's list, will never be sold in that bookstore unless something miraculous happens somewhere else and the bookstore buyer hears about it.

Most bookstore and chain buyers will order titles in proportion to their positioning on the publisher's list. In the smallest stores, only the top books may be bought, or books on subject matters that have a following among the customers of that store. In larger stores that can and do represent most of a list, the books that are bought in the largest quantity will be shown face out on the bookstore shelves. The books that are bought in ones and twos will be spine out, which reduces their chances of being seen by the browser. Books bought in small quantities for spine-out display usually experience a high return rate. So do books by best-selling authors that are oversold because of past accomplishment or inflated expectation. Shopping-mall bookstores, now on the wane, introduced book buying in the 1970s to many people who were intimidated by bookstores and afraid that if a clerk asked them what they wanted, they'd be paralyzed for an answer. But these mall stores could sell in quantity only the "big" books, displayed in "dumps" up front or on the narrow ends of display islands, called end caps, which are rented by the publisher and therefore available only for titles high up on the list that have a budget for in-store promotion.

Display space is not the only thing rented. The books themselves are really rented rather than bought by the bookstore because they can be returned, usually anytime up to one year from the time of purchase. So when a publisher or editor represents that a book has "sold" 10,000 copies, it means that 10,000 copies have been placed in stores on the equivalent of consignment, subject to return. And the hard fact is that about 40 percent of new books, especially novels, are usually returned and remaindered, meaning sold for salvage value, with no royalty to the author.

The size of the first printing as announced to or by the sales reps or in print to the trade is often greatly exaggerated by certain publishers. The bookstore buyer isn't always fooled. The largest exaggerations are for the "biggest" books. The same is true for the size of the advertising or marketing budget. The books that will sell best are almost always the books that the publisher pushes or promotes the most, a decision you now know was made prior to publication. The absence of print advertising for a book is a wound to the author's pride more than a detriment to sales. Few books sell as a result of space advertising. The key activities for selling books are publicity and visibility where books are sold.

Can any outside influence affect the positioning of a book? Yes. Licenses to major book clubs are almost always arranged at least four months prior to publication. A main selection at the Book-of-the-Month Club or the Literary Guild can influence the positioning of a book somewhat. That happens to several dozen books a year, most of which have already been positioned high on the publisher's list, which may be one reason the book clubs picked them. After all, books heavily promoted by the publisher have a better chance of selling to book club members. Selection as an alternate by a major club or by one of the hundred or more clubs that are smaller than the Literary Guild or Book-of-the-Month Club will usually not influence a book's positioning.

Most first-time authors—and others, too—are so happy to have a publisher accept a book that they don't think much about positioning, or don't know about it, even though that positioning will influence the fate of the book significantly. Now that you know, is there anything you or your agent can do to influence your book's place on the publisher's list?

Obviously the advance obtained for the book means more than just money. If anyone working for the publishing firm says the advance does not influence positioning, he is lying. Is this lie commonplace? Yes. Are authors gullible in this respect? Yes. Even experienced authors? Yes. And agents? Remember that an agent has to be something of a confidence builder. If all he can get for the author is a modest advance, he wants the author to be happy nevertheless, so he will encourage the author to believe the editor who is saying that there is more hope for the book than the size of the advance would indicate.

If you are promised promotion or advertising for your book, it would help if that ends up in your contract as a commitment, at least as to a minimum. Editors move around, and an absent editor's verbal promises of a year ago are written on sand in a sandstorm. Don't be surprised if even the best agents can't get a contract commitment for advertising or promotion, because it is rarely forthcoming.

An agent can try to keep the paperback rights free for competitive bidding. If two paperback companies like the book well enough, competition could drive the price up. And the hardcover publisher might—just might—adjust the book's position on the list.

Once upon a time most editors could be counted on to support a book they acquired through the publishing process. Editors with good in-house reputations were relied on by others in the organization. Today, the predominant influence is from the sales side of the firm. Still, some editors have a way of charming salespeople into glancing at a manuscript. Some marketing directors actually read all or part of a manuscript that a reliable editor is enthusiastic about. If your agent can get your manuscript into the hands of such an editor, your chances for good positioning are greater. The outcome often depends on which editor within the house receives the manuscript. Many agents prefer to submit a book to the highest-ranking editor they know well, but books bought by the head editors are often delegated to editors lower in the pecking order who will have less influence on the publishing process. It can be said that a book's positioning is determined not only before the first review appears, but much earlier, when the agent submits it for consideration. In fact, the reputation of the agent doing the submitting matters. There are reportedly nearly 1,000 literary agents in North America alone, but fewer than a dozen have clout. An editor will seize and quickly open any package arriving from such an agent, who will probably be known to have big-name or recently successful authors in her stable.

A point you don't want to lose sight of is that publicity is the most cost-effective means for letting the public know a particular book exists. Nothing prevents the author with energy and personality from stepping forward to promote his own book if the publisher is not doing enough. Whatever the publisher does, in the author's eyes it will never be enough, and the author is often right.

Publicity Primer

by Michael Taeckens

Michael Taeckens, a poet, is publicity director for Algonquin Books of Chapel Hill, a division of Workman Publishing.

A first publication can be just as nerve-racking as it is thrilling—turning in your manuscript is like entrusting your baby to a sitter for the first time. It's no wonder you have a million qualms and just as many questions: Once my book is published, how will it fare against all the other books out there? Will it sell at all? Will the media pay attention to my book? What is a "publicist," anyway? Will mine pay attention to me?

While these questions can create a whirlwind of doubt and panic, the truth is that you, the brand-new author, can play a crucial role in making your book successful. If you are willing to work effectively with your publicist and actively participate in the promotion of your book, your publishing experience will be a fruitful one.

First, let's understand exactly what the publicist does. If you are publishing with a mid-sized or large publishing house, chances are you will have one key publicist assigned to your book, with other publicists providing backup. There are many strategies your publicity team will employ in promoting your book to national and local magazine, newspaper, television, radio, and Web media. These may include:

- Scheduling **publicity calls,** or face-to-face meetings with editors and producers. These meetings, held each catalogue season, allow your publicist to "pitch" your book directly to those who are making the decisions.

- Mailing **galleys,** or bound page proofs, of your book to a carefully formulated media list. Once the galleys arrive at the publisher—anywhere from four to eight months in advance of the publication date—your publicist will send them out to the names on that list, including pre-publication magazines. (Prepublication periodicals, which librarians, booksellers, and publishing professionals subscribe to, focus on the publishing industry and on reviewing new books; the main ones are *Publishers Weekly, Kirkus Reviews, Booklist*, and *Library Journal*. "Blurbs," or favorable quotes, from reviews of your book will be sent to online booksellers such as Amazon [amazon.com] and Barnes & Noble [www.bn.com] for posting on your book's "pages.") The galley package will also include the publication date, a description of the book, and any blurbs from individuals and/or prepublication reviews. The press release will be enclosed with the galley.

- *Writing **press releases**, or one- to two-page pitches for your book.* These are used to capture the media's attention and to give a condensed version of why you and your book are of interest. Generally, the publicist will emphasize your book's "hook" or "handle" and present it in a catchy way. Sometimes, a publicist will see potential in his author as a "human interest story" and will write a separate press release that is sent to features editors for "off the book page" publicity (editorial coverage aside from book reviews). Press releases are mailed with the galleys, sometimes in press kits (see below).

- *Creating **press kits**, or folders containing pertinent information about a book and its author.* Press kits typically contain a press release, author photo, author biography, and any favorable prepublication reviews or other publicity. Sometimes they include "talking points"— bulleted items the author can talk about in an interview—or a Q&A with the author.

- *Mailing the **bound book**, or the final product.* Bound books usually arrive four to eight weeks in advance of publication. The publicist mails them to targeted media, including some of the same media that received galleys.

- *Arranging an **author tour**.* If your publishing house has agreed to send you on tour, your publicist will book readings for you at various bookstores, libraries, and/or literary events, to start on publication date. Author tours vary in size and location, but whether your tour is large or small, national or local, your publicist will select the best venues for you and your book. In some instances your publicist will set up a "media satellite tour" in lieu of or in addition to a traditional tour. A media satellite tour consists of an interview with you at a radio or TV station, which is then available for broadcast by various shows around the nation. Because media satellite tours are always handled by external, specialized companies, they can be rather costly.

Okay. That's what you can expect your publicist to do. Now here are some strategies you can use to make your working relationship with your publicist effective.

1. Pay special attention to your author questionnaire, one of the most important tools for marketing and publicizing your book. When your publicist is getting ready to mail your galleys, this is the first item she will consult. On it you will be asked to supply any media contacts you have, media sources to whom you want your book sent, awards you want your book to be considered for, and a "big mouth" mailing list, or a list of prominent individuals you would like to receive your book. Because this questionnaire is so vital, be sure to do your research and fill it out with full and complete information, including addresses of all the individuals you list. If you acquire new information after you have turned your questionnaire in, be sure to let your publicist know.

2. Trust your publicist's expertise. Publicists are experts at compiling broad and well-targeted mailing lists; they are trained and experienced in pitching books not only to all major magazines, newspapers, Web sites, and TV and radio shows, but to subject-specific media as well. Publicity departments have comprehensive media databases that allow them to search for media by subject, editor title, and geographic location, to name just a few criteria. If your book is about dogs, your publicist will pitch your book to pet editors and media focused on animals.

3. Keep a pocketbook calendar (preferably in both digital and paper format). Ask your publicist ahead of time to provide you with a schedule of when your galleys and bound books will be mailed out. Make note of these dates in your calendar. If your publisher is sending you on tour, be sure to mark down all of your travel and reading dates and times. Keep your itinerary and any other materials your publicist sends you with your calendar—and never forget to take them with you on the road.

4. Let your publicist do the work by requesting that he inform you of publicity as it occurs. This way, he will contact you to let you know when reviews, interviews, and feature stories are confirmed. You won't have to ask whether something is happening and you will be up to date with all information.

5. Maintain weekly contact with your publicist, but don't call and/or e-mail her every day. You and your book are not her only responsibilities. Naturally, you will have questions and/or concerns, but instead of relaying these to your publicist in a piecemeal fashion, take some time to collect all your thoughts and send them at one time. It may sometimes take a couple of days for you to get a reply, but you will eventually be answered. Your publicist should give you biweekly progress reports to let you know what she is doing and what publicity is in the works. You will be able to tell from her regular communication with you just how devoted she is to your book. If you are not hearing from your publicist at all, let your editor know immediately.

There are also some things about your publicist and the publicity process that you will want to keep in mind:

1. Publicists, just like agents and editors, are excessively busy and always juggling a number of projects simultaneously. In your mind, your book is, of course, the one that matters. But to your publicist, who is working on anywhere from ten to thirty books at once, every single book on his list matters and deserves equal time. Because of this, there is no way he can give any one author undivided attention. Don't take it personally.

2. Publicity results are never guaranteed. Book-review editors typically receive 300 to 500 books a week—that's 15,600 to 26,000 books a year.

Your book will therefore be competing with hoards of other books for a limited amount of review and feature attention. Because the market is so oversaturated, it is literally impossible for every book to attain the recognition and success that it deserves. Truth be told, a lot of a book's success is based on a combination of hard work, timing, and sheer luck. There are books that receive little to no publicity and hit the best-seller lists, and books that get reviewed far and wide and sell few copies. The amount of publicity or sales a book gets is rarely equal to its worth. And keep in mind: You have already reached an enviable level of success just by publishing your book.

3. Have realistic expectations. If you've written a collection of short stories or an experimental novel or a how-to book, chances are that it won't hit the best-seller lists. However, these kinds of books can be successful without best-seller status. There are aficionados for every book genre out there—and if there's an audience for your book, there's a chance it can sell well. It's your publisher's job to find your audience and make sure that audience is aware of your book.

4. Treat your publicist in the manner you want to be treated. At times you may feel angry, hurt, or confused if a review doesn't come through, but the last person you want to blame is your publicist, the very person responsible for standing up for your book. It is important to remember that publicists have no control over the media. All they can offer is their best effort.

Now, last but definitely not least, there are a number of things you can do on your own to help promote your book:

1. Get your name in print. First-time authors who have the most success-ful experiences with their books are those who frequently publish in literary journals, magazines, and newspapers. The more you publish, the more likely you are to garner media contacts and get your name recognized—both of which will help you get more publicity. Write op-eds, short stories, personal essays, book reviews, travel pieces— anything you can to get your name in print. If you have an agent, ask her for help in getting your pieces published.

2. Make sure people in your community know about your book. Many authors build their literary reputations in their own region, where local support is strong. Introduce yourself to your local booksellers, librarians, and book-group leaders and make sure your marketing or publicity department sends them galleys. In your author questionnaire, list names and contact information for all of the local media that cover books; your publicist will then send them your galleys and books with material highlighting the fact that you are a local author. (Important note: *Never* contact the media yourself; it will only serve to annoy both your publicist and the person you are contacting.)

3. Ask your family, friends, colleagues, and acquaintances to read your book and post reviews on Amazon's and Barnes & Noble's Web sites.

4. If your publisher isn't already doing it for you, get postcards made that advertise your book. Chances are, if you are willing to pay the money your publisher will take care of getting the postcards produced, and may even send them out to the media. If your publisher can't do this, there are hundreds of postcard companies out there; you can find them by doing an Internet search. One of the most reliable companies is 1-800 Postcards (www.1800postcards.com/), where you can get a minimum of 5,000 full-color postcards for $250. Ideally, the front of your postcard should reproduce your book's cover. On the back, be sure to include the title, your name, and the name of your publisher—and double-check the spelling. Once you have the postcards in your possession, mail them to everyone you know. Keep some with you at all times to hand out to people you meet.

5. If your publisher is not sending you on a tour, ask if he will coordinate one for you if you pay for the expenses. If not, you can arrange your own tour with some advance planning and relatively little money. You'll need to contact the events coordinators at bookstores and libraries at least three to five months in advance of your publication date. You can easily book readings in your hometown and throughout your state by letting the events coordinators know you are a local author. If you have friends and family members in other areas of the country, have them contact their local bookstores and libraries and see if they would be interested in having you read.

———

With all of this information under your belt, you're one step ahead of other debut authors. You can confidently enter into a relationship with your publicist, knowing ahead of time her responsibilities and how you can work most effectively with her. And you'll also know what you yourself can do to help promote your book—and help it achieve the success it deserves.

How to Win Friends and Influence Booksellers

by Kate Whouley

Kate Whouley, a bookselling consultant, is the series editor for the American Booksellers Association's Fundamentals of Bookselling.

Picture a room full of booksellers at an annual convention. At the front of your standard-issue convention meeting room is a dais and skirted table; seated are three panelists and a moderator. The topic is "Does the Book Pay Rent?" The discussion is about how booksellers can create a unique and personal selection in bookstores while still making sure every title contributes something to the bottom line. The room, however, has a few strays—among them, a first-time author who asks, apropos of nothing that has been discussed, "Can each of you tell me how you decide to have an author event?" It is her second non sequitur of the hour, and this time, the moderator smiles, and in her most friendly yet firm moderator voice, says, "Gee, I think that's another panel."

When the program ends, the author approaches the panelists. To do what? Pitch her book at yet another inappropriate moment. Laboring under the mistaken belief that proximity to booksellers will lead to book sales, this author is not making friends. And if she's influencing booksellers at all, it's to convince them not to stock her book. Yes, this is a true story. In fact, I was the moderator. This anecdote made me think about the empathy gap between authors and booksellers. Why, I wondered, in pursuit of the same goal—selling books—do so many writers make this sort of faux pas when it comes to interacting with booksellers? It occurred to me that while any number of novels and a

truckload of nonfiction titles can help a bookseller understand something about the writing life, not too many writers have much opportunity to learn about what it is like to be a bookseller. Here's the chance
to find out. Imagine this . . .

The day dawns. You get up. Listen to NPR while you drink your
coffee, maybe scan the paper for any book coverage. Shower, dress, and
check your e-mail. Print out *PW Daily*, an e-mail newsletter that lists,
among other book news, titles scheduled for media attention, and make
a mental note to ask someone to check your stock on those books. Walk
to your bookstore, haul in the stack of newspapers and the small pile of
quarters a few of your regulars leave in exchange for an early paper.
Count the drawer, make the bank deposit. Open the store, help a few
customers with odd requests, download any orders you have waiting on
the Web site. At 10 A.M., your store manager, Jan, arrives, followed by
your HarperCollins sales rep, who is there to sell you his company's fall
list. You've already looked over the catalogues (last night in bed), so you
figure you'll be able to get through the buy in a couple of hours. (You're
not counting the titles, but if you were, you would discover you plan to
make decisions on 850 titles that day.)

Your afternoon begins with the noon arrival of Leo, a part-timer,
and tuna on rye, courtesy of HarperCollins. You are eating at your
desk, sandwich wrappers and water bottles competing for space with
the jackets the rep is still producing between mouthfuls. Refueled, you
talk about what titles you'd like to promote, and your rep checks on
your co-op money. ("Cooperative advertising" means promotional
costs are shared by bookseller and publisher; the publisher's contri-
bution is usually a percentage of the bookstore's purchases from that
publisher.) You fill out some forms and make some notes for your promotion file. You make a pitch to have a big-name author; the rep tells
you they are being very conservative with the tour. You'll need to put
together a package to convince the HarperCollins publicity department that yours should be one of twenty stores nationwide to host an
event. By 2:30 your rep is on his way, and you're back on the sales floor.
It's your favorite place to be, and you don't get out there very often
during the heavy buying seasons. You locate an obscure book for a
regular—you actually bought a single copy with this very customer in
mind—and ring up a couple more sales, chatting with the customers
about their selections.

Jan is placing a wholesaler order; Leo is just returning from a change run. Time for you to pay some bills. You retreat to the back room and your computer, cut checks for some publishers, decide to return some stock to others so you won't owe as much. While the checks are printing, you review your computerized inventory records and compile a list of titles that haven't sold a copy in the last ninety days. Once the return list is generated, you go out front again, pass it to Leo so he can pull the books. The back door buzzes. UPS is here. After you sign on the electronic line, you help the UPS man stack the shipment in your back room. You decide to unpack the fourteen boxes yourself, partly because you can enter the shipment into the computer more quickly than Jan or Leo can, but also because after nineteen years as a bookseller, you still feel a little bit like a kid at Christmas when you open a box of new titles. You never know what will be inside that box or, even better, inside the books inside the box. This is an odd truth, for it is also true you ordered these very books yourself about four months ago. But the real book—the real ideas in real type, bound and jacketed— is a world apart from a cover shot and a blurb in a publisher's catalogue, and after all these years, you still like yours to be the first pair of hands that hold it.

You're a bookseller. It's maybe the only job you've ever had, and it is certainly the only job you've ever loved. You look forward to your days, packed with people and books—not to mention more phone calls than you could ever hope to return, endless paperwork, too many hours in front of a computer, plenty of heavy lifting, and constant, often bizarre interruptions. Still, you love your work. You like buying books before they are books, betting on what will sell in your store. Once, your car mechanic told you you'd make a good stockbroker, because you aren't afraid to take calculated risks, and you asked him if he was suggesting a career change so you could afford to repair your radiator. On days like today, when the bills exceed the receipts, you figure you'd also make a good private eye; you're always tracking down the I-don't-know-the-title-but's, with a single, usually misleading clue. But before you can pursue this depressing line of thought, the intercom rings, and you go up front to help with the late-afternoon rush. A customer needs a recommendation, and you get to do what you love most of all: put the just-right book into the hands of a grateful customer. You close with Leo, though you weren't intending to stay this late. The rush kept going into the evening, and you didn't feel right leaving him on his own. You grab a galley the Harper rep left for you and head out the door, yanking twice to make sure the lock is engaged. Leo offers you a lift home and you accept; it's been a long day and you have yet to greet your spouse, your kids, your cats. Tomorrow is another busy day, but you try not to think about that. Leo's talking about the book he's reading now, and you are all ears. His tastes are so different from yours. That's at least half the reason you hired him. He's great on the sales floor, and every book he reads and shares with you is another entry into your personal database, under the category of Books I Have Not Read Myself, but Which I Can Recommend to the Right Customer.

Now that you've been a bookseller for a few pages, you have a sense of just how hard you have to work, just how much you must cram into a single day, but maybe you don't know just how smart you'll need to be to stay in business. Consider this: A successful bookseller ends up with about $2.30 in profit for every $100.00 in book sales. That's because the cost of books, freight, rent, payroll, and all the other assorted expenses in a well-run store take up the remainder of those sales dollars. To keep your business head above water, you must be an outstanding financial manager as well as an excellent reader and genial salesperson, not to mention a savvy event planner, thoughtful marketer, and very good personnel manager.

Ready to quit your job as a bookseller? Okay, you can go back to being a writer, but think back on your day as a bookseller and answer this: How present are you, the author, in the day of a bookseller? Of course you are there, by implication, in almost everything a bookseller does. You, after all, have written at least one of the books a bookseller will decide whether to order, stock, promote, or return. But unless you are the capital-*A* author on the twenty-city tour that booksellers are fighting over, you, the person who is the small-*a* author, do not inhabit the center of the bookseller universe. That place is claimed by the most important person in a bookseller's life: the customer. For while it is true that without authors there would be no books, it is also true that without reading customers there would be no need for books, booksellers, or authors.

Once you understand that customers hold pride of place in a bookstore, you are on your way to becoming a friend to a bookseller. With any luck, you already frequent your local bookseller's store not only as a writer but also a reading customer. That's the best place to start influencing booksellers—at your local bookstore. Booksellers are connected through regional and national associations, and one thing they talk about when they gather together is what they are reading. They also share their passionate recommendations through a program sponsored by the American Booksellers Association called Book Sense. About 1,200 ABA-member bookstores are part of Book Sense, which compiles Book Sense 76, a bimonthly selection of bookseller favorites that are promoted through in-store displays, newsletters, Web sites, and a published list.

How do you the small-*a* author have a shot at making the list? First write an excellent book. Next, share it with booksellers in a way that acknowledges what you have already learned: that customers matter most; that booksellers are as smart as they are busy; that they deserve your respect for the hard, good work they do in the world, and your thanks for placing your book into the hands of reading customers. This means, for example, that you won't do this:

AUTHOR: I'm wondering if you have a particular book. *Big Bold Cat?*

BOOKSELLER: [*checks inventory; does not see a listing*] Gee, I don't have it in stock at the moment. Would you like me to see if I can order you a copy?

AUTHOR: Oh, I don't need a copy. I'm the author.

What's wrong with this transaction? First of all, you didn't fess up. Even worse, you were pretending to be a customer. At this point in the nontransaction the bookseller knows you are going to tell her, through words or actions, that she *should* be stocking your book. Meanwhile, she knows nothing about it, hasn't heard of it or you, and has no idea that it is the excellent (if underpromoted) book that you the author know you have written. The bookseller is naturally leery. Do you know how many times a week a bookseller gets harassed by self-published authors with books of little or no appeal to his market? At this moment, you're looking worse than a cold call. You're here, live, in person, creating a backup at the cash register.

Here's a better scenario. You approach the bookseller with a copy of your book in hand, maybe a copy of a good review tucked inside and a handwritten note, asking her to consider stocking it for the store. You give her (that's right, *give*—for free) the book to read. You let her know where she can get copies to sell—either from your publisher, or from one or both of the large national book wholesalers, Ingram or Baker & Taylor. You thank her for her valuable time. And before you leave the store, you buy a book.

Sadly, you may not have an independent bookstore in your neighborhood. But it's likely that you do have a bookstore of some kind within driving distance. If that store is owned by a corporate chain, there's still a good chance it is populated by good booksellers who care deeply about excellent books. They may not have the ability to make buying decisions, but they are only a phone call away from the home office. It's possible that by writing an excellent book, and being a good customer, your local connection will mean an opportunity for your book to be considered chainwide.

Of course, not every bookseller is local, and you can't be a customer in every bookstore in America, and you'd like your book to sell in as many bookstores as possible. Some of the same rules apply to distance-authoring. Respect booksellers' time and their work, approach them honestly, and, if you are lucky enough to be on tour, cooperatively. Yes, this may mean answering questions from out of left field when a bookstore hosts you for a discussion, or worse, being unfailingly polite and upbeat when only your three second-cousins show up for your book signing in Twin Falls, Idaho. If the line of customers wraps around the block, be happy to sign books until your arm falls off, and after a ten-minute break, sign some more for the store.

Remember, too, you have friends and relatives to enlist in the national (or if you think big, international) cause. With any luck, they frequent bookstores far from your home and they are proud of you. Give them a lesson on the straightforward, respectful approach to the booksellers. (It's even worse when that exchange ends with the noncustomer saying, "I'm the author's mother.") Ask your mother, her friends and yours, and any relative you would invite to your funeral to *buy* a copy of your book, to order it if it isn't stocked, to become customers, and to feel free to share their good reviews of the book with their local bookstore.

———————

Okay, time to go back to being a bookseller. It's almost midnight. The kids are asleep. So is your spouse. The cats are snuggled in beside your feet, and your bedside light is on. You're reading. It's a galley of a new book by a local author. And it's good—*really* good. Already, you have a list of customers in your head who you know will want to read it. You're feeling that thrill of discovery, that sense of being the link between books and the people who read and write them. Oh, there's nothing like a good book. Except perhaps a customer who can't wait to read it.

How Lucky Can You Get . . .
and Other Things No One Tells You

by M.J. Rose

M.J. Rose, a novelist and journalist, has written more than 150 articles on the publishing industry.

No question about it, Carl P. was one lucky writer. At thirty-three, four weeks after sending out two dozen queries, four agents called asking to read the manuscript of his first novel, *Lucky Boy*.

Two weeks after that, his first-choice agent offered to represent him.

Let's call the agent Lucy. Typically, Lucy gets more than 200 queries a week, so this was indeed a lucky break for Carl. Within a month of signing with Lucy, Carl had a $75,000 offer for *Lucky Boy* from one of the better publishing houses. At Lucy's recommendation, and with excitement, Carl accepted the offer.

To celebrate, Carl's editor, let's call her Pandora, took him to lunch at Michael's in midtown Manhattan (where everyone in the biz lunches). Over sparkling water, she spoke of her vision of Carl's novel, how much faith she had in his talent, and how excited she was to launch his career.

Pandora promised Carl that her imprint was devoted to "building a writer's career," not just "buying one book." And that the marketing and promotion budget for his book was high and designed to build him a readership.

And then they talked about how hard it is to get published and how tens of thousands of manuscripts a year go unsold. In the last two years alone, 70,000 authors have self-published, and who knows how many have just given up because they couldn't get that one big break that Carl had been handed on a china platter along with his roasted free-range chicken.

He felt as lucky as the boy in the title of his book. But Carl's luck was about to change.

The first sign of a reversal of fortune came three months later, when Pandora's assistant called Carl to discuss the edits on his manuscript.

"I thought I was going to be working on this book with Pandora," Carl complained to his agent after the first few working sessions with Julie, the twentysomething junior assistant, went badly.

Lucy calmed Carl down, convinced him that the assistant was Pandora's pet and not to worry. "Not a word goes out without Pandora's approval," she promised. But as time went on, it became clear that Julie didn't understand the book. Most of the changes she wanted didn't make editorial sense to Carl.

And then Carl saw his cover, which he felt misrepresented the book.

Lucy agreed, but convinced Carl to accept the cover anyway because the publisher was excited about it, and Carl was lucky that the publisher was excited. It just wouldn't be smart to make a fuss at this point in the process.

Two months later Carl saw his book's listing in the publisher's catalogue for the forthcoming season. It wasn't the full page that Pandora had told him he'd be getting. Nor did it list the ten-city tour or the national advertising campaign that had also been promised at lunch.

When he called Lucy to complain about this treatment, she didn't return his phone call or e-mail for two days, and when she finally did it was to tell him not to panic. Everyone at the house loved the book, and he was worrying for nothing. "This is a tough business; you are so lucky. Now's not the time to complain," Lucy said.

This was not the last time he'd hear those words in the next eight months. No matter what the problem—the publisher only making 100 advance reading copies instead of the 500 promised, the book's launch being postponed to the next quarter, yet another edit from the junior assistant—no matter how upset he got, the refrain he heard over and over was "But you are so lucky. Your book is being published. That's what you need to remember."

Except Carl didn't feel lucky anymore and when he pleaded with Lucy to get on the phone and call his editor and straighten out the various messes, Lucy finally admitted that she didn't want to put her relationship with Pandora in jeopardy.

When *Lucky Boy* came out there was little review attention and initial sales were less than stellar. Carl felt anything but lucky. "I turned into the redheaded stepchild and my book just disappeared," he told me.

As authors, are we just so lucky to be published that we should shut up and stop complaining? Or should we be angry? Or is there a more productive way to navigate this strange land called publishing that does not resemble any other business model out there?

What's the Problem?

Part of the problem is the fact that it is so damn hard to get published.

"I felt a groveling attitude not only toward my first publisher but toward my first agent, a woman who sold every one of my novels, but who nevertheless told me at every turn that I was lucky to be published at all, let alone to have an agent," said Ada L., the author of six published books.

It took years of prodding from Ada's writer friends before Ada found the courage to ditch her agent and find a new one. Why? She was afraid to call her original agent because the agent couldn't have a conversation with Ada without getting in that "luck factor" phrase at least once.

Is it any wonder that writers' primary attitude is one of gratitude when our agents, editors, and countless other writers who are desperate to be published all keep telling us how lucky we are? Even seemingly positive news reemphasizes the luck factor. When Oprah picked a book for her book club, other writers talked about how lucky that newly anointed author had been to be plucked from obscurity. When *Today* and *Good Morning America* choose a book for their book clubs, every publicist and editor—and again, every writer—talks about the luck of the chosen one. After all, with more than 130,000 books published every year, you have to be more than a damn good writer to be anointed by reviews. You have to be lucky.

Ada L. suggested to me that writers don't always feel empowered because they aren't really in on the process. "We don't negotiate, we don't know which editor is looking for which product. We're removed." For some reason these are the rules and protocols writers have always followed.

Here's a thought: We're the writers, aren't we? Let's rewrite the rules!

"I was told I would never get a review in a major newspaper and not to even try," Jane T., a midlist author, said. "I tried anyway, contacting the paper myself, and when I got the review—a rave—guess what I was told by my publicist? I was *lucky.* 'And please don't do it again' because I was making the publicist's job harder."

ICM literary agent Lisa Bankoff points out that there is also a fear factor exacerbating the problem. She reports having phone conversations with dissatisfied authors who complain about unresponsive publicists, ill-conceived book jackets, or a lack of advertising. "Often, they're absolutely right to feel that the publisher could be doing a better job of it, paying closer attention, offering more meaningful consultation. That said, I've had many of those same phone conversations end with the client begging me not to repeat any of it to the editor. God forbid, the squeaky wheel might get replaced instead of oiled."

That fear is part of why we crawl away, convincing ourselves we should be grateful instead of acting on our anger. If we get anything— one ad in a major newspaper, a four-city tour, three weeks of decent co-op placement in the chains—we consider ourselves blessed. We've heard of too many cases where books, sometimes despite a big advance, are dropped or just die from a publisher's lack of interest.

So, like neglected children, we're thankful for every small favor.

In Their Defense

John Glusman, editor in chief of Farrar, Straus & Giroux, sympathizes with authors and blames a marketplace that is more competitive than ever. "As a result of consolidation in the industry, there is less of an emphasis on quality and more attention paid to the bottom line. That makes the stakes higher and puts more expectation on certain books to perform," Glusman says.

Publishers aren't out to destroy writers, but publishing a successful book is very much a guessing game. Agents don't mean not to return our calls, they are just overworked. And publicists aren't the devil's spawn who think we are lunatics. They are for the most part overburdened with too many books to push each month. At the same time, the amount of review space in magazines and newspapers has been cut by 25 to 50 percent in the last two years. There isn't time to do a good PR job on every book, which is why writers should learn to do some of their own, or save some of their advance to hire an outside PR firm.

Glusman reminds authors that sometimes decisions seem personal when they aren't. There are actual problems in publishing today. "There is less and less media attention for books, and everyone is becoming anxious. The shelf life and book review space and the attention span of the general public are shorter. And the relatively long time it takes to produce a book makes it even more difficult."

Author Elizabeth Benedict (*Almost,* Houghton Mifflin, 2001) says that while your book is the center of your world, to an editor it's one of two dozen books she's working on that season, and she knows that not all of those books are going to be smashing successes.

"I imagine that editors keep some distance between themselves and writers so that if a book doesn't take off, the editor can retreat a bit more gracefully, instead of having an author who feels as though the moon has been promised but not delivered. Maybe this feels to some authors as though the publisher wants them to feel 'grateful' instead of involved," she says.

One way to combat this feeling as an author is to have realistic expectations. Simon Lipskar, a literary agent with Writers House Literary Agency, suggests that when a publisher has paid less than a $25,000 advance to an author for a first novel, it's foolish, no matter how great one's fantasies, to hope that the publisher will print 50,000 copies in hardcover, run an expensive (and often pointless) ad campaign, send the author on an expensive (and often pointless) author tour, and so on. "It's the author's part of the bargain as a professional to know that, in most cases, these things will simply not happen. Asking for them, begging for them, demanding them: This is part of what leads publishers to react with an attitude that implies that the author should shut up and take what's being given."

If an author can instead balance expectations against the realities of what the publisher will or won't do for his book, then the cycle that leads to feelings of resentment and frustration can be put off from the start.

Lipskar is not suggesting that authors should simply stand back and let publishers do what they're going to do. Rather, he says, one has to be realistic about what the publisher is going to bring to the table and then say to oneself, "Okay, so what am I going to do to sell copies of this book?" Authors who are less frustrated with the process and their publishers are usually of two camps, the best-sellers and those who get beyond this us-versus-them mentality.

This latter group of authors—who do take control—realize that a book is not dead after three months as publishing wisdom dictates, and they get creative. The authors who do not rely on luck tend to have more positive publishing experiences and feel less angry at the outcome.

What to Do?

Ultimately, we all have to realize this basic truth: If writers don't write, publishers have nothing to publish. And if they don't publish, they don't have a business and we don't have a career.

They can't do it without us and we can't do it without them.

"Without the fruits of your labor, none of us would have jobs," says ICM's Bankoff. "I'd have no deals to commission, editors would have time to do nothing but refine their own prose, and the legion of promotion, marketing, publicity, and salespeople would be forced to invest their energies in other pursuits." The editor and the agent, Bankoff says, are on a shared quest, and it's one only the writer can satisfy. And yet all too often what should be a partnership is just not treated as such.

It begins with the very way authors communicate (or rather don't communicate) with their publishers: An author deals with an agent who deals with an editor. The editor in turn deals with the rest of the house, and then reports back to either the agent (if it's business) or to the author (if it's editorial).

The channels are not very clear.

FSG's Glusman suggests that the author rely on her agent to make this process go more smoothly. "It's a big universe, with a lot of different players in it," he says. "The process itself is fairly simple, but there is a lot of competition, and every author feels it. An author's agent should be his or her champion, run interference, and get involved when there are issues."

Amy Bloom (*Normal: Transsexual CEOs, Crossdressing Cops, and Hermaphrodites with Attitude*, Random House, 2002) suggests we not be fooled by the nice stuff that precedes signing a contract and that we should proceed through the publishing process with the right attitude. "One can be appreciative without being subservient. Objectively this is a business, and publishers are not our parents or our friends. We sell them our goods, and they pay for them. We all need to concentrate on doing business in a positive and supportive way. In a way that does not cause pain."

Whomever you talk to—authors, publishers, or agents—everyone agrees: It all goes back to the agent. You must have an agent you can trust.

Being Grateful Is a Two-Way Street

If all the parties involved can have respect for one another's roles, then the idea of being grateful doesn't seem as onerous or troublesome.

In an ideal world, editors and publishers would be genuinely grateful to be publishing and authors would be genuinely grateful to be published by the people and companies who publish them and agents would be genuinely grateful to be working on behalf of the talented authors they represent.

In fact, many people are. Lipskar, for one, says he is. "Yes, relationships sometimes get strained, and I certainly know high-handed editors, agents, and authors who all think they're bigger than the process. And authors should absolutely be leery of agents and editors who from the outset treat them with disdain. But 'being grateful' can be a positive way of approaching a process that is often fraught with tension, as opposed to a sign of codependency and weakness."

Afterword

I am the author of more than 150 articles on the publishing industry, but I have never written an article for which so few authors and publishing professionals were willing to speak for the record. More than 50 agents, editors, and authors I contacted refused.

We are in the business of communicating, and so this silence is alarming. The widespread hesitancy to speak about these issues is almost as significant as the issues themselves.

"I don't think I have any right to complain about the things that are wrong—and there is a lot wrong—because I've been so lucky with how my career has gone," says one best-selling writer whose name every reader and every bookseller knows. "I'd be afraid to jinx it."

Not enough said, but as clear a communication as I've ever read.

SECTION 4

Meeting Your Public
(and Getting Them to Buy Your Book)

Publicity for Your Small Press Title

by Robert McDowell

Robert McDowell, a poet, is the publisher of Story Line Press.

The Big Picture

When my first collection, *Quiet Money*, was published by Henry Holt & Company in 1987, I had little understanding of how to promote a new book of poetry. My attitude, writer to publisher, was: "I wrote the book, you accepted it; now you sell it." I looked forward to giving readings and expected that I would be paid for many of them. I wondered if Holt would compensate me for travel, perhaps provide per diems, too. Though I was fortunate that the book was widely and well reviewed, I was disappointed that few reading opportunities came my way. I never did get a response to my question about travel and expenses, and three weeks after my book appeared, my editor left the company.

If only I had known then what I know now! If I had, I would have worked harder to read at bookstores (even to audiences of two or three people, because you are really reading for the store's buyer, who may reorder and even hand-sell your book to customers). I would have approached more libraries and schools, whether or not they had speaker budgets. I would have courted bookstore- and neighborhood-based writing groups and reading clubs, gladly accepting remuneration in the form of tea, coffee, and homemade cookies. Instead, I did next to nothing. Oh, I collected and treasured my reviews; I read when invited, though invitations never overburdened my mailbox. As the book took its crucial baby steps into the world, I languished. Why? Perhaps I was lulled by the reviews into a false sense of the inevitability of great success. It's likely I didn't really know what to do, and that even if I had known, I would have been sabotaged by my opinion—where did it come from?—that promotion wasn't really my job, wasn't, in a way, even necessary.

After twenty-five years of working as an editor and publisher of, first, *The Reaper* magazine, then Story Line Press—selecting, editing, producing, and promoting more than 200 volumes of poetry, fiction, drama, creative nonfiction, and criticism by others—I've learned that promotional opportunities and responsibilities exist at every level of book publication. The successful author must be involved in every way. In 2001 the University of Pittsburgh Press accepted my new book of poetry, *On Foot, In Flames*. Thinking of the writers I had published at Story Line, I realized that I needed to put into practice for myself those things I was always telling them to do. To help myself do this, I sketched out a list of the steps that authors and publishers must take together to publish a successful new book.

The Questionnaire and Lists

Once contracts are signed, the serious work of dealing with preproduction material begins. Publishers usually give authors a questionnaire to complete in order to collect information that will assist them in better marketing the book. The questionnaire asks the author to look at the book-to-be in visionary, critical terms. How would the author describe the book's potential audience? How does this book compare with popular current books (this is especially important in fiction and nonfiction). If the author has already published books, what was each of those experiences like? Where has the author lived and worked and studied? What contacts can the author provide that might lead to readings, workshops, conferences, reviews, awards? What is the author willing to do to promote the new book?

New authors should keep in mind that the support team, the staff-people working for the publisher, do not already know everything about them and their work. That's why it is always best to approach the questionnaire as if the people reading it know nothing about you— whether you've published one book or twenty. I also remind myself over and over that the publisher's staff are not ciphers, nor are they servants who live to draw my bath and prepare impeccable martinis. They are usually underpaid, dedicated people who, like me, want to produce and promote my book in the most efficient, effective way.

When filling out my questionnaire, I agonized over the three paragraphs I wrote to describe the book. I knew that some of what I'd write might very well provide the publisher's sales reps with the "hooks" they would rely on during their calls to bookstore accounts. Hooks describing a book are essential. When a sales rep calls on an account, she or he spends about three minutes on each publisher in the distributor catalogue (small presses rarely have their own sales force; they are often sold into stores by companies that represent a number of publishers, such as Consortium or Publishers Group West). In that brief time, the rep must describe all the new books the publisher plans to bring out in the upcoming season. In my book's case, the hooks included: (1) publisher of a well-known press; (2) coeditor of *Reaper* magazine; (3) a leader of the Expansive Poetry movement; (4) westerner; (5) author and editor of well-known, critical volumes and anthologies; (6) third book of poetry. I also listed the names and addresses of every reviewer who had written about my first two books of poetry. I prepared mailing labels for 200 poetry reviewers I hoped the book would go to. I attached to the questionnaire a sheet of "bullets" from earlier reviews of each of my books (a bullet is the one pithy comment that best characterizes a particular review), and longer interviews and articles on my poetry and related endeavors in the field. I worked with a photographer who prepared a CD from which we could print a limitless supply of black-and-white and color 3-by-5 and 5-by-7-inch author photos. I attached my standard résumé and a half-page biography. I included jacket comments graciously provided by poets whose work I had long admired—Kim Addonizio, Maxine Kumin, and Chase Twichell. Finally, anticipating the publisher's mailing of postcard announcements and an order form, I attached, on labels, my personal mailing list of 700-plus names.

I learned the value of an author's personal mailing list in my fourth year at Story Line, when we published Colette Inez's *Family Life*. A normal response to a direct mailing of a flyer–order form is 2 percent. Inez's mailing list of over 500 names netted a response of 25 percent. That translated into 125 copies of *Family Life* sold before the book had even landed in bookstores. Publishers love developments like that. I asked Inez how she had assembled her list (at the time, my own personal list was a measly 150 names, many of them family and friends).

She explained that she constantly added to her list by asking for the addresses of people who attended her readings or took classes from her at conferences. She thought of her list as a living organism, a constantly expanding constituency. And that's exactly how it seemed to us at Story Line, too. From that time on, I encouraged Story Line authors to work on, and work, their personal mailing lists. As one of our sales reps put it, "The author is the most effective salesperson you will ever have."

The Book Inside and Out

Two common sources of anxiety for authors are the book's design and the editorial process. Decisions about the cover and format of the book are the responsibility of the publisher. An author will usually be asked to provide input, and he or she may even suggest a cover image. But, more often, the cover image, along with the typeface and layout, is selected by the publisher and the book's designer. Publishers know which images will and will not reproduce well and which typefaces are easiest to read. Their selections are based on aesthetic and marketing principles that have evolved over many projects. For example, a poetry, fiction, or nonfiction series may have a uniform cover design (as New Directions and the Pitt Poetry Series did for many years) developed by the publisher's marketing staff as a way to distinguish the books as both appealing and recognizable on bookstore shelves.

Another issue is whether to publish a hardcover or paperback first edition. Like many authors, I once believed that a paperback edition somehow suggested an inferior publishing event. It isn't so. Of course, a hardcover book is lovely to behold. But no book is penalized today for appearing in paper rather than in a cloth edition. Even fiction, unless a mass-market trade paperback deal is already made before first edition publication, is not hindered by paperback-only publication. Libraries now purchase paperbacks and apply their own stiff boards to protect the books. Bookstores are much more likely to order more copies of paperback than cloth books. And it is more cost-effective for publishers to produce paperbacks. Cloth binding more than doubles the cost of producing a book. In most cases, the end result does not justify the added expense.

While the design work is under way, the author will most likely be engaged in a discussion with the editor regarding line alterations or more substantive changes to the manuscript. Authors can resent this stage, resisting change of any kind. Disagreement and negotiation are fine, but general reluctance or a blanket refusal to accept an editor's suggestions will probably create strained relations. The editor almost always has more experience than the author, and it is pointless to upset one's most important professional connection.

My editor for *On Foot, In Flames*, Ed Ochester, caught an embarrassing grammatical error, suggested a couple of line changes, and asked me to eliminate a poem he found not credible. I did not want to lose the poem, which after all was the seven-page result of hours and hours of hard work, but because I trusted Ed's professional experience I agreed to the changes and cuts he suggested. The editorial process, and my collaborative role in it, improved my book, resulting in a stronger product for the marketplace.

Editorial issues need to be resolved as quickly as possible. I gave myself no more than two weeks to complete the work and have it all back in the publisher's hands. If one can wrap up the work even sooner, so much the better. Publishers require more lead time than authors usually imagine. In today's climate, once a book is accepted one should count on at least a year's passing before its publication; indeed, two and even three years is not unusual.

Press Kits and Tours

Few publishers are going to be able to assign to you and your new book an exclusive publicist. An author may hire her own. Professional publicists are especially helpful in setting up radio and television appearances; they can often get through to those sought-after media people who will rarely answer an author's phone calls or letters. But it is financially difficult, if not impossible, for most authors to travel this route (when I checked, the price range was $5,000 to $20,000). In most cases, the publisher's publicist, while working on several titles, will be delighted to offer support and will step in to handle specific requests (such as nominating you for an appearance at a regional trade-book show).

Maria Sticco, the publicity director at Pitt, carefully read my new book and continues to partner effectively with me in my marketing efforts. But it is first and foremost up to me to manage this area.

Knowing this so well, I spent the year during which my book was in production working to prepare and disseminate support materials and set up readings, signings, and workshops. For my press kit, I purchased hundreds of two-pocket folders for 29 cents each. Into these I placed the press-generated postcard and order information, my 3-by-5-inch author photo, and three pages of reviewer bullets from my earlier books. As a reviewer and publisher, I have seen hundreds of press kits, and the reviewer comments typically included are so uniformly positive, so bland in their upbeat sameness that one's eyes glaze over. So I decided to include a few stinkers at my own expense. (My favorite has to be the *Choice* notice of my second book, *The Diviners*, which concluded with a death knell: "Not Recommended.") I also included a long article from the *Dictionary of Literary Biography* on my poetry, a résumé, and a brief biography. Once reviews appeared (the first usually come from *Booklist, Publishers Weekly, Library Journal,* and *Kirkus Reviews*), I included copies of them in the kit as well.

As soon as the book was available (about seven weeks before the publication date), I bought 200 copies. I wanted to signal to my publisher that I was committed to the new book and that I intended to get behind it in every way the publisher's staff and I could think of; I also wanted to include a copy of the book in almost every press kit I mailed. Of course, I wondered if I was buying too many copies, but I can report that three months after the book's publication, I had to order another 100.

I sent out press kits with appropriate letters to teachers and writing program coordinators who might invite me to read or conduct workshops. I sent them out to librarians and select media people. Not only does a good press kit increase your chances of being invited somewhere you would like to go, it solves the problem of getting your hosts the publicity materials they will need if they decide to bring you in.

Because publishers have limited advertising budgets, I also assumed some of the responsibility of print ads. Pitt ran several ads in trade journals announcing its spring 2002 list of four books of poetry, which included mine. I had ads designed for my book alone, then paid to run them in consecutive issues of *APR* and *Poetry*, two magazines with an audience of poetry readers. Had my collection been one of essays or short stories, I would have researched various literary magazines and chosen to advertise with those that had the largest audience of readers who I suspected would appreciate my work.

The Launch

Because I had long-standing invitations to appear at the Writer's Garret, in Dallas, and at Lamar University, in Beaumont, I launched *On Foot, In Flames* in Texas. I had to be in New York the following week, and with the help of fellow writers and organizers Ram Devineni, Kate Light, and Diane Simmons, I set up three readings and a school visit, to take place over a period of five days.

After returning home to Ashland, Oregon, I spent nine days driving 1,600 miles through eastern Oregon and Washington. On that trip I taught twenty-two classes at five high schools and one middle school, gave four evening readings sponsored by small local libraries, and read at Auntie's Bookstore in Spokane. One night in Fossil, Oregon, I read at an assisted-care complex for senior citizens. Others in the town of 500 attended, but most of my audience was over the age of seventy. It was a great audience, and I sold a dozen books after the reading.

The next night, in Condon, Oregon, the library where I was scheduled to read was closed for renovations. The alternative space turned out to be the second-floor landing of the Condon Hotel. Only the librarian and two older women showed up. I read for thirty-five minutes to them and to hotel guests, coming from and going to their rooms, who would pause for a time to listen. I thought of something I often say to writers—that selling serious literature at times comes down to selling one, two, or three copies at a time. I sold one book that night, and even though the author in me could have easily retreated to a humiliating place, the marketer and proselytizer in me was proud of that sale. My poetry had just taken one more small step out into the world.

Some of my readings and appearances have involved remuneration. Many have not. When this is the case, I pay for my own travel, room, and board. At Story Line Press, we must ask our authors to accept as much of these responsibilities as they possibly can. As an author, I do the same for the sake of my new book, which I know will quickly vanish if I do not make every effort to place it in the hands of readers, new and old, one by one. I have recently completed a novel I am optimistic about. Because it is fiction, with a potentially larger audience than poetry, I have prepared materials similar to the press kit described earlier and used these to court agents. Yet even though I hope the right agent and publisher will combine to bring me a larger advance than poets hope for, I know that if the book is published, I will perform the same tasks and be willing to take on the responsibilities laid out here concerning my recent book of poetry.

Presenting your new book to the public is really no different from presenting yourself every day. The irony lies in offering what is so personal, and offering it mostly to strangers. Always there is the gulf between what you are doing—promoting—and what you are delivering—the offering of a sacred act performed in solitude. How well you straddle that abyss, how you leap from side to side, determines how sustained and sustaining your life as an author will be.

Techno Promo:
Are You Ready for Digital Marketing?

by Catherine Wald

Catherine Wald is the author of The
Resilient Writer: Tales of Rejection and
Triumph from 20 Top Authors

For authors, the Internet tantalizes and terrifies. While we're tempted by the Web's seemingly limitless potential to help us build our reputations and reach new audiences, we're also afraid of getting hopelessly bogged down in technical complexities and losing ourselves in cyberspace. Is the Web a boon to writers, or is it a technological vacuum that will suck up hours that would be better spent on our writing? Do we really want to use the Net to become our own publishers and promoters, or is all that stuff better left to the pros?

The answer, experts say, depends on your goals, not to mention your comfort level with the technology and the amount of time you want to spend. But whether you seek to post basic information about your work or to drive noticeable increases in book sales, there are several ways you can build a presence that reflects your own personal style and helps you connect with readers in a way that feels comfortable to you.

First of all, don't be daunted by the Web's vastness. Try viewing it as a collection of small, intertwined neighborhoods rather than as a monolithic metropolis. "If you treat the Web like the biggest place in the world, you won't get anywhere," says novelist and e-marketing expert M.J. Rose. "If you treat it like a tiny town where you're going to be able to meet all your neighbors and borrow sugar from them, you're going to be successful."

Building a Home Base

So where do you begin? To live in a neighborhood, the first thing you need to have is a home, and that's what a Web site is for. Your site serves as a place to house critical pieces of information about yourself and your work, but it's also the return address you use on your e-mail "signature," which ideally includes the name of your book and a few laudatory words from a reviewer. "When you're out on the Web promoting yourself, you need to have a home base that you can refer people to," says Moira Allen, editor of the e-newsletter and Web site Writing-World.com.

If you have an affinity for technology, Allen says, you can save money and build a site yourself by learning HTML and a program such as Microsoft FrontPage. Yahoo (www.yahoo.com) and EarthLink (www. earthlink.com), as well as sites such as www.register.com, offer relatively inexpensive packages for hosting Web sites that include templates and management software. If you aren't tech-savvy, you can hire a Web site designer to do the work for you.

But however you choose to create your site, think carefully about your objectives and the image you want to project. "The Internet is flooded with sloppy, unimpressive, cutesy, and trivial 'writer' home pages," explains Allen in *writing.com: Creative Internet Strategies to Advance Your Writing Career* (Allworth Press, 1999). "As a professional, you want to say something more than, 'Hi, my name is Bob, click here to read my stories, click here for a picture of my dog.'" In addition to this suggesting a lack of professionalism, she says, readers are turned off by sites that have so many graphic bells and whistles that they take forever to download, or sites that are nothing but one big ad for your book. "People get on the Internet to find information—and people who want to shop generally go to a store," Allen says.

Web sites that succeed, she says, offer "a reason for readers to come, and a reason to tell a friend to come, and a reason to link to you—whether it's excerpts from your book, articles, or poetry." A typical Web site, she explains in her book, should feature an inviting, easy-to-navigate home page, some kind of table of contents, a photo and bio, and annotated links. It can also include selections from work-in-progress, background information about the subjects you write about, writing tips, and previously published articles. To get ideas, visit other author sites and take notes about what you do and don't like.

Once you've established your site, you can start exploring other on-line venues where your work can appear. Allen recommends e-zines, which, she says, typically do not use exclusive rights, meaning you can publish the same story or poem in more than one. "There are tons of literary e-zines out there that probably attract a very different audience from literary print publications." (For more information about e-zines, try www.freezineweb.com or www.zinester.com.) As a plus, many e-zines feature contributor bios that link back to authors' Web sites.

Reaching Out to Readers

Once you've built your house and settled in, it's time to get to know your neighbors, particularly those who may be interested in your work. The good news is that "with the Web, you can go in search of your readers and you can talk to them directly, for free," says M.J. Rose, who proved the effectiveness of doing just that when she self-published her rejected novel, *Lip Service*, and, reaching out to one reader at a time, marketed it via the Web so successfully that she went on to land contracts with Pocket Books and the Doubleday Direct book club.

Begin your search, Rose suggests in her book *How to Publish and Promote Online* (St. Martin's Griffin, 2000), coauthored with Angela Adair-Hoy, by defining your target audiences as narrowly as you can. In other words, hone in on women in their forties who have read Proust, for example, rather than all women who read books. "For every niche you can think of," she says, "you can find at least one newsgroup, e-zine, newsletter, or listserv on the Web targeted to that group."

To find these people, start by typing words or phrases describing them into the major search engines. Then follow the links, making a list of relevant sites and communities as you go along. Armed with this list, you can begin approaching them individually—asking them to review your books, link to you, reprint your articles, or invite you to host chats.

Or you could begin in a more low-key way, by simply joining a handful of online communities—discussion groups such as e-mail lists, newsgroups, forums, or live chat rooms. Spend a little time listening in without participating, Rose advises. Then pick three groups that you feel comfortable with and slowly begin to take part in discussions without promoting your work, but always keeping the name of your book in your e-mail signature. "After about five or six weeks, people will start to ask you about your work, and the ones who like it will spread the word in the marketplace."

Readers respond because they love to deal with authors directly instead of through intermediaries such as publishers. According to Rose, "An author talking directly to a reader has a much greater impact on that reader than an ad or a review would have. Until a few years ago, the only way to talk to an author was on an author tour. But now anyone can e-mail an author and the author can immediately write back. This affords the authors amazing abilities to build relationships with readers."

Rose promises that authors willing to put two to three hours a week into Web promotional efforts will see results—as long as they have dedication and patience. "You have to look at this as a long-term investment of time," she says. "It's a wonderful process, but if you expect to start selling things right away, you're going to be frustrated."

If You Build It, Will They Come?

In most neighborhoods, heavy traffic is considered a negative, but on the Web it's the key to visibility and survival. As cocreator and coeditor, with Diane Boller, of *Poetry Daily* (www.poems.com), Don Selby knows all about building traffic: *Poetry Daily* had over 5 million visitors last year, and it gets about 22,000 visitors in a typical day. "Our audience is people you would expect—teachers, poets, librarians, students, and others connected with the poetry profession—but it's also heavy-equipment operators, homemakers, doctors . . . even a woman on a research ship in the Antarctic," says Selby.

Selby sees the Web as an effective tool for both publishers and poets to get the word out about their work, but he cautions that maintaining an active Web site and continually directing readers toward it requires an ongoing commitment of time and energy. "It is the case on the Web that you may build it, but people may not come," he says. "Although the Web is easy to get started on, and inexpensive relative to other sorts of things one might consider to publicize their work, it nevertheless is serious publishing work."

To attract visitors, he says, you need to learn how the major search engines work, and how to get—and keep—your site listed as prominently as possible, so that when surfers type in "poet" or "historical novels" or "short stories," your URL will pop up toward the front of the lists. Then, he adds, "To be visible on the Web and to encourage people to come back once they've found you in the first instance, you need to change content frequently—whether it's sample poems, reviews, or other writing." This constant refreshing not only keeps readers coming back, it also signals to search engine "spiders" that your site is updated frequently, which in turn helps your ranking in the search engines. You can also send out regular e-newsletters and other reminders to keep first-time visitors coming back.

Writers and poets who want to do well on the Web need to learn to think more like publishers, and that's all to the good, Selby says. "As writers and poets try to do things on the Web, they will learn a little more about what publishers are up against." As a result, he says, "authors, poets, publishers, and editors will be jointly on the same page about how to make the most out of the resources they have available."

Meanwhile, those who get involved in the Web need to budget their time carefully. "And then, one hopes that you're not too exhausted to do what you really do, which is to write," cautions Selby.

For Those Who Would Rather Be Writing

For authors who would rather be writing than learning the ropes of Web design, publication, and promotion, there are places like BookZone (www.bookzone.com) and Authors on the Web (www.authorsontheweb.com). These sites offer built-in traffic and publicity through newsletters, contests, and already established online links to important literary and book-related sites—and authors can pick and choose among these services, depending on their budgets and needs. For example, author and screenwriter John Blumenthal, whose self-published *What's Wrong with Dorfman* won critical acclaim in 2000, chose BookZone to design and host his site because, he says, it had a good reputation and "I'm close to computer-illiterate." But because he considers himself an entrepreneurial type and enjoys doing his own promotion, he didn't sign up for those added services.

On Site: Three Approaches

Those writers who have built their homes on the Web are using graphic and editorial approaches that are as individual as their writing styles. As editor of *January Magazine* (www.januarymagazine.com), a respected book-related Web site that draws about 15,000 visitors a day, Linda Richards has visited countless author URLs, and she's excited by what she sees.

"The Web gives authors a direct connection to their readers that they've just never had before," she says. "I think a lot of authors understand this very well and have used this relatively new medium to touch their readers in entirely new ways, evolving what works for them as they go along."

To demonstrate how different successful author Web sites can be, Richards picked three examples from "hundreds of authors I could have just as easily mentioned."

- Booker Prize–winner Margaret Atwood, author of *Blind Assassin* (www.web.net/owtoad): "I think the site works well because of its sort of homemade quality. This is an author who sells a lot of books, and yet has chosen to create a site that seems very reflective of her personality: She's very down-to-earth, very businesslike, and of course, not one to mince words. Her site reflects those things, and you can find your way around it without a lot of bells and whistles."
- Nick Bantock, author of the *New York Times* best-selling *Griffin & Sabine* trilogy (www.nickbantock. com): "Since he's a visual as well as a literary artist, he has done a good job of creating a site that is not only informative, but that really reflects his art and even offers the opportunity for usable samples of that art. He's got some download-able and printable ex libris there that are just brilliant."
- Diana Gabaldon, author of the *New York Times* best-selling *Outlander* series of time-travel romance novels (www.cco.caltech.edu/ ~gatti/gabaldon): "Diana Gabaldon has used the various aspects of the Net to create her first books and then her readership. She's done this not out of manipulation, but out of deep talent and great passion." The site includes interviews, book excerpts, and information about upcoming book tours.

Getting Personal with Readers

For Linda Richards, the Web is less about overt marketing and more about fostering communication between writer and audience. "To my mind an author's successful use of Internet technology is not about 'sell.' It's not about technology. It's about communication. The success factor doesn't rest with sex—Java mouse-overs, Flash animations, or an extremely expensive site—but rather with how well the author manages to connect with readers. The authors who are using the medium most successfully understand that the Internet is simply another way to reach people and the one that they can have the most control over."

With that in mind, successful Web sites focus on providing information and fostering relationships. They're the perfect venues to offer readers in-depth details and enticing extras—for example, ideas you didn't have room for in your latest book, thoughts that arose in between the writing and the publication, a chapter that was cut from the book, even an excerpt from your book as a teaser.

Ideally, Richards says, Web marketing should be an integral part of an author's promotional efforts. "The Web isn't the moon. It isn't a different planet. It's a vast reflection of our own communities—all kinds of people reside there. It's also a very literate medium; a lot of Web users read and buy books. So I think it's important for all aspects of the publishing industry to stop trying to put Web marketing in a box. It should be an important component of any book's marketing plan."

Writers, she adds, should also take advantage of the one thing the Web can do that other, more traditional venues can't: It allows authors "to fill the gaping hole that used to exist between the publisher and the reader. The Web makes it possible for an author to interact directly with readers—and that's a pretty powerful tool if used correctly."

Bookstore Appearances and Speaking Engagements

by Jacqueline Deval

Jacqueline Deval, formerly a director of publicity for many years, is the publisher of Hearst Books.

Setting up local bookstore appearances and other speaking engagements can be a productive way to get involved in your publicity campaign. Even if you have a publicist who is active on your behalf, you can track down leads that she probably won't have time to research.

Bookstore events are an important part of building your readership. If the events are not heavily attended—average attendance is as low as ten to fifteen people—the book still enjoys visibility through displays and store promotions leading up to the occasion. Your book also benefits from increased awareness among store managers, which can lead to hand-selling. And you've begun to develop an audience as the people who attend the event will talk about your book. Admittedly this type of grassroots effort is time-consuming, but if you are an unknown writer, here's where you can start to build your readership.

Speaking engagements at nonbookstore venues can also deliver larger audiences for you. Host organizations might include universities, corporations, libraries, museums, YMCAs, garden clubs, fraternal groups, and so on. Usually, these require a longer booking lead time than bookstores do, so start your research and outreach five to six months before you expect to visit a particular market. Of course, some speaking engagements can be set up with a shorter lead time, but if you have the luxury of time, use it to your advantage.

A word of advice if you are arranging your own bookstore and other appearances: Make sure to schedule them to take place *after* your book has been published, so that books can be sold at the events.

How to Set Up Bookstore Signings

According to *Publishers Weekly*, publicists work through the home offices of Barnes & Noble and Borders to set up 6,000 chain bookstore events a year. In addition, independent booksellers and the chains' local store managers set up thousands more.

Your publicist will probably set up some bookstore appearances for you. But you can continue to appear at bookstores after your official campaign is over. You may supplement your publicist's efforts by setting up events for which he will not have time. Be aware that bookstore chains do not pay for travel or serve as publicists for individual authors.

Once you obtain a list of stores to contact (and you can find store locations at www.barnesandnobleinc.com/store, www.booksamillion.com, www.borders.com, and www.booksense.com), send the information to your publicist to find out if your choices are appropriate. After checking with the sales reps, the publicist will give you an assessment of whether the stores are capable of mounting good events. Give your publicist at least a week to get back to you with this information. If you hear nothing, then proceed to set up your own events. Also ask your publicist to provide you with copies of the press release and extra book jackets. You'll probably need one or two jackets for every signing you arrange.

When you're ready to set up the events, contact the local stores directly. (Don't bother contacting the home offices of the major chains, as the event planners prefer to work directly with the publishers.) Ask the store's events coordinator if you can schedule an event at the store. Describe the sort of appearance you envision, whether a reading, a lecture, or a question-and-answer session. Avoid bookstore events where all you do is sign books. Let the coordinator know how long you are prepared to talk. It's best to plan for a twenty-minute presentation followed by questions and answers. Let the events manager know if you have a local mailing list; this makes you a more attractive candidate.

Once you've booked an event, follow up promptly with a letter or an e-mail confirming the arrangements, accompanied by a press release, a photograph of yourself, a book jacket, and any other information that the bookstore can use in displays, mailings, and other promotions. Tell your publicist about the forthcoming event. She should then notify the local sales rep. Better yet, inform the publicist by e-mail so that she can easily forward the information to the appropriate sales rep.

Arrange the bookstore event six weeks to three months in advance. This allows the events coordinator sufficient time to list your event in the store's newsletter and calendar. The events coordinator may ask you if co-op money is available to promote the event. (Co-op monies are matching promotional funds paid by publishers to booksellers. The amount of co-op funds to which a bookstore is entitled depends on how much business that store transacted with your publisher during the previous year.) Because you cannot know what co-op is available, ask the events coordinator to get in touch with the publisher's sales rep. Your publisher may allow a small amount of money to be spent on co-op programs, which might include a newsletter mailing to store customers (costing as little as fifty dollars), a small store-produced ad in the local paper or on the radio, or refreshments at the signing. As you might expect, publishers are less liberal about co-op spending during times of economic recession. If the funds are not available, the store might not cancel the event if it has already made a commitment to you, though it will not have as many resources for promotion. If the store asks you to pay the co-op charge, politely decline the opportunity. Co-op marketing is a way for booksellers to get money out of publishers: Authors shouldn't have to foot this bill.

If you're planning to appear in all the local bookstores in your community, schedule your events far apart so that you're not appearing at a chain store a couple of days before you appear at the independent bookseller down the street, or vice versa. Because booksellers are competitive, timing events too closely will only anger them and that will not help your book. Separate your appearances by weeks or months.

Let us suppose that you set up a hometown bookstore appearance. You probably know many people in your area and can provide the store with a good-sized mailing list. Give the store a copy of the list, printed, on labels, to send out notices about your appearance. If the store is not prepared to take care of the mailing, make up a simple flyer and send it out yourself. You can use your mailing list more than once. Some authors will list all their appearances in one flyer. Others will send sequential mailings.

Ask the bookstore's events coordinator if he plans to contact the local newspapers and other publications to get the event mentioned in the listings sections. If not, ask for a copy of the store's media list and make the calls yourself. Getting listed is a pretty straightforward procedure. Call the local papers and ask for the calendar or listings editor. Then fax, mail, or e-mail the information as the editor specifies. Ask if the paper can use a photo, and if so send one.

Go to the professional-development area of www.bookweb.org, the Web site for independent booksellers. Click "Marketing Tools" and you will find information about promoting bookstore events, sample media and calendar listings alerts, and pitch letter templates. Then check out www.netread.com. The site e-mails a free events calendar for any zip code you desire. Even if you have a good and active publicist, take the time to list your own events. Publicists trust the bookstores to properly get event information into calendar listings and instead concentrate their efforts on securing feature interviews.

Bookstores often have ties to community groups. Ask the events coordinator the names of local groups or associations that the store will notify about your appearance. If you have ideas about specific groups in the area that might be drawn to your event, then contact them directly. Ask if they are willing to notify their members about your event. Pitch them the idea of cosponsoring the event (at no charge). If they go for it, ask for a copy of their mailing list (on labels), which you will give to the store to send invitations. The invitations should, of course, mention the name of the cosponsoring organization. In this instance, everyone gains an audience.

Make Your Appearance a Success

Your principal obligation as a speaker is to engage your audience. You want to inform and entertain, and ultimately motivate listeners to buy a copy of your book. Use humor or eloquence, surprise or pathos—anything that will capture your audience's attention. Whatever you do, do not bore.

Unless you are a brilliant spontaneous speaker, you should practice what you are going to say before you appear at a lecture or reading. Some authors speak too long; others deliver lengthy passages in a monotone, numbing the audience. Instead, consider your audience's interests. If your book is a novel, read short segments of your text and, in between, discuss various aspects of your book's development. If your book is nonfiction, then create a short talk based on the key themes of your work. A straight reading of nonfiction almost never works. These other suggested approaches will help you connect with the audience. No matter the content you select for your appearances, remember to look up and make eye contact. Raise your voice so that the person farthest from you will be able to hear you. Remember that the carpeting and surrounding books can absorb or mute your voice.

Prior to your events, you might listen to tapes of writers whose readings of their work you admire. Practice your own presentation style until it sounds as smooth, natural, and entertaining as theirs. Another sensible tactic is to attend bookstore readings and evaluate what you find effective in other authors' presentations.

The novelist Edna O'Brien has a gorgeous, resonant voice and an Irish accent. She is a dramatic and mesmerizing reader. So is Toni Morrison, who creates a charged atmosphere at her readings. Nikki Giovanni is an impassioned reader of her poetry. Frank McCourt and T.C. Boyle are successful and engaging speakers. For utmost effect and beauty, first prize goes to Dylan Thomas. Listen to an audiotape of his captivating and resonant voice presenting his poetry. This sort of private education is essential if you are planning an extended reading tour and have little experience in giving readings.

Relax about the prospect of bookstore appearances. Even if you are unpracticed at public speaking, you will eventually hit your stride with audiences. The old saying is true: No two audiences are alike. Each has a distinct, individual personality. The trick to managing them is to be yourself. Then there will come that magnificent moment when, as you stand in front of a room of strangers, whether a handful of people or a crowd, and speak about your book, you will feel their avid interest in what you are saying. Their engagement will be palpable. They will be putty in your hands—and made to laugh or cry or sigh in empathy with your characters. When this magical moment arrives, you have to be strong: Do not be greedy and speak for too long. It is best to cut your talk a little short. Leave the audience wanting more, which is of course the art of the seducer—as well as the art of a successful author on tour.

The Book Signing

You should arrive fifteen minutes or so before the event is scheduled to begin. The store manager will greet you and show you where you will be reading. Bookstores are well practiced at running these events. They provide all the necessities: lectern, microphone, or perhaps a table and chair if you are only signing books. If your appearance takes place in a city where your sales rep lives or is visiting, then the rep will probably attend the event.

If you are an unknown author, the crowd could range anywhere from a disappointing handful to a happy group of fifteen or more. For authors who have written topical works of nonfiction, the crowd can become significantly larger. For example, Susanna Kaysen's appearances for her memoir about mental illness, *Girl, Interrupted*, attracted many people who identified with her experiences. At the time, Kaysen was an unknown writer, but favorable review coverage and the subject matter made her bookstore events a hit. Similarly, Mary Karr, author of the memoir *The Liars' Club*, attracted large audiences based on the terrific review coverage and her feisty and appealing perspective on her dysfunctional family.

This should go without saying, but during the question-and-answer period, you should treat the audience with the greatest respect. Always. Even someone who asks a loopy and long-winded question. Remember, you need them so much more than they need you. I once witnessed a famous literary writer address an audience member with contempt, telling the poor man that he had obviously missed the entire point of the presentation. No one deserves that treatment. Such a bully was that author that I could feel the audience wilt, and no one asked any more questions. To my mind, the author got his just reward. His nasty behavior certainly did not motivate me to read or buy his books.

Your greatest fear about your public appearances might be that no one will show up. Sometimes appearances fail to attract an audience because of competition from a local event or bad weather. Keep your chin up, keep smiling. Perhaps do what one resourceful friend of mine did. He became a volunteer bookstore clerk and assisted customers. Whatever you do, do not complain to the bookstore staff. You will only alienate and embarrass them. If you do, you will lose the support of a bookseller who might have talked to customers about your book long after you've left the store.

An essential part of your job is to keep the bookseller feeling motivated and interested in you. After all, the store booked your appearance because your book was expected to appeal to customers. Take this opportunity to get to know the store staff. Again, they might become your allies in a hand-selling campaign once you've left the store.

Let's say you tour five or six cities, and only about twelve people show up at each reading. You may come away wondering whether all your effort was worthwhile. As you see it, you're selling only a handful of books at a time. But behind the obvious, what you are accomplishing is building an audience. With the handful of people that showed up and bought and read your book, you have created a baseline audience upon which to build for your next book. Finding an audience can be a slow growth process. Sometimes it requires long, hard work. But with persistence, you can reach the payoff.

On one occasion, a friend of mine showed up at his own reading and found that the bookstore had made little effort to promote it. The store was located in a mall in Atlanta. Making the best of a bad situation, this author stood outside the store and started to drum up attention, noisily, for his book. He called people over and invited them to come inside to hear his reading. Big on personality, he soon gathered twenty or so people for the reading, and even convinced two strangers to buy copies of the book before they'd even set foot in the store. He knew that if he didn't get busy and try to make some success out of the event, then his time and effort would have been wasted.

You will decide for yourself if you feel comfortable with showmanship when it comes to building an audience. Remember that shyness does not sell books—unless you're able to create a Salinger-esque mystique. To thwart shyness, remind yourself that you're not promoting you. Rather, you are promoting your book and the wisdom, service, or entertainment that it offers. If it helps, you can even think of yourself as promoting reading, not just your book.

How to Give a Rousing Reading

by Tom Bradley

*Tom Bradley is a novelist living in
Nagasaki, Japan.*

It's official, no doubt about it. We have returned to Homeric times,
when writers had to recite, and recite well, or risk being buried in
flung tableware and beef bones. Swelling legions of authors exhaust
their vitality before the public. And if you've been exposed to the regular plague of such literary burlesques lately, you will understand the
need for a bit of judicious advice on how to give a reading.

Writers are understandably concerned about getting published in
the best places, and after that, getting rave reviews from the highest
critical entities. But once those chores have been accomplished, there's
something else you need to lose sleep over: how to elicit and sustain
worshipful reactions from mobs of rowdy listeners.

Truman Capote gave the best performance I have ever attended. It
took place in the Far West, where the men are big and the lecterns pro-
portional. You could only see the upper half of this little old man's head
as he read strictly from his very early stuff, the nice lyrical things about
being reared by crazy aunties and grannies in the Deep South. At the
end of every selection, he would stride out from behind the lectern,
raise his book over his head, and give it one good shake. It was a gesture
that even his detractors would have had to call mighty. He waved his
work high in the air, as if to say, "Think what you will about me and my
life. This is the only thing that matters." Everyone in the room was
moved, especially the scribblers—the majority of whom had only
shown up to be obnoxious during the question-and-answer part and to
jeer at this "little lapdog of the rich and famous." We gave Truman
Capote a standing ovation that night.

If you love somebody's work, you'll find uncanny enhancements in the most affected delivery, the reediest voice, the plainest face. Capote demonstrated that, to the satisfaction of thousands. On the other hand, one wonders how Gerard Manley Hopkins rendered his own "sprung rhythm," and whether it would have been possible to sit through a couple of hours watching him do it.

In a strictly technical sense, Jorge Luis Borges was the worst I've ever seen. The great Argentinean was deep in his dotage, and arrived on the arm of this academic type, a self-proclaimed Custodian of the Author's Immortality Before the Fact. Whenever somebody asked Borges a question about his artistic development, or his childhood, or anything more complicated than "How do you like the weather in these parts?" he'd say, "I'll let my esteemed colleague answer that one," and slip off into dreamland. And this colleague would simper, "Well, you know, it's only a theory of mine. I haven't published it yet, but . . . ," and proceed to psychoanalyze the human being seated onstage next to him as if he were already dead. It was more surreal than anything in a Borges story.

The one we had come to see didn't actually read anything. But at one point his blind old eyes lit up, and he interrupted his colleague, and he started talking about the stroll across the tree-lined park that had brought him to us that night. He said it was already reconstituting itself in his memory as more fictional than real. Everybody in the place was a Borges fan, and we all knew exactly what he meant, or thought we did, and that one short utterance gave us everything we had come for. We supplied the magic from our recollections of his books, which are all that matter now that he's dead, anyway.

Assuming you haven't quite reached the status of legend in your own time, as both Capote and Borges did, there are practical matters that need to be addressed before you powder your nose and make your debut. Vocal quality, it has to be said once and for all, is about 82 percent of everything—at least for those auditors who haven't come around to worshiping every syllable that bears your name, regardless of delivery. Drama students are taken through a daily regimen of wrenching weird noises from their throats and noses: squeaks and grunts and hoots and screams—the equivalent of a rousing game of hockey for the vocal cords. But you don't need to formalize it to that extent. It helps to be raising children, who require those sorts of noises several times per hour from at least one parent.

I've been told that my voice is good. Whether that's true or not, it definitely carries far and wide without much effort on my end of things. My theater friends tell me that being gigantic is an advantage. I'm six-foot-nine, and weigh more than three hundred pounds. (Can't help it: basketball family, you know. My father holds a plausible claim to having invented the hook shot when he was a pro in Chicago, way back in the olden days; my second cousin Bill Bradley played for the Toledo Toots or whomever, and then went on to become one of the next presidents of our nation; and my Mormon nephew Shawn Bradley is currently the NBA's premier shot blocker or something. I have no idea what team he plays for, but he's seven-foot-six, so he gets to be in Bugs Bunny movies. It's not fair.) That extra span of lung and trachea acts as a resonator. Also, slipping into a little superfluous avoirdupois doesn't hurt: That surplus unction oozes straight to the larynx, enriching and lubing things up. So equipped, I can fill up a big hall with myself with no strain. Like Thomas "Fats" Waller said, "All you gotta do is give me air and I fill it, one way or another, yes, yes."

Even if you haven't been so blessed, and you're short and scrawny, you should always stand (Capote did). And shove that lectern aside. If it's bolted down, stand in front of it. Or on top of it. And even if you don't have time for daily throat hockey, you must avoid microphones altogether. Certainly never allow yourself to be handed a mike without a stand.

Obviously, none of this advice applies if you're writing domesticated realism in the intimate and soft-pedaled mode, bathed in muted tones, imbued with "transparency of style," with simple declarative syntax, no intimidating polysyllables, all democratic and "pure," manageable by all and sundry, "real-time fictions" offering reassurance and comfort to moral valetudinarians, featuring ordinary characters whom just about anybody can gently condescend to, doing ordinary things, just as you'd do in your daily life if you, too, were a member of the nebbishim. In that case you'll need to ask someone to lug a comfy chair onto the stage for you, and equip yourself with a brown ceramic cup of chamomile tea and fuzzy bunny slippers, and a mike with one of those spongy muffling things over its glans.

For everyone else, those reciters born with at least a normal budget of animal vigor, it's advisable to be drunk. But not too, lest you lose sight, literally, of the page. Personally, I've always been able to tune a wine drunk more finely than a spirituous one. Beer's out of the question. Upper-gastrointestinal eructations are the bane of any vocal performer, and frequent visits to the urinal tend to interrupt the flow of your plotline. Wine's the thing, as long as there's some okay cheap California stuff around. If necessary (and if it fits in with the milieu—isn't too disruptive of the ambience and so forth—and doesn't seriously violate local licensing laws), don't hesitate to tote your own in. A nice screw-top jug of Carlo Rossi red is just about right.

Once you've arrived at a style of vocalizing, there remains the small problem of your entrance. If you can do it without making your hosts too angry, it's always best to politely forgo any offers of an introduction. And intros from your own lips are even worse. We've all squirmed through too many interminable preambles—necessary because the works themselves are couched in private language, dealing with private matters that the authors are too coy or lazy or theoretically constricted to elucidate in the body of the work. These intros are never composed or rehearsed, but are supposed to be emphatically spontaneous, and every other syllable is "um." In deliberate reaction to that abuse, the canny author won't say anything at all, but will climb up there and just start reading recital pieces that have been shaped into self-explanatory and self-contained wholes. That's with a *w*.

Should you show up early and mix, or create a mystique by showing up late? This all depends upon the size and mood of the gathering. If it's small and relaxed enough so there's a plausible chance of schmoozing and glad-handing everyone, you should be there before the doors are unlocked. With a big crowd it's always better to be tardy—not so much for "mystique" as to avoid getting chummy with just one clump of the audience and then being tempted to elicit most of your cheers and guffaws from that quadrant of the room. That always looks like you carted in your own claque, or paid a bunch of ringers to come in from the taverns. (Not a bad idea, come to think of it.)

Speaking of drunken spelunkers, I love hecklers and interlopers of any kind, and never get enough of them. I encourage people to jump up and chatter or giggle or scream right in the middle of everything. It almost never happens, of course. I even love the passive-aggressive types with the marathon "questions" designed to exhibit themselves and their erudition. Many writers pride themselves on their ability to stall out these motormouths with humiliation techniques. But I'm never mean to them. I give them the Mother Teresa treatment.

Now, my cruel streak is just as broad and deep as the next selfish, conceited author's, and I've occasionally let that streak show. Indiscriminate kindness is by no means my strong suit. But as it's an abstract quality, quite alien to me, and something that I have observed mostly from the outside, I'm actually very good at faking it. Normal people are much more impressed if you treat these long-winded interlocutors gently. Like a good junior-high-level writing teacher, you should hear them out with infinite patience, then rephrase their verbosity succinctly and elegantly and make it sound as though it might actually make sense. Then answer it to the best of your earnest, sincere ability. And if you can encompass all this with a soft, almost epicene voice (try to sound like that movie star–martial arts expert who appointed himself the Dalai Lama's bodyguard) . . . well, among numerous other benefits, it will just about melt any potential sex partners in the audience, if that happens to be a consideration.

Many writers are perplexed by the question of whether they should read novel excerpts or short stories in the "live format." On one occasion, John Irving solved that perplexity by dragging us through what must have been an entire book. He went on for the better part of a night, and lost one or two fans in the process. I, on the other hand, have never faced this excerpt/short story dilemma, and I'll tell you why: I've never written a short story in my life.

All the things I've published in magazines are adaptations knocked together from separate parts of larger works, carefully shuffled and adjusted to follow Poe's formula for the short story (the "singleness of expression," the "economy of means," making it consumable in a single sitting—just the right length so people's buttocks don't get tired, and so on). I recite only these "shorties" and fob them off as integrated excerpts lifted whole from the novels. But I don't think it's intolerably dishonest of me. Nobody's ever asked for his money back. Didn't Picasso or somebody say that art is lies? It's true even if he did say it.

The point is that we're engaging in a performance. And without the primeval shape of the completed tale, the rising action, climax, and denouement, you miss the opportunity to draw the full dramatic potential from your hour upon the stage. The most you get is puzzled silence and a few anticlimactic throat-clearings from the peanut gallery. "Literary events" are theater, not literature per se, which has taken place mostly in silence and solitude since literacy became widespread enough to present a market.

As far as making your literary selection goes, you'll find every detail of every audience's response etched forever in your memory—not just laughter and jeers, but even squeaking chairs and coughs. Whenever you reread the passage, the recollected sounds will accompany every word as it passes under your eye. Keep that in mind if you decide to publicly present the same stuff more than once. Don't be surprised if the Des Moines teenager materializes in the Pittsburgh front row and yawns on that certain subordinate clause.

The key is to be drawn into the story with all the absolute concentration and intensity and devotion that, in your fondest and most megalomaniacal fantasies, you wish every reader would bring to your work. And to do that, a big part of you has to shut out the rest of the room completely. Your own ideal reader would be someone who reads exactly as you do when you come to a new book by an author whom you admire virtually without reservation, when you are willing, during this first reading at least, to suspend critical judgment and be swept away into this writer's heaven or hell or purgatory or limbo.

One of the most difficult things that public readers have to do, and continually remind themselves to do, especially prose writers, is to speak slowly. Selfishly consume what the socialized, diurnal self would consider an inordinate amount of the audience's collective life span. But if you become your own ideal reader, that ceases to pose any difficulty. You naturally relish each sacred phoneme, unless your writing sucks and isn't worthy of that much attention in the first place. But that's a different topic.

When the last word is declaimed and the lights come back on, and when all tomfoolery is set aside along with my mocked-up "shorties," I go home where there's no peanut gallery except in my imagination, and I sit down to write what I am increasingly coming to consider *closet fiction*—as radical as that may sound to the devoted followers of the public reading circuit. Like that little lapdog I mentioned earlier, I base my self-respect on the paper product, because the mass of bone and soft tissue that gets dragged to the lectern will be silenced and invisible soon enough.

Slam Your Way Across America

by R. Eirik Ott

R. Eirik Ott, a poet, is the author of the chapbook series The Wussy Boy Chronicles.

In the heyday of punk rock, little garage bands armed with duct-taped guitars and as much passion as raw talent skirted the mainstream rock world by setting up their own network of true believers. They slapped together shoestring tours with the help of friends of friends they'd never met, blew their last wads of cash on used vans and pawn-shop amps, and hit the road, playing house parties for twenty kids at a time and hoping for just enough gas money to get to the next town, the next gig, the next series of couches they'd be crashing on.

The same energy is in full effect in the underground performance poetry scene. More and more poets are getting fed up with the standard routine of sending their poems to the literary magazines listed in *Poet's Market* only to reap a pile of rejection letters months later. They're photocopying their own chapbooks of poetry, burning their own CD recordings, and hitting the spoken-word highway just like their punk-rock brethren.

Thanks largely to the widespread popularity of competitive poetry slamming—the full-contact sport of spoken word—a loose network has spread its way through America one college town at a time. Clusters of performance poets, slam organizers, hosts, and venue owners trade missives via e-mail and Web site postings to keep one another informed and in check, and they meet regularly to figure out what the next step forward should be.

In case you've never experienced what has been called "a bona fide cultural force" by the *New York Times*, a poetry slam is like a lyrical box-ing match. Five judges are randomly chosen from the audience and tasked with rating each performance on an Olympic scale of 1 to 10. Readers sign up open-mike style and are called to the stage one at a time to perform one original poem within three minutes. Each poet is scored, and at the end of the slam whoever has the highest score is declared the winner.

You can imagine the kind of criticism this sort of thing gets. Literary critic Harold Bloom dismissed slam poets as poetasters "declaiming rant and nonsense at each other" and the burgeoning poetry slam scene as "the death of art" in the *Paris Review* (spring 2000). Former poet laureate Robert Pinsky pooh-poohed poetry slamming during a November 1999 segment of *60 Minutes*, claiming performance-based slam poetry didn't hold up to the classic works in the literary canon. The elitist sniping hasn't stopped the spread of poetry slamming and the steep rise in popularity of the form, however, nor has it stopped it from becoming what the *Daily Oklahoman* called "the hottest thing to hit poetry since Ginsburg's *Howl*."

Imbued with a punk-rock do-it-yourself attitude, the network of slammers has spread from coast to coast, linking and organizing an impressive circuit of more than 100 venues in the United States. The central organization is a nonprofit corporation called Poetry Slam, Inc., which runs a popular Web site at www.poetryslam.com and organizes a yearly gathering of more than 500 poets and thousands of fans from around the country called the National Poetry Slam. PSI and its nationwide poetry slam community have become the best route for a relatively new and unknown poet to organize a performance poetry tour.

That's exactly what I did in the summer of 2000. I had just graduated with a degree in journalism I was eager to ignore and had nothing holding me back from hitting the road. So I logged onto the Internet and started e-mailing everyone I knew in the poetry slam scene, and within two weeks I had booked more than sixty gigs across twenty-seven states spread over four months. I dubbed my tour Couches Across America, threw my belongings into storage, and hit the road for an endless summer of couch surfing, poetry slamming, Greyhound-bus riding, groupie shagging, and spoken word madness. (Okay, maybe not the groupie shagging part, but I was ever-hopeful.)

I sold nearly 1,000 self-published poetry chapbooks at $5 each, plus got paid between $25 and $100 per feature, which not only funded the entire tour but left me with enough in the bank to relocate to Seattle afterward. Along the way, I was able to scare up enough publicity about my tour to fatten my clip file with articles from the *Los Angeles Times*, the *San Jose Mercury News*, the *Utne Reader*, the *Dallas Morning News*, the *Sydney Morning Herald* (Australia), the *Ottawa Citizen* (Canada), the *Daily Oklahoman*, and countless tiny little papers scattered all over the United States.

Obviously, someone who is completely unknown and unconnected to the poetry slam community can't just send out e-mails and expect a tour to miraculously form. Most organizers of poetry slams won't give you the time of day if they don't know you or at least know someone who knows you or, at the very least, know something about the scene that spawned you.

What made the task of booking a tour easy for me was the fact that I had been performing poetry and organizing spoken-word events for nearly ten years, plus I had made a name for myself within the poetry slam community by being a part of the 1999 San Francisco Poetry Slam Team, cochampions (with Team San Jose) of the 1999 National Poetry Slam in Chicago.

You don't have to be part of a national championship poetry slam team before you can mount a moderately successful tour, but there are definitely steps you need to take before hitting the performance poetry highway.

Here, then, is a thumbnail guide to what it takes to work up to booking a solo poetry tour punk-rock style using the network set up by poetry slammers around the country.

1. First, you have to be really good.

No book or magazine article can help you with this, although there are plenty out there that would love for you to believe they can. The last thing in the world I want to do is unleash a Shatneresque horde of third-rate street poets upon an unsuspecting world, so make sure you are really good at what you do. (Be honest: If you suck, your tour will suck and no one will invite you back for more, plus you will give every other performance poet following in your footsteps a bad name.)

2. Put together a chapbook of your very best work.

Anyone with access to a typewriter and a photocopier can put together a little book of poetry at the nearest Kinko's. Add access to a computer and a design program like Adobe PageMaker, and you can have a snazzy little collection that people will actually line up to buy. Having a decent chapbook is crucial because its sales can fund your entire tour, plus it works as a calling card, networking tool, and show souvenir all at the same time.

3. Make a name for yourself in your local scene.

Even a punk band like the Sex Pistols was an unknown local band at one time, so you've got to build a fan base in your hometown. Hit every open-mike poetry reading in town, from staid Barnes & Noble readings to poetry slams in smoky college bars. Your mission at this level is to score featured readings in the most popular spots in town and to heavily promote them just as a band would promote a show, with a flurry of flyers, handbills, and, most important, stories in the local paper.

Getting media coverage will take some convincing on your part, otherwise your only mention in the newspaper will be a sentence in the back of the calendar section. Connect what you are doing locally with the growing poetry slam scene nationally. Concentrate on developing a relationship with the people who can help you out the most—such as the writers and editors on the entertainment staff of local newspapers. (Do not forget college and university papers! Student reporters are always hungry for a good entertainment story that involves something other than movie reviews and the same old bands.)

Once you have been rewarded with ink, you will have ammunition for the next step.

4. Create a press kit.

This is your extended résumé telling the world (especially reporters and the organizers of poetry readings) who you are and what you can do. Every press kit has essential elements: clips from newspapers, especially reviews and interviews featuring you and your work; an audio recording of your poetry in action, preferably on a CD but at least on a good-quality audiotape; a copy of your latest chapbook; a performance résumé telling of your featured gigs and publishing experience; a press release with the essentials—dates, times, places for the tour you are promoting, as well as contact information; and a dynamic color photograph of you performing in front of a crowd of cheering fans.

This last one is especially important. Do not under any circumstances supply a photo of you in a cardigan resting your elbow on your knee and your chin on your fist. Such a photo only cements the widely held belief that poetry is boring. Make sure your photo displays all the energy and emotion of a great rock 'n' roll shot in *Rolling Stone*. Including a compelling photo increases the chance that an editor will be interested in publishing an accompanying article, so make it a good one emphasizing that you are not just a poet, but a *performance* poet. Even better, provide more than one photo to give the publication more design flexibility.

If you really want to get professional, you can put together a Web site with all this information, featuring scanned photos, MP3 recordings of your work, text versions of your best pieces, your bio, links to online stories covering your work, and ordering information for your chapbooks. The easier it is to get information about your work, the easier it is to write a story about you that will spread the word.

5. Get out of your hometown.

And bring your press kit with you! You'll never know how good you are until you take your act on the road, so visit nearby readings and strut your stuff for new audiences. Finding a reading is as easy as finding a college with a nearby coffeehouse, but you can get an idea of where poetry slams are held by visiting www.poetryslam.com, the official site of Poetry Slam, Inc. You can find information on all the regularly scheduled slams across the country, plus the friendly folks running the Web site will gladly direct you to additional people running readings in your area.

Don't be afraid of road-tripping several hours just to read for a crowd of fifty people. Again, this is how you develop a reputation outside your little hometown, so do a bang-up job, leave a copy of your press kit with the host of the reading, and ask to be considered for a featured reading sometime in the future. If you blow away a new audience, chances are the host will be very eager to book a gig with you.

Once you get that gig, start promoting the hell out of it. Draft up a press release with all the information about your gig and send it along with a copy of your press kit to every newspaper in town, then follow it up a few days later with a phone call. You can get contact information for just about any newspaper in the country by visiting the newspaper's Web site. If you score a featured article, you can add it to your press kit, and believe me, the more clips you have, the better, because it shows that you mean business.

At the gig, be sure to kick up a sweat and sell a lot of chapbooks. Make certain that every single person in that reading goes away with either a copy of your book or something else with your contact information on it. When I toured, I printed up stickers with my Web site and some punk-rock graphics and handed them out for free. If someone didn't have the money to buy my chapbook that night, he or she could always go to my Web site and order one online. Ask the host to spread the word about your abilities. Poetry slammers are a tight-knit bunch, and they connect on the Internet regularly. As you perform featured readings in more places, your performance résumé will grow more and more respectable, as will the list of hosts you can use as references.

6. Attend a national poetry slam.

This is the Woodstock of spoken word—the premiere showcase of the performance poetry form—and it is a must for any wanna-be poet interested in rock-star status. It's an annual five-day festival of spoken word events and competitions mixing fifty-six four-person poetry slam teams and their entourages with standing-room-only crowds of poetry fans. Bring a big box of chapbooks along with you, because hundreds of poets exchange them like trading cards. You'll come away with a suitcase full of independently produced chapbooks by people from all over the country, which then expands your list of contacts for touring. And be prepared for some of the most amazing performances of poetry you have ever seen. When I was in the finals of the 1999 National Poetry Slam in Chicago, the audience numbered more than 3,000, and the roar of applause for every poem was deafening, just a whooping mass of screams.

A word of caution: Don't get into this for the money. Remember, some of the best punk rockers who ever lived never made enough money to quit their day jobs. But you can bet they did more in a summer of road-tripping in the back of a van than most people can imagine doing in a lifetime. Punk rockers hit the road with nothing but three chords and the truth, and hard on their heels are performance poets who are eagerly stripping away the numbing barrage of stimuli and laying bare the essential ingredients for an engaging evening of expression: a mouth, a microphone, and a cheering audience.

Who needs a poem in *The New Yorker* when you can be a rock star?

SECTION 5

Jobs in the Field:

Lots of Reward, Little Pay

So You Want to Start a Literary Magazine?
Rebecca Wolff

Editing Lit Mags Online
Guy Shahar

How to Start a Reading Series
Fran Gordon

Tales of a Literary Saloon Keeper
Melvin Jules Bukiet

Balancing Act: Teaching Creative Writing
Hilma Wolitzer

So You Want to Start a Literary Magazine?

by Rebecca Wolff

Rebecca Wolff, a poet, is the editor of
Fence *and the publisher of* Fence Books.

Presumably you have been struck by lightning. You have had an idea: It has dawned on you that there is a terrible void, a dearth, a yawning chasm in the literary landscape whose dimensions, proportions, and significance only you can fathom, and which is shaped exactly like a literary journal (as opposed to a writing group, reading series, or Web site).

This idea, this burgeoning literary journal, now struggling against the confines of your fevered vision like a particularly determined chick inside a particularly sturdy egg, could evolve in several ways. You may know exactly what kind of writing you are interested in publishing. To say "good writing" is generally not enough—there are, according to the Council of Literary Magazines and Presses (CLMP; www.clmp.org), more than 600 journals being published annually in the United States, each of which, on some level, claims their content is "good." What you need is a specific editorial vision of the *kind* of good work you plan on publishing. Take, for example, the journal *3rd bed* (www.3rdbed.com). The editors of *3rd bed* admire writing that traces a lineage back to the Surrealists, even to the Dadaists. This is the niche it fills, the need it has met.

Your journal may evolve instead in terms of how you envision its audience: Is your journal of specifically regional interest, like the *Connecticut Review* (www.ctstateu.edu/univrel/ctreview/index.htm), which is housed at the University of Connecticut and publishes writers mostly from that state, including high school–age writers? Or is your journal intended to speak, either by virtue of its aesthetic policies or of its format and distribution, to a very specific group of people, one almost exactly the size of your Rolodex? Many worthy journals arise out of the publisher's desire to publish his or her own writing, as well as that of his or her friends/community, and to hand-deliver the results—the handmade journal *Skanky Possum* (www.skankypossum.com) is one particularly brilliant example.

Once you've settled on your journal's identity, it's important to be able to articulate it—hence, the mission statement: a concise, one- or two-sentence description of your journal's raison d'être. If your journal is to be run, as many are, as a nonprofit organization, this is an absolute prerequisite, as every grant application will request a mission statement. If your journal is to be run by the skin of your teeth, out of your own back pocket, this is still a very good idea, as the question you will be asked most often, when you mention to a friend or an interested author that you are starting a journal, is: What kind of journal is this to be? Why, in effect, must there be another journal in this world?

Necessarily, you have come upon the answer to this question after having immersed yourself in a sampling of what is already being published by other optimistic, creative, hardworking publishers like the one you hope to become. I say necessarily because it *is* necessary, in order to publish a journal worth the paper it's printed on, to understand the field you are entering, the context into which your entry will march. Ideally, you have even spent some few months or even years working at an already existing literary journal. This will not only help you to understand the time and energy necessary for the project, but also to have a sense of the exact nature of the task. It may even dissuade you—you may decide simply to add your energies to an existing journal, if in fact there is already one whose mission coincides satisfactorily with your own.

But once you have determined that your journal simply *must be*, there are a few decisions to be made.

Finances

Now that the creative vision of your journal (hereafter to be referred to as *The Absolutely Necessary Review*, or *TANR*) has hatched, so to speak, you must decide how to tend to it financially. Will you rely on your personal resources and go it alone? Or will you need help? If so, is there an institution available to you—such as a community center, arts organization, or even a university—that would sponsor *TANR?* Do you wish to incorporate as a nonprofit organization, so that you may apply for grants and solicit donations from private foundations and individuals? Or perhaps you will attempt to support it by means of advertising sales, subscriptions, and the occasional fund-raising event.

Many journals, like the one I edit, *Fence,* acquire nonprofit status. This route, much like the decision to start a journal in the first place, is neither to be taken lightly nor for granted (no pun intended). The 501(c) (3) moniker means that you offer a public service worthy of support by charitable institutions and even possibly by the government. If you are a nonprofit you spend an awful lot of time providing evidence, in the form of grant proposals and financial reports, of your worthiness of this support.

Nonprofits are also required to form a board of directors, a group of interested (and, ideally, affluent) people who will help maintain organizational and financial stability. The board has both legal and financial responsibility for the organization, and can make decisions without any input from the editor. (It also has the power to put a new editor in place at any time.) The process of attaining 501(c) (3) status is lengthy and full of paper, and should ideally be performed for you by a lawyer. *Fence* was lucky enough to obtain the services of an organization in New York City called Volunteer Lawyers for the Arts. Visit http://arts.endow.gov/artforms/Manage/VLA2.html for a state-by-state list of similar organizations in the U.S.

Many journals, both nonprofit and otherwise, have a patron or, sometimes, "publisher." These lucky journals—*Tin House, Grand Street, Open City,* and, now, famously, *Poetry,* for example—are supported in large part by wealthy individuals or private foundations endowed by individuals. The degree of editorial involvement desired by this publisher or benefactor will vary considerably from journal to journal—if the benevolent publisher is yourself, then this will never pose a problem. *Grand Street* is such a journal; its editor, Jean Stein, is both its publisher and its patron. If, on the other hand, you find yourself in a relationship of dependency with a patron, issues can arise, most notably: What exactly does the patron want in return? Editorial input? Social prestige? To be published in your journal, or to publish his friends? It's important to sort out exactly what your patron expects from his relationship with *TANR.*

If you plan to raise money for your journal, on whatever scale, the first thing you ought to prepare yourself to do is to become an event planner, one who can organize readings, either singly or in series; launch parties; parties with readings; benefit readings with wine and cheese; and fancy fund-raisers with famous writers. *Fence* funded its entire first print run with a benefit reading featuring four wonderful poets and a novelist. Event planners are resourceful people. You will rack your brain for what are called, in any industry, your "connections": people or organizations you have access to who can provide you with or help you locate free stuff—free venues, free wine, free catering, free printing of your invitations, free mailing lists for your invitations, and so on. If you are a nonprofit your board of directors should be helping you to accomplish some of this, either by throwing the fancy parties or by locating potential funders.

Submissions

Writers love to be solicited. For your first issue, go wild with letters. Invite everyone you've ever admired, or fantasized about publishing, including former teachers. Depending on your decisions concerning your audience, you may wish to include lots of well-known, even famous writers (read: big draws, names to put on the back of *TANR* so that people in bookstores will pick it up and not put it down immediately), or you may wish to entirely avoid such names and exclusively present the work of writers known only to you and your immediate circle. The thing to do is to know what you want and why you want it, and to understand the consequences. A journal that does not feature any (or many) well-known authors, whatever the realm of their notoriety, will not sell on the newsstand, and will have difficulty finding distribution. More about this later.

After your first issue has come out, you will swiftly begin receiving unsolicited submissions. Again, depending on your desires, you may want to list *TANR* in such publishing resource books as *The Poets Market*. Be aware that if you do this, *TANR* will soon receive such a tidal wave, a tsunami even, of unsolicited and often inappropriate submissions. More effective, perhaps, is to circulate complimentary copies of your new magazine to writers and other significant figures you want to be aware of it. They will pass the word on and probably send work themselves.

While many journals employ interns to open and sort through mail, I have always considered it a pleasure and a duty to actually read the entire slush pile (an unflattering term for unsolicited submissions), or at least to divide it among *Fence*'s editors. This is because it is inherent to *Fence*'s mission that we publish a significant amount of work by writers who are not part of any particularly prominent circles, scenes, or cultures.

At *Fence* we have four poetry editors, including me. About every four months, the stack of submissions is divided among us first according to whom they are addressed and then to whose pile is biggest (we try to even them out). We each read our pile and reject what we feel comfortable rejecting, then make copies of the work we are interested in publishing or at least discussing with our fellow editors. We each mail these copies to the other three editors about two weeks in advance of the date set for our editorial meeting. At the meeting we employ a highly sophisticated system of cajolement, seduction, and harassment in order to try to convince the other three editors of the value of our favorite poems. The resulting mélange of accepted work is generally successful at representing the mélange of our editors' actual tastes and concerns.

We operate with a publishing backlog, at this point, of at least a year, which allows us to use a bit of hindsight in curating the issues; we attempt to create an even gender ratio—that is, our only demographic concern aside from an abiding desire to publish writing we like by writers of color as often as it comes our way. Because our response time has lengthened from one to sometimes as many as six months, we welcome simultaneous submissions; it's only fair.

Copyright and Contracts, Author Fees

Most journals obtain "First North American Serial Rights," which means that they have the right to publish the work first and that the rights revert back to the author upon publication. If the poem or story is subsequently anthologized or published as part of a collection, *TANR* should be acknowledged on the copyright or acknowledgments page.

A contract is a good idea, as it will help to avoid any future confusion as to what exactly has been agreed to by the author. This document can easily be mailed out as part of your acceptance letter. Contractual considerations for the publisher include: Do you wish to obtain permission to post the work on your Web site, if you have one? Do you wish to be able to reprint the work in any anthology you may publish later—such as *The Best of TANR*? At the very least your contract should ask for a current correct address for the contributor, including an e-mail address, and a signature assigning first serial rights. The contract should also state that the author must provide *TANR* with a digital file of the work and a biographical statement, within a certain time, and delivered to *TANR* in its preferred mode (by e-mail, regular mail on a disk, other). If *TANR* is lucky enough to be able to pay its authors, the contract should state its rate of payment and the approximate time the author can expect to receive this payment. At the very least the contract should promise payment of one free author copy (the standard is two free copies) of whichever issue the work appears in.

Production

Desktop publishing has changed the literary landscape—it is now feasible, even quite easy, for one person to edit, design, and lay out for production an entire book or journal. If you are design-savvy, and handy with such programs as Quark, PageMaker, In Design, Photoshop, then you will be many steps ahead of the game. If you are savvy but not handy, then you will need to either take a course or to find someone who is handy: a production editor who can work with you on the design of the magazine and then lay it out. If you are neither savvy nor handy, you will need to hire a designer, who will come up with some ideas for the look of the magazine—"trim size" (width by height), what the pages will look like (fonts, text styles, and so on), a title design or logo—and work with you on arriving at a final decision.

Journals range in their production values: They can be photocopied and stapled; printed on an antique, hand-cranked letterpress and hand-sewn; professionally offset-printed and machine-bound with what is known as a "perfect binding" (many commercial magazines are printed this way; they have a flat spine on which can be printed the title, date of the issue, and so on). Of course you must take into consideration practical matters such as production costs and readability when choosing a design, but also remember that the physical look of the journal should convey the kind of aesthetic statement you wish to make.

In beginning *Fence*, I first came up with the title; for reasons I hope are obvious, the image of a fence, and those who sit upon it, was correlative with my goals as an editor. Hot on the heels of the title came a design imperative: I wanted readers to be attracted to *Fence*'s size and to the image on the cover; I wanted them to wish to hold it in their hands and look inside, and to be moved by the clarity and confidence of its interior layout just as the layout serves to present the writing confidently and clearly.

The production schedule for a journal such as *TANR* goes something like this: For an issue that you want to come out in, say, early May, your editorial deadline should be about three months earlier—in this case early February. This means that by February 5, all contracts have been mailed out and received back from the authors, along with the works in digital form, which are ready to be poured into your template. First, you must decide in which order the work will appear in the journal and inform your designer. The designer (or you, if you have the skill) will pour everything in and, within a week or so, provide you with a version that is ready for you to start proofreading. This could either be an actual hard copy or a PDF file for you to print out yourself, depending on the benevolence of your designer. You proofread this "first pass" against your copies of the original submitted work to make sure that errors in formatting have not occurred in the translation into digital information. You make your corrections—as well as any desired changes in formatting, such as last-minute switches in the order, or a decision to move a poem into the middle of the page instead of justifying it against the left margin—and return the pages to the designer, who inputs the changes and prints it out again and returns it to you: the second pass. It is now approximately March 10. It is wise to bring in at least one set of fresh eyes for the second pass, as they will invariably catch errors you have missed. Once you have retrieved these changes from Fresh Eyes, passed them on to your designer, and received a new printout (March 15), it is time to check all the changes you have requested (the foul copy) against the new copy: the third pass. At this point ask your designer to create individual PDF files of the poems and stories and e-mail them to your contributors with a note requesting that they get back to you with any corrections (*not* revisions—the time is long past for such things) in a few days—for example, by April 1. Some journals still send out printed galleys to authors. Either way, the author changes should then be entered and a fresh copy printed out. You or another set of Fresh Eyes should proof the author changes against the fresh copy, one more time. When you have ascertained that everything is as it should be, it's time to get the thing together on a disk and ship it off to the printer: It is now April 5.

Printing

Regardless of your chosen format, you will need to find a printer. Perhaps Kinko's will be your printer, if you are going low-budget; perhaps you will seek out the services of a local artisan with a letterpress in her barn. But if you are intent on creating a journal that can be distributed nationally—that is, by a distributor—you will need to find a printer who can produce a perfect-bound journal.

After sampling quite a few printers, I chose Westcan Printing Group, in Winnipeg, Manitoba (toll-free at 866-669-9914) for *Fence*. You want to find a printer that is accommodating and helpful as well as accurate and timely. Undoubtedly, you will want to receive at least three bids on your job: Most printers now have electronic quote forms on their Web sites, wherein you submit your "specs"—trim size, print run, number of color/black-and-white pages, shipping information—and they in turn submit to you an estimated cost. It is not always wise to go with the lowest bid; you'll want to see samples of printers' work and make a choice based on quality rather than budget.

Your chosen printer will get what is called a "blueline" back to you within two to four weeks (April 19 to May 3), depending on the size of the company and its schedule. This blueline stage is crucial in terms of your ability to get *TANR* out on time: You must check over these bluelines (it's your last chance to fix errors; it will cost you something per each page that must be corrected) quickly and get them back to the printer as fast as possible. Once they receive the bluelines and make any corrections necessary, they will begin to run the job, and *TANR* should be ready to ship sometime around May 13 to 23.

Distribution

Only you will be able to judge how important these last two subjects are for the success of your magazine. It all depends on your mission. Some journals, as noted, are distributed by hand. Some are distributed only by the U.S. Postal Service, publisher to subscriber. One worthy "distributor," Small Press Distribution (www.spdbooks.org), in Berkeley, California, is actually a wholesaler and relies on its catalogue and Web site to distribute magazines, rather than on sales reps, as a true distributor does. On the other hand, many of the larger distributors, such as Ingram Periodicals, are more accustomed to dealing with larger periodicals, such as *Time* and *Rolling Stone,* and will have difficulty understanding that when they fax you a print order, they are reaching your home telephone. Similarly, they will have difficulty understanding the care and attention that *TANR* requires in order to ensure that it reaches its audience. I have personally discovered that in this instance, as in most others, it is useful to be a squeaky wheel. I have developed a friendly telephone relationship with my account representative at Ingram, and have been able to effect many changes for the better concerning the actual destination of those precious 770 copies of *Fence* that are distributed to Ingram's 400 or so bookstores and newsstands across the United States.

It can be very difficult to get a new journal distributed. Once approached by a publisher, a periodicals distributor such as Ingram or Bernhard DeBoer, Inc., will ask you to fill out an application form providing information about your journal, such as trim size, frequency of publication, and category of contents (literary, romance, gardening, whatever). They will also request that you send ten to fourteen sample copies of the current issue of the magazine, which they will cleverly deposit in a few of their stores, somewhere in the U.S. If they sell an acceptable number of copies within an acceptable time limit, they will accept your journal for distribution.

It is virtually impossible to find distribution for a journal before it has published at least one issue. How do you make use, then, of your first issue? The best thing to do is to send a selective but far-reaching mailing of complimentary copies. Send them to writers you admire, potential future funders, other magazine editors, press venues such as newspapers and radio stations with literary features, and anyone else you think should know of the existence of your new magazine. This way *TANR* will get into the hands of at least some readers and, if you're lucky, the buzz will begin.

Promotion

Fence was conceived with active promotion (or publicity, or marketing) as a prerequisite of its success. I wanted to reach as many readers as possible. This is what I desire for the writing we publish; this is what I see as the raison d'être of this particular journal: not to be known and read only by a lucky band of insiders, but to become part of a very large conversation, or dialogue, among the many different writing communities at play.

With this in mind, we have coordinated and participated in as many readings, conferences, panel discussions, talks, festivals, and other gatherings of live bodies as possible. To accomplish this you must research literary events in your area, or in areas that you want to target for potential readers of *TANR*. I highly recommend this as *TANR*'s best means of promotion: There is nothing like actually meeting people and talking about your magazine to help create a sense of excitement and actuality about it.

There are other more expensive and less friendly means of promotion. If you can afford it I highly recommend advertising in other literary and industry magazines—some will even agree to an advertising exchange where each magazine runs an ad for the other. Press releases are another way to get the word out, but keep in mind that they are only as effective as your mailing lists. E-mail announcement lists are not actually expensive to use, but beware: They can be very time-consuming to create and maintain and can often annoy people if they are used injudiciously.

As a last word, *TANR* would do well to become a member of the aforementioned CLMP, a service and advocacy nonprofit that is a wealth of information and advice on all of the above subjects and more. CLMP runs workshops, mentorships, and panels on small-press literary topics such as distribution, promotion, contracts, interns, and fundraising.

Long live *TANR*.

Editing Lit Mags Online

by Guy Shahar

Guy Shahar is the founding editor of the Cortland Review.

Among the vast array of resources the Internet has made readily available to the literary community is the online magazine. With basic computer skills, anyone, it seems, can launch one. This fact leads to the biggest disadvantage of online publishing—credibility, or, rather, the lack thereof.

In the early days of the Web, before present-day coding standards and high-speed access, the medium was limited to text and was delivered via a slow modem line. Few people had computer access in their homes. Online space was expensive, and the Internet was mostly the domain of universities, whose students and professors posted the majority of content. Many would-be authors began to "self-publish" on the Internet. Before long, free Web services offered everyone the opportunity to post pages, and creative writers, born overnight, crowded the Internet with drivel. As the Web further developed, vanity presses entered the game and began using the Internet for their various pay-for-publishing schemes. Understandably, the legitimate literary community turned its back.

Online journals also have the disadvantage of, well, not being books. The screen lacks the uniformity of the book, a portable object designed for the sole purpose of reading—its margins are justified, line width is manageable, the font is easy on the eyes. On the screen you are forced to contend with an overwhelming number of factors: glare, refresh rate, contrast ratio, brightness, and so on. While most Web sites are designed with readability in mind, their design is affected by many factors. The look and size of the text changes based on different screen resolutions and color depths. A Web site may use a font not available on your computer, and your computer will be forced to select a substitute. Even if the font is compatible with your computer, your particular Web browser and computer operating system may render it completely different from the way it was intended to be seen.

So why would anyone launch an online- over a print-format magazine?

For starters, there's cost. Theoretically you could publish an online magazine without spending a dime. Publishing a print magazine, on the other hand, involves the cost of paper, printing, and distribution, which can be expensive. While most print publishers must charge for their publication as a way to partially recoup expenses, online publishers don't.

Because online journals aren't limited by the number of copies they can afford to print or by the breadth and reach of their distribution channels, they enjoy the potential for a wider audience than print magazines. Anyone with a computer and Internet access can read an online journal anywhere, anytime.

Having a Web-based magazine also means that back issues are readily available. In addition, readers have an unparalleled capability to search. If a reader is looking for an obscure word or phrase he remembers from a particular piece published five years ago, he can search for it, and let an online search engine take on the task of sifting through the Web to find it. This takes place in a matter of seconds, as compared with scanning and skimming through printed material page by page.

On the editorial side, technological enhancements can ease the burden of operating a journal. At the *Cortland Review* (www.cortlandreview.com), an online literary magazine founded in 1997 where I serve as editor in chief, we use a database-driven system that automates the publication process and workflow—from user submissions to reader evaluations, from acceptances to galley changes to publication- and search-engine indexing. Automation removes a lot of the time-consuming work for our volunteer staff. Today's advanced Web servers, robust databases, and sophisticated programming languages are powerful tools.

Due to the nonlinear, link-based architecture of the Internet, online editors can add a host of special enhancements unavailable to print editors, such as audiovisual features. A sound recording or video clip of an author reading her poem or story can add immense value to a reader's understanding and appreciation of her body of work. The site can also provide a link to an author's work elsewhere on the site or on another Web site—possibly a different online magazine, or an online bookstore where interested readers may purchase the author's work. Amazon.com and BarnesandNoble.com offer affiliate programs that give a percentage of sales to sites that refer customers to them. Online features such as "send to a friend" or "comment on this work" have become commonly used applications on many Web sites. Some journals even provide the author's e-mail address so readers may contact him directly. The reader's engagement with the work doesn't have to end with the text.

Getting Started

Let's say you're convinced: You've committed to starting your literary magazine online. The first thing you'll want to do is find a place for your site to live. You'll need a URL. This address is what users will type into their browsers so they can get to your journal. Now, you *could* obtain an address from a free online service, but something like "www.somefreeservice.com/members/pages/yourmagazine" is not easy for readers to remember (or type). Be professional and purchase a domain name (i.e., www.yourmagazine.com) for your magazine from an official domain-name registrar (godaddy.com charges as little as $6.95 per year for a domain name registration).

Next you'll need a Web host—a server connected to the Internet that will store your Web pages and display them when readers type in your address. Again, this can be done inexpensively through free services. However, many of these will infuriate your readers with pop-up ads and banners, destroying any effort you've made to look professional. Do your homework: Research some reliable Web hosts (tophosts.com or webhostsonline.com are good starting points, or you can run an online search for "web hosts"). If you want a site without frills, you can probably find an adequate Web hosting plan for under $10 a month. If you want to have audio and video clips on your site, the price will vary, as your hosting plan will require more disk space and bandwidth to allow your readers to download them.

A strong design is crucial. In the early days of the Internet, interesting content was enough to hold a reader's attention. Today you need a well-organized Web site with a compelling design to present your content in the best possible light; this means you'll want an attractive, organized layout appropriate for your subject matter. Above all else, it must be easy to read, preferably with black text on a white background and plenty of margin and white space for it to breathe. Why is this so important? If you want readers to remain on your site for any length of time (referred to as site stickiness) you want to make it as comfortable a place to be as possible. A sure way to discourage stickiness is with small colored type on a textured background that no one can stare at for more than a few seconds without getting a migraine. Throw in a few flashing or blinking widgets, and you'll blind your readers. I've visited many magazines that had interesting content, but due to poor design I had to give up trying to read them. Avoid this by looking for a good Web site designer, or if you're going to design the site yourself, read up on the basics before you proceed (goodpractices.com and webmonkey. com are good resources, or you can run an online search for "web site design").

Your site must have an intuitive navigational structure and an intelligent hierarchy of content. Readers who are unable to find what they're looking for on your site in the first three seconds will leave—no matter how pretty your design or how compelling the work you publish. You *must* make sure your site is easy to use. One way to test your site's usability is to invite friends or volunteers to make their way around the site and to record their experiences. If navigating your pages becomes second-nature even to first-time visitors, you've got a winner.

Establish a set publication schedule and stick to it. Nothing screams amateur louder than a magazine that adds new content at the whim of the editor. The *Cortland Review* publishes one issue and one feature quarterly. Thirty thousand readers visit our site each month, and they expect our new issues and features to appear on a regular basis. While we may not always publish on the exact date we proposed, we shoot for it every time. So should you. This will also help you establish a regular readership.

A successful magazine requires a lot of time and effort. Finding time to edit, time to read, time to create HTML pages, time to set goals, time to define a vision and style and follow it, and time to keep redefining it will lead you to look for a staff—and you need great people. The staff is the foundation of a journal. It's crucial to have people to discuss ideas with, share the workload, and set goals. If you don't have a list of eager friends ready to take the plunge with you, an online message board for writers might be a good place to start your search. Find volunteers who are passionate about writing and share your vision to create a journal. At the *Cortland Review*, nearly all of our senior staff consider the *Cortland Review* their "third job." Most have full-time jobs and family responsibilities.

Remember that online staff members can feel isolated and unappreciated, so occasionally find excuses to bring them together to get a better sense of themselves as part of a team. Good management skills apply in the real world as well as the virtual one. At the *Cortland Review*, with staff members scattered across the globe, we routinely have online chats when in-person get-togethers are not possible.

Luckily, operating an online journal can be done without real estate. The *Cortland Review* office is online, and we have a private Web site or intranet, which is nothing more than a regular Web site to which access is restricted. This enables our staff to log in from anywhere in the world, chat, post messages, review/comment on submissions, manage galleys, and so on. It's our virtual office, and, aside from cost savings, it allows us to employ a variety of individuals who live in other states, and in some cases, other countries. We're all connected by the same medium through which we also publish our magazine.

Online publishing is hard work. There are many ways to go about it and many obstacles to overcome. Along with all the technical aspects of setting up a strong Web site, don't forget content. Seek out and publish the very best work you can find. These days more and more quality journals are appearing online, and many established print journals have launched online counterparts. The Internet is becoming a viable source for good writing; make sure your online journal contributes to the cause.

How to Start a Reading Series

by Fran Gordon

*Fran Gordon, a novelist, is the director of
the PAGE reading series in New York City.*

For as long as there have been writers, there have been public readings. In 19 B.C., Virgil slipped out of his own crowded poetry reading in Naples to avoid fervent admirers. Today, many writers realize
that admirers are integral to their success. Readings not only offer an
opportunity for writers to promote their work, they also create a supportive environment for otherwise solitary writers to interact with their
readers. A reading series, in which writers from a shifting roster read
aloud new work on a particular day every week or month in a venue set
aside for just that purpose, can help create that supportive environment
and nuture it into becoming a community of writers and readers who
all thrive on the pleasures of the written and spoken word. And the
longer the reading series runs—some have lasted for decades—the
tighter the bonds of that community will grow.

Initiating a reading series takes work, but it's a rewarding endeavor.
The community you build will long outlast any single event's individual
ovation.

Picking a Venue

Before picking a venue, consider how much money you want to spend
(probably none) and what tone you want to set—elegant, populist, Beat,
new-but-in-the-know. Venue options, even in a small city, are only
really limited by your imagination. Check out local public spaces, community halls, university auditoriums, the town hall. Is there a room that
would comfortably seat thirty people and might be available once a

month? How about trying centrally located bars, coffee shops, libraries, restaurants, or art galleries? Visit any venue that appeals to your sensibility (intimate, formal, bohemian) at different times during the day and night and at various points in the week to learn the hours when the establishment has the fewest customers. Almost every venue has a few hours of downtime; any semiquiet time will do.

If you choose to run your series in a bar, you want a night when business is slow. Sunday and Monday nights are generally reading-friendly, as are Saturday afternoons. The bar's owners should be glad of the additional business, and the writers won't have to shout to be heard. Coffee shops have been the venue for many memorable series, including the legendary Limbo series, which hosted such writers as Bret Easton Ellis and Colm Toibin in Manhattan's East Village in the early 1990s. I have even heard of a reading series that took place in a deli. The owners did not read or write in English, but they were smart businesspeople who believed in the power of literature—and the power of the dollar; the deli's revenues increased threefold during the readings.

Restaurant owners may not be amenable to readings that might interrupt their customers' dining experience, but they often have separate rooms for events or large parties, which could be used if available. If you can schedule your readings well before the dinner hour, and not during the fray of table service, the owners may, in many cases, be supportive. If your audience doesn't generate income for the owners by ordering food or drinks, it may be necessary to charge admission or set a one-drink minimum as a way to compensate owners for holding your reading series on their premises.

Setting and Maintaining the Tone

When looking for the perfect venue for your series, think about the kind of writers you want to host (established, emerging, experimental) and the age and type of audience you expect (college students or professional adults with disposable income). These decisions will help set the tone of your reading series. Then choose your venue with an eye to creating an atmosphere that is consistent with the program you intend to present.

I direct the PAGE reading series at the National Arts Club (NAC), which is housed in a national historic landmark, the Samuel Tilden mansion in Manhattan. With its stained-glass ceilings and hand-carved wood fireplaces, the NAC provides a quiet and formal atmosphere. Typical PAGE fare has included events such as a reading of T.S. Eliot's *The Waste Land*, led by Paul Muldoon, with Richard Howard, Brenda Shaughnessy, and Mary Karr.

Manhattan's legendary Ear Inn, which has hosted Saturday afternoon readings since the late '70s, is a completely different environment. The Ear Inn is the kind of traditional Irish tavern that can be found all across America—small, dark, and intimate, with great pub food and cheap beer. Poet Michael Broder, director of the series, has hosted a wide range of readers, from the illustrious (Jane Cooper, Marie Ponsot) to the rapidly rising (Kathleen Ossip, Mark Bibbins) to the emerging but not yet known. Whether you want a cozy tavern or a historic site, finding the right setting for your series is crucial. The question is: Once you build it, will they come?

Enlisting Readers

You've nailed down the perfect place, now you need to find writers to read their work so that you can attract an audience to fill the seats. At this point you will have decided what type of writer you want to feature. Perhaps you'd like only a specific type: poets or political essayists or biographers. This type of specificity can help you promote your series (more on promotion later). Perhaps you'd prefer to invite a wide range of writers. A varied selection of published authors is sure to bring a wider audience to your events. But be realistic: If your series is located far from a major metropolis, your author wish list and your actual bookings might be sadly disparate.

A good place to start looking for writers to participate in your series is your local university. The university's course bulletin and its Web site should have plenty of information to kick off your research. To begin with, find out who teaches on the faculty. If a creative writing program is in place, there will almost certainly be guest lecturers coming to campus. "Piggybacking" an extra reading onto an existing author tour is an inexpensive, effective way to give simultaneous exposure to an author, her new book, and your new reading series.

Local authors are often a sure bet, not only as dependable community readers but as links to the literary community at large. A published author living in your town probably has friends or colleagues who could read with him and will bring a small crowd along to listen. A reliable source to find out who your local authors are is your bookseller. And because booksellers receive publishers' advance catalogues, they are also knowledgeable about which authors are planning book tours for the upcoming season. If a publisher is already planning to send an author to your hometown, talking that author into one more reading shouldn't be that hard a sell.

Another good way to draw in area writers is by publishing a call for submissions in your local paper. This is also, of course, a bit of extra publicity for your series. Briefly (and enthusiastically) describe your series, the venue, and the kind of work you're looking for. Then wait for the submissions to roll in. Get a friend to help you read and select writers from the batch—you may find a handful of great, undiscovered writers in the process.

Don't be afraid to aim high. Contact writers you admire, even if you think they'll say no. Some writers prefer to be contacted through their agents or publishers, while others don't mind being (politely) contacted directly. All publishers and many individual authors have Web sites with an e-mail option. *Publishers Weekly* often notes authors' tours and lists contact information for agents and publicists. You can also send a letter to an author's agent or publisher expressing your admiration for her work and asking if she would consider reading in your series. One letter is sufficient. Be sure to include your own mailing and e-mail address along with your phone number. Of course, you must first be a reader of literature yourself to run a successful reading series: Be sure you're familiar with an author's work before requesting her participation. You might also stress—to authors, agents, or publicists, as the case may be—that there will be books sold at the event, and that it will be well publicized. This demonstrates that you run a professional series.

Once you've enlisted one strong writer per scheduled reading, ask each writer if he or she would like to choose a friend or colleague to participate as well. If the writer is also a teacher, invite him or her to read with a protégé (published or unpublished). This kind of pairing can generate a buzz among certain circles—just the kind of publicity you need, but limit the number of readers at any one event to three (unless you're hosting a special party). Combining authors whose genre or subject matter is similar is another smart way to group writers. I hosted a wonderful night featuring Patricia Volk, Vivian Gornick, and Daniel Asa Rose, all authors of memoirs. Although their perspectives and styles were vastly different, they each read about family, which gave the reading a cohesiveness that the audience really responded to.

If possible, it's always good to give your readers an honorarium. Some series charge admission at the door and use all or part of these receipts to pay participating authors. Consider approaching local businesses and asking them to underwrite your series. (You then, of course, acknowledge their generosity on all your mailings and flyers.) You can also apply for grants from arts organizations in your area. (Contact your state arts organization for funding opportunities; Poets & Writers, Inc., provides matching funds for readings in New York, California, and the cities of Chicago and Detroit.) Do not despair if you cannot afford to pay writers, most will be happy with a well-attended and successfully publicized event where their books are available for sale.

Getting the Word Out

Begin publicizing the series by listing the schedule of readings in local newspapers, popular city-specific publications like *Time Out New York* (which doesn't charge for listings), and by posting eye-catching flyers on area bulletin boards. If you have access to the services of a graphic designer, create a logo for your series and use it on all your press material. Contact community outreach staff at your local radio station— they might be willing to promote the series on the air, particularly if you're willing to plug the station at the event. Send them a press release with the date, time, and location of your readings, along with brief profiles of upcoming writers and excerpts of any positive reviews of their work.

E-mail is a cheap and effective mode of publicity. Of course you will have begun developing your own mailing list. (Start with friends, family, and members of any local organizations you may belong to.) Approach fellow arts organizations and ask if they would be willing to give you an e-mail list, or at least swap theirs for yours. Send out an announcement of your reading a few weeks in advance, and then resend it a day or so before the event as a reminder. Do not send more than two e-mails. At the end of each reading, ask audience members to leave their e-mail addresses, as well as those of anyone they know who might be interested in the series. Your own list will expand quickly, and even if all the people on it don't attend each reading, your mailing will generate interest in the series. Do whatever you can to fill the seats, but remember that even a modest crowd at a reading can help boost book sales for an author. Word of mouth is still your best promotional tool.

Hosting the Event

It's a warm Thursday evening and your local café is filling up with spirited literary enthusiasts and three excellent local writers. You've researched, planned, and publicized your way to an organized, successful reading. Now what?

Hosting a great reading means better attendance next time, so remember to impose fairly strict time limits on the authors—the limitations are in the best interest of everyone. The most successful readings leave an audience wanting more. I learned this the hard way. I once assumed that a writer would know, with just one reminder from me, that twenty-five minutes was optimum reading time. By forty-five minutes, a colleague was tapping me on the shoulder whispering "Stop him." After fifty minutes, I, along with half the crowd, was tapping my wrist to indicate time. It was uncomfortable for everyone and might have been avoided had I stressed the time limit before the reading. Try to observe these guidelines: No single-author reading should exceed forty minutes, and no ensemble event should exceed an hour to an hour and a half.

Be sure that you consult the author first before enlisting her to field questions at the lectern after a reading. A successful Q & A session is not something you can plan for, and is dependent upon, among other things, the caliber of questions asked by the audience, and the author's level of engagement with them. If an author seems to be having fun, you may want to allow the session to go on for fifteen minutes or more; if not, limit the session to five minutes.

Make sure that the author's books are available for sale at the events and encourage the author to stick around and sign copies for audience members who want to buy her book. Most independent booksellers will be more than willing to send a clerk down to set up a table and sell books. If your local bookseller is short on staff, ask if you can borrow a box of books and sell them yourself, or try calling the publisher—they may send over a box themselves.

Whether you fill 20 seats or 300, you've created a place where important literary voices can be heard—and a community that will continue your publicity for you.

Tales of a Literary Saloon Keeper

by Melvin Jules Bukiet

Melvin Jules Bukiet is the author of seven books of fiction. He teaches creative writing at Sarah Lawrence College.

Down and In, Ronald Sukenick's sweet memoir of the New York avant-garde from the 1950s through the 1980s, views its subject through the mirrored glass behind the bar of each decade's preeminent watering hole. Yet the literary lush life goes further back, to Hemingway and Fitzgerald at the Café Deux Magots in Paris and further still to the days when Samuel Johnson held court at London's Turk's Head Tavern. I'd like to think that it also goes up and on—that is, upstairs and onward from the 1990s into the 2000s, at the bar that I co-own, KGB.

Set among Manhattan's East Village tenements and off-off-Broadway theaters, the building where KGB is located had been the headquarters for members of the Ukrainian Labor Home who left the USSR after the revolution and eventually settled in the United States. My friend Denis Woychuk, children's book author and lawyer for the criminally insane (viz. his *Attorney for the Damned*), was practically raised in the building, so when, in 1993, the octogenarian founders became disinclined to handle the premises, they turned it over to him to use as he wished, to produce and share revenues.

That's where I came in. Denis invited me to examine the second-floor social club, which had allegedly been built during Prohibition as a speakeasy and where Lucky Luciano was a regular way before the Reds took over. It was a small but beautiful room with a dark wood bar, stained-glass cabinets, tall windows, and faded red velvet banquettes. Like Judy Garland and Mickey Rooney confronted with an empty barn, we immediately said, "Let's put on a show." What sort of show we'd just have to improvise.

With an investment approximating the cost of a used car, KGB formally incorporated as Kraine Gallery Bar, Inc., though the gallery part of our original vision never materialized. Denis, I, and a bluff-tempered, tale-spinning behemoth of a man who had run security at a famous disco were the main partners. Tracy (name of a cheerleader, body of a fullback) was going to manage KGB for a percentage. To this day, I can't blame him for "losing" several months' worth of receipts and nearly wiping us out.

Dismayed, but not destroyed, Denis and I bounced the bouncer and forged onward. In our hands, the character of the place gradually changed to a more bookish joint decorated with manifestos and Russian film posters we dredged out of the archives in the basement. Ironically inclined writers seemed to enjoy the air of Muscovite decrepitude and filtered in out of the pan-artistic neighborhood woodwork. Literary agent Jennifer Lyons organized a monthly gathering of young editors, and one of these led to a boozy book party when W.W. Norton published *Next* (1994), an anthology of twentysomething journalism.

After the hubbub, an editor from the *New York Times* Style section decided to write about KGB. The history of the bar and its quirky owners, who didn't have the faintest idea what they were doing, provided an irresistible angle, and a piece appeared on Sunday, July 10, 1994, titled "No Spies, Just Book Lovers."

But more vital for us than the delightful text was the accompanying photograph. The *Times* had sent a camera downtown one random day when I had opened the doors early so that a friend of a friend, Frank Browning, author of *The Culture of Desire*, could read from his work. Frank's frowzy image hunched over a lectern appeared on several million breakfast tables and our phone rang off the hook with people wanting to know when the next reading was.

Having neither the time nor the ability to organize such an enterprise, I still recognized a constituency when it stared me in the face. But how to satisfy that constituency? This was before Barnes & Noble started putting dozens of writers a month into its stores, and there was clearly a need for something less hallowed than the 92nd Street Y's walnut-paneled auditorium in which Nobel laureates regularly appeared. I tacked the *Times* article on the bulletin board outside the MFA division of Columbia University and scribbled across the bottom: "Literary Director Sought for Reading Series. Good Position. No Pay."

Enter Dirk Standen and Ken Foster. Ambitious students who yearned for a project outside academia, not to mention free books and a reason to call editorial types, they both applied for the position. "You're partners," I said. Their mandate was simple: Make something happen, bring in a few bodies, and have fun. Dirk and Ken were young, their taste was young, and they immediately tapped into a vein of longing among their peers.

The first reading was by Elizabeth Wurtzel and Lawrence David. Riding high on the notoriety of *Prozac Nation,* Wurtzel drew an SRO crowd, read from her chronicle of wanton despair, and answered questions from the adoring audience. Standing behind the only bar in the world I'm allowed to stand behind, near the vodka well, I couldn't resist asking the last question of the evening: "Would either of you care to address narcissism in our time?"

David, the author of the novel *Need,* flushed and stammered, but Wurtzel just batted her enormous eyes and said, "I'd like to, but I'm too self-obsessed." That set the pattern for further events: reader reads, owner insults. Oh, not always, only on occasion—when deserved and when the vodka well ran dry.

Some readings were spectacular, some tedious. Sometimes readings drew poorly due to the weather or the World Series. Other times authors brought entourages that stayed on, carousing till the wee hours when Sinatra replaced Nirvana on the jukebox, at least partially because of the swiftly established policy that readers drank free. It was the least we could do for them, since we never paid the writers, just as we never charged the audience.

More parties happened, although Knopf passed on our suggestion to throw one for Ivan (Denis's borzoi and KGB's unofficial mascot) when he appeared on the cover of the publishing house's spring '95 catalogue. An editor from Knopf who was moving to Russia threw herself a party instead. Word of mouth spread.

The *Nation* had a party. Rick Moody, Lucy Grealy, Elissa Schappell, and Rebecca Goldstein read. There was a New Orleans night.

And the media descended. *The New Yorker* mentioned us in a special fiction issue. The *Wall Street Journal* devoted a spread to the bar about as large as the bar itself. A music video was shot there. Foreign tourist guides listed us. *Story* magazine hosted a reading that allegedly led to the discovery of Junot Díaz.

Walter Mosley, Sigrid Nunez, and Jonathan Franzen read. Contributors to the *Breast Anthology* read.

When *GQ* called to ask if we could arrange a private reading by Donna Tartt to celebrate her story in its next issue, we were glad to oblige, and equally glad to leak the event to the publishing reporter at the *New York Observer.* Suddenly that pale orange weekly, that arbiter of cultural hotness, referred to us as a "den of literary lion cubs," and we were off. Instead of us having to justify ourselves and convince or cajole people into reading, publicists were hawking their lists to Ken and to Fran Gordon, a fanatical devotee of the early readings who had taken over Dirk's place in the operation by 1996. Soon it seemed that nobody who was physically capable of climbing the steep staircase turned us down.

On tour with a new book myself, I finally understood why KGB is so pleasing a place for other writers to read. First, it's small, so it's always crowded. Second, there's no pressure to sell books, and thus the success of a reading is not measured in financial terms. Most important, it's a good audience, willing to allow writers to try untested material. Liquor helps. Cigarettes help.

Michael Chabon (swoonsville) read and so did Amy Homes (gasp) and students from the NYU writing program.

Mind, Denis and I were still amateurs. I write novels and book reviews, used to edit fiction for a national magazine, and teach writing at a wonderful liberal arts college—all pursuits somehow connected with a life in letters—but I had never thought of being a literary impresario, and certainly not as a side effect of whimsical participation in a bar. We went through a series of disastrous thieving bartenders, invested in an ice machine, plugged up the bullet hole in the window that appeared after hours one night, and persevered.

I introduced Gordon Lish and his magazine, the *Quarterly*, and we sparred—verbally, though for a moment it seemed likely to develop otherwise—for an hour. I swear that all I said in my introduction was "flat sentences, feckless characters, nonexistent plots; I don't understand how these writers manage to get up in the morning, let alone put pen to paper." The *Observer* reported on the encounter in its gossip column.

For a while there was ill feeling between KGB and a competitor, Limbo, a Johnsonian coffeehouse that held readings two blocks away.

Readings, however, are not automobiles. If you buy a Ford, you don't generally buy a General Motors, too, but if you go to one reading in the East Village that you like you'll probably go to another. Together with Limbo, KGB hosted "A Moveable Read" that took the entire audience from one venue to the other.

Of course, we faced problems, ranging from temperamental egos to a strain on the overused plumbing. Once a beer keg deliveryman lost his balance at the top of the stairs. Man and keg tumbled down and took out the landing like a bowling ball walloping tenpins. We improvised a wooden bridge over the chasm, sued the distributor, and settled for a lot of free beer. Once there was a stabbing; here's the terrifying but fortunately nonfatal situation: girl and new boyfriend bump into unhappy old boyfriend.

In a reversal of that gruesome romantic tangle, KGB's inamorata at the *Observer* aimed to prove that the pen was crueler than the sword by changing our description to "kiddie slacker hangout" when she listed a reading by David Foster Wallace. So be it; the press makes you and the press tries to break you. But the *Observer* missed the real story that night. Since we usually have two readers on any given evening, the interesting question was whom to pair with the author of *Infinite Jest*. Instead of trying to find a second author of an equally weighty book (the building might have collapsed), we offered this coveted spot in a bound-to-be-attention-getting bill to our bartender, Dan, who read from his bizarrely compelling, painstakingly researched work-in-progress titled "The Nazi Murder of John F. Kennedy."

By 1997 a poetry series curated by David Lehman and Star Black commenced at the bar. If the fiction writers tended to be more experimental, the poets were better known. John Ashbery, Mark Strand, and Charles Simic read.

The *Times* returned several more times, once for a lovely Metro section feature; and once, even more flatteringly, it mentioned us en passant in the City section. Interviewing someone who conducts a smaller reading series, the paper of record quoted him as saying, "We're not KGB, but we try." It was the very offhandedness of the reference and the fact that it required no explanation that was the greatest acknowledgment. After all, if he had invented a new soda and said "We're not Coca-Cola, but we try," the *Times* would not have felt compelled to parenthetically identify the latter as "a beverage made in Atlanta."

No question about it, renown has its rewards. In 1998, William Morrow thought we were enough of a brand name to publish *The KGB Bar Reader*, an anthology of fiction that had been read at the bar. And in 2000, Morrow published *The KGB Bar Book of Poems*. Similarly, along with the bar's success came personal success for both Ken and Fran, who obtained book contracts and left us to pursue private projects. They were replaced by Daphne Beal and then by Jon Wei and Rebecca Donner, also recent MFA students who will enjoy the use of our soapbox until they too finish their own books.

In addition to such pet projects as the Five-Year Plan ("Drink all you want for $10,000") and an Open Microphone Thomas Pynchon Imitator Contest (won by novelist and *Los Angeles Times* book critic Jonathan Levi, who premiered an operatic version of his story "The Scrimshaw Violin" at the bar in 1999), the readings have expanded from fiction on Sundays and poetry on Mondays to journalists one Wednesday a month, and more idiosyncratic events than I can recall. When Denis and I meet, we get grandiose and dream about franchising KGBs in second-floor walk-up holes-in-the-wall across the country, maybe grow as vast and domineering as our namesake.

Owning KGB has provided me with the opportunity to meet writers I admire, help lesser-known writers, and give literature one more home in the world. Fortunately, the bar is as far from my own home on the Upper West Side as any spot in Manhattan. Otherwise I might be tempted to make more than my approximately bimonthly appearances, which could pose a hazard to domestic tranquility. I prefer it like this; with three children and a few more books to write, I don't spend much time in bars these days, no matter how cool they are.

What's coming up in this new decade and, presumably, several beyond, when perhaps we will merit inclusion in some successor volume to *Down and In*, I'm not particularly sure. That will be determined by what the novelists and poets of today and tomorrow write. In the meanwhile, communism is gone from the Kremlin, but this is our party and we'll read if we want to. KGB has been the best toy I've ever had. Someday it may even show a profit.

Balancing Act:
Teaching Creative Writing

by Hilma Wolitzer

Hilma Wolitzer, a novelist, has taught creative writing for more than thirty years.

That old saw "Those who can, do; those who can't, teach" doesn't apply to teachers of creative writing, like me, who manage to do both. Our related, parallel careers usually result from a combination of financial necessity and a desire to be useful. Most of us learn early on that Write at Home, Make Big Bucks! is only another advertising lie.

Actually, teaching isn't among the highest paid professions, either, and there's a lot of skepticism about the usefulness of creative writing workshops. When asked if I actually *believe* in them, I have to say that I don't, at least not in a religious, do-or-die sense. We all know of successful writers who've never attended any of the burgeoning programs around the country, and even condemn them as breeding grounds for a particular kind of "workshopped" mediocrity. The first thing they might learn at one of the programs they scorn is that *workshopped* is neither an adjective nor a verb. And many writers who claim to be completely self-taught are members of less formal professional cliques that regularly pass their work around. The American poet John Ciardi once said, "Every writer I can think of was at some time a member of a group, whether it was the Greek agora, or the Roman bath, or the French Café, or the English University." Sometimes it's not exactly a group, but merely one or two literary friends who offer each other opinions and suggestions on work in progress. Ezra Pound and T.S. Eliot are notable examples of mutual influence. Hemingway and Fitzgerald also traded manuscripts and hands-on advice, and George Sand sought comments from Balzac and Flaubert, before and after publication.

Not everyone has access to genius, though, or even to like-minded novices, and asking the available but uninformed, like one's family, what they think of your story or poem may invite both personal and professional catastrophe. Your mother will probably love it just because it's yours; a competitive sibling might profess to hate it for the very same reason. And ulterior motives are likely to inspire the solicited judgment ("It's really great! Can we go to sleep now?" or "A sestina? I thought you were making dinner") of most lovers and spouses.

Writing is solitary but not necessarily lonely work, especially for fiction writers who enjoy the society and "collaboration" of their characters, those voices living in their heads. But the energy and self-confidence that drives one to finish a manuscript can evaporate as soon as it's done. I remember wondering if my own first story, written long before I'd ever met another writer, *was* actually a story. Euphoria gave way quickly to self-doubt, and finally to despair. I decided to enroll, rather belatedly, in a university writing workshop, which involved financial juggling, finding a baby-sitter, and commuting from the suburbs to the city. It turned out to be a sound decision for me (after a shaky start, but more about that later), and although it was cheering to read that Virginia Woolf questioned whether her brand-new work (*To the Lighthouse*) was "nonsense" or "brilliance," she probably didn't have to leave Bloomsbury to find out.

The kind of response to written work that impels and informs a good revision should ideally come from one's peers, those people frequently found in well-organized, well-run workshops. Despite the naysayers, accomplished writers who might not have developed as admirably or as early on their own emerge regularly from writing programs. The alumni lists from schools like Columbia University and the University of Iowa are truly impressive. Raymond Carver was grateful to find himself in a lesser-known university workshop (at Chico State in California), led by John Gardner. Gardner, who said, "Even in the best writers workshop one is likely to learn more from one's fellow students than from one's teacher," was equally pleased to discover Carver. Teachers learn in the workshop, too, as they're reminded, by their students, of the long patience writing (and rewriting) requires, the particular thrill of finding the right word, and the courage necessary to discard material that doesn't work. I've witnessed, in various workshops I've attended and led, the mutual benefits to teacher and student, and the metamorphosis of raw, nervous promise into polished work. So I count myself among those who believe that writing *can* be taught, but only to writers—that is, gifted, motivated people who simply need direction, encouragement, and the company of other writers.

John Gardner was right about the importance of one's fellow students, but the leader of a workshop must help to create and sustain an environment in which work flourishes. The classroom is merely a microcosm of the larger world, where bullies, saboteurs, or narcissists may threaten to take over. The atmosphere should be friendly and casual, but certain rules must be in place. It's of primary importance to remember that the work belongs to the writer. In addition to oral responses, I encourage handwritten comments from workshop members on their fellows' manuscripts, and offer my own, too, often suggesting radical changes and even alternate words. But I always write them in pencil, to emphasize that they *are* only suggestions. All written comments should be signed; that helps to keep them thoughtful and honest.

There must be mutual respect among all the members of the group, and professional standards of criticism, no matter what anyone thinks of anyone else. The *manuscript* is to be criticized, not the writer. No one comes to a workshop to be insulted, to be told he's an insensitive or lousy writer, any more than he wants to hear that he's ugly or a bad dresser. Negative comments about someone's work, even when they're leavened by constructive suggestions, may not be easy to take, either, but at least they're appropriate responses.

Competition should never be fostered. Of course some submitted work is better than others—talent isn't distributed democratically—but I try not to compare various students' stories because it's not a contest. Each person should be "competing" only with the most recent draft of her own story, attempting to make it better (or, as Grace Paley says, "truer") in the next revision.

The workshop is something like a courtroom, where everyone should be given the chance to express opinions and ideas (offer evidence) about the manuscript under discussion. But the writer (defendant and jury) should simply listen and absorb the criticism until the others have all spoken. Then he may have the opportunity to ask or answer questions or to explain things that weren't understood.

The instructor, too, has to remember not to be a bully, a saboteur, or a narcissist. That is, she can't impose her own writing voice on her students or insist that her opinions override everyone else's. But she can lead them into thinking analytically about their work, by asking certain questions: What is this story about? Do I care about the characters? What were the writer's intentions, and were they fulfilled? Is the language accurate and interesting?

One of the best writing workshops I ever attended (as a visitor) was a fourth-grade class in a public school, where the kids were presenting their personal journal entries. The teacher had each student read his or her work aloud, followed by oral responses from the others. She wisely divided those responses into two parts: "comments" and "suggestions." The comments, which came first, were mostly positive: "I loved it!"; "I almost cried at the end"; "I know exactly how you felt" (that shock of recognition every writer strives for!); and even "Your posture was really good." The suggestions, about both content and writing style, tended to be more critical, and directly and indirectly encouraged revision. The praise they received first seemed to help these very young writers handle any ensuing disapproval of their work. Although I agree with their teacher that everyone learns more swiftly through positive conditioning, adults don't always have to be soothed first if the negative remarks are fair and constructive. I hate to use touchy-feely terms like "share" and "safe place," but a good workshop is a place where writers are comfortable about showing (sharing) their work and expressing their opinions, and may feel safe from devastation, if not from disappointment. When I lead a group I usually start off by saying that our collective purpose is revision, not suicide.

Most of us who teach creative writing consider it a worthy profession, but maybe we're not the best ones to judge. After all, it's what we do for (sort of) a living, and self-preservation probably affects our judgment. When I was a new (but hardly young) student, I wasn't so sure. At my first session of Anatole Broyard's Introductory Fiction Workshop at the New School for Social Research (now New School University), in Manhattan's Greenwich Village, I was called on to read my work aloud. It was scary, to say the least. I was a housewife and mother who prided myself, rather defensively, on life experience, as opposed to academic training (which I lacked), and who drew freely on my own domesticity for fictional material. Following the first dictum of all the books I'd read on craft, I was writing about what I knew; the story I read to the group that night actually took place in a supermarket. But the very first comment from a classmate was that it was the most boring story he'd ever heard. I was ready to give up all literary pretensions and ambitions and head right back to the kitchen and the nursery, but Broyard (who later became a daily book critic for the *New York Times*) urged my workshop critic to say *why* he thought the story was boring, what I could do to make it better, and, most crucially, if there was anything at all he liked about my writing. Broyard even offered an example of a line *he* admired. In that awful, wonderful moment I learned something about my story—maybe it wasn't perfect, but it wasn't hopeless, either—and something even more vital about teaching creative writing: Work should be constructively analyzed, not simply judged. My supermarket story was eventually published (after many, many drafts), and a few years later I become a teacher myself.

Balancing the demands of writing and teaching is pretty tricky. Both occupations take a great deal of time and concentration, and similar kinds of psychic energy. I'm one of those writers lucky enough to be able to read other writers' work when I'm in the middle of my own writing project without feeling corrupted (or interrupted) by their external voices. Reading has always been a spur for my writing (language sparking language), and reading student work seems to hone my editorial skills. I just have to be disciplined about the number of hours devoted to student work, in and out of the classroom, and to my own writing.

Recently I asked the members of my undergraduate fiction workshop at Columbia what value, if any, they placed on the experience. A lot of hands went up. One man said that the workshop allowed him to deal honestly with his fears as a writer, especially whether he should actually think of himself as one. A woman claimed that she felt forced to commit time to her writing because she knew she had to regularly turn something in. Another woman, with a history of failed starts, said she was compelled to finally *finish* a story. Several people admitted to feeling starved for feedback before they'd joined the workshop, although the most useful criticism they received there only confirmed their own worst fears about their writing. The advantages of community were stressed by almost everyone, especially about how heartening it was to read other students' early drafts and see them struggling with similar, and sometimes worse, problems. Despite efforts to avoid it, jealousy and even a little Schadenfreude probably darkened the community from time to time, but a blend of honesty and charity seemed to prevail.

As such a late-blooming writer myself, I often wonder if I might have jump-started my career sooner by attending a writing workshop when I was my students' age. Although I continue to comfort myself with thoughts of the life experience I'd accumulated first—the raw material that I still distill and use in my fiction—I know now that *all* experience is useful to a writer, including the lively give-and-take of a workshop. To avoid solipsism and the limitations of the imagination, writers must leave the rarefied air inside our heads from time to time. We do this when we read, certainly, in all of our social and familial contacts, and when we work at something other than our writing. I've held several different jobs in my life, and although a few of them—like babysitting, waiting tables, bookkeeping, and steaming feathers in a hat factory—may seem like unlikely sources of creative inspiration, they were all instructive about how we live, which is at the very heart of storytelling. Teaching creative writing is, in some ways, just another job, but with a few really terrific and relevant perks.

Afterword

Why I Write

by Robert Phillips

Robert Phillips is the author and editor of more than thirty-two books of poetry, fiction, and criticism.

A student once asked Flannery O'Connor why she wrote. She replied, "Because I'm good at it." An interviewer recently asked me the same question, and I had no snappy, single-minded reply. Rather, it evoked a variety of responses. I recalled Dylan Thomas's wonderful note at the beginning of his *Collected Poems*, stating that his work was written for the love of Man and in praise of God, and that he'd be a damned fool if it wasn't. I have no such high intentions.

I write because it makes me happy. My friend Delmore Schwartz defined the object of poetry as "the ascent of joy." Nothing—well, *almost* nothing—makes me as happy as when I have completed what I feel to be a good and original piece of writing.

I write because I have a strong desire to objectify what is indispensable to my happiness. Apparently I also write because I have a strong desire to objectify what is indispensable to my unhappiness. One critic of my first collection of short stories commented, "Fifteen short stories, and not a happy ending among them!" In this sense perhaps I share the worldview of Thomas Hardy. A woman was having tea with Mrs. Hardy, and inquired, "Did Mr. Hardy have a good day of writing?" Mrs. Hardy replied, "Oh, I'm sure of it. I could hear him sobbing all afternoon." My colleague, the esteemed fiction writer Daniel Stern, once quoted a friend, "You have to understand, having a good time is not my idea of having a good time."

I write to exercise my demons. When I was young, I used to rack my brain for subjects to write about. Now that I am older—much older—I

237

write about the things I can't get rid of, the things that haunt me. I'm not talking about nightmares. I'm talking about life events and traumas that I wish I could get rid of, once and for all, to close them off between two covers and put them on a shelf, never to be thought about again. I'm reminded of the saying attributed to Jesus in the Gnostic Gospel of Thomas:

> If you bring forth what is within you,
> What you bring forth will save you.
> If you do not bring forth what is within you,
> What you do not bring forth will destroy you.

One of the most cynical definitions of a novelist I ever read is from Georges Simenon, who said, "A novelist is a man who doesn't like his mother." In my case, I was a young poet who didn't like his father. We all have grudges. But there is no less attractive an artifice than grudge-work. I've written a number of such pieces. One early poem, called "The Mole," was about my father. I didn't send it back home, of course, and figured that in that small town of 3,000 he'd never see it. A year later he was sitting in the dentist's office. He picked up a limp old *New Yorker* and encountered it. He told me, "Bobby, that poem hurt worse than the dentist's drill." There perhaps is an inevitability here. Writing on John Crowe Ransom, W.D. Snodgrass remarked, "How could one be a first-rate artist without offending, deeply, those he most loves?" And Truman Capote, reacting to his closest friends' horror at their depictions in his novel *Answered Prayers*, responded, "I'm a writer, and I use everything. Did all those people think I was there just to entertain them?"

Nevertheless, I am happy to report that years after *The New Yorker* incident, I was able to write a very positive poem about my father and our relationship. I sent it to him inside a Father's Day card. He got in the car and rode up and down the road, showing it to all his neighbors. It was a healing experience for both of us. Auden says poetry makes nothing happen, but he's wrong. Tennessee Williams's psychiatrist told him in a session, "You will begin to forgive the world when you've forgiven your father." This is true.

I write because it gives me focus. There is a famous anecdote about an old lady's dying. She raises her head from the deathbed and says to her family, "If I'd known it would go by so fast, I would have noticed more." It seems to me that a writer's job is to notice, and to put his or her observations and conclusions down for others to share. The greatest poverty, said Wallace Stevens, is not to live in a physical world. And yet in a world of strip malls and tract houses, fast-food chains and AstroTurf, our environment has become neutral or invisible. It is the role of the writer to create splendor from the world that surrounds us, even if it is Interstate 110. Literature should make us look freshly at our tired world. Writing is a way of seeing, not of saying, things. Another woman, Lady Mary Wortley Montagu, uttered these last words on her deathbed: "It has all been very interesting!" Lady Mary was a writer. If you don't know her collected letters, you should.

I write to create beauty. For some years I have thought beauty alone gives significance to life, that art is the crowning achievement of human endeavor. I of course am not alone. William Faulkner once stated that he would rob his mother, if necessary, to create a work of art. "The 'Ode on a Grecian Urn,'" said Faulkner, "is worth any number of old ladies." Somerset Maugham stated, "The only purpose that could be assigned to the teeming generations that succeed one another on the face of the earth was to produce now and then an artist." Henry James was in the same boat with Faulkner and Maugham (and what a boat ride that would have been). James proclaimed, "It is *art* that makes life, makes interest, makes importance. . . . I know of no substitute whatever for the force and beauty of its process." James's word *process* is important: You create not just for the result, but for the release in the making.

I write because writing never bores me—unlike that low-scoring game, soccer; or fishing, painting by numbers, bowling, and the films of John Cassavetes.

I write because it was the one thing I could do better than my older brother, who was a football and basketball star, and who looked like the young Gregory Peck. Also because it was the one thing I could do better than my younger brother, who played the trumpet. He looked like Troy Donahue.

I write because writing is sexy. Making a poem or story is like having a love affair with yourself. As Woody Allen says, "I was the best I ever had." The poem or story or novel is a love affair between the writer and words, between him- or herself and the subject. Readers come in only a long time later, as witnesses to the wedding. In between there are the secret affairs of revision, submission, acceptance, proofs.

I write because writing is renewal. Heracleitus said the sun is new every day—and so am I, if I write something new.

I write to find out who I am. But in order to find out who I am, I must first find out who I was. So I reflect on past experiences and examine them. Ultimately I try to shape them and draw a conclusion. Poetry is a moment's monument, according to Dante Gabriel Rossetti. What I find out about myself is often a surprise. Which perhaps is one mark that a piece of writing is a good one. To quote Robert Frost, "No surprise for the writer, no surprise for the reader." Picasso said it another way: "If you know exactly what you are going to do, what is the good of doing it?"

I write because it is a positive force. It keeps me off the streets. Flannery O'Connor said, "People without hope don't write novels." Philip Larkin, that sourpuss contemporary poet, said, "The most positive act in the world is writing a poem." Keats called poetry a form of prayer, and so it is. Writing gives the writer all kinds of hope. There's hope you'll live long enough to complete the book, hope you'll find an agent, a publisher, an audience, get reviewed, get reviewed well, perhaps even win a prize or fellowship. Novelists can even hope for reprint sales, book club sales, and movie rights.

For the born writer, there is something positive about writing every day. (One cannot make a writer out of a born dentist.) But how does one write daily? Baudelaire defined inspiration as "working every day." O'Connor, in an interview, confessed, "If I waited for inspiration, I'd still be waiting." O'Connor said she went to her writing desk every morning, and if anything came to her, she was there to receive it. This is contrary to the popular conception of a writer as someone who has to wait to be struck by lightning.

I write because it gives me a sense of identity. I'm ink, therefore I am. My colleague at the University of Houston, Cynthia Macdonald, once remarked that writers become writers because they weren't invited to the party. Once you become a writer, you may get invited to parties. But of course that is not what Macdonald meant.

I write to explore vicariously lives different from my own. My work includes poems about gangster John Dillinger and serial rapist Ted Bundy, stories about charwomen and illiterate farmers. What these works give me, I hope, is greater breadth, a moving away from the purely subjective into the objective. As good as the novelist Jean Rhys was, one finally tires of all her stories and novels about herself, and welcomes the one final novel in which she became the first Mrs. Rochester, the madwoman in the attic.

You will note that all my motives for writing are personal ones. I've rarely written for a cause, or to attempt to effect a change. I don't have a political bone in my body. I never could have assayed the likes of Stowe's *Uncle Tom's Cabin*, which helped bring about the Civil War, or Upton Sinclair's *The Jungle*, which reformed the meatpacking industry. My map is an interior one, not that of the greater world. Probably that is a great limitation. Perhaps not. I take solace in Howard Moss's division of poetry into that of the window and that of the mirror. Walt Whitman's was a window, Emily Dickinson's a mirror. Who is to say which is the greater poet? I once was asked to contribute a new poem for an anthology about the 1960s. Think of all that happened in the '60s: the Bay of Pigs, the Watts riots, the explosion of the first hydrogen bomb, the assassinations of both Kennedys as well as Malcolm X and Martin Luther King. . . . So what did I write about? Janis Joplin. If poetry is, as Wallace Stevens thought, a response to the daily necessity of getting the world right, we must ask, whose world? In my case, the world of rock was as central as the Cuban missile crisis. Chekhov said artists and writers should engage in politics only enough to protect themselves from politics. Messages, I believe, are for mailmen, not poets. I agree with Mallarmé, who said, "Literature is not written with ideas, but with words."

You may notice, as well, that making money is not among the reasons why I write. Not every writer feels this way. Delmore Schwartz once exclaimed to John Berryman, "Literature doesn't matter! The only thing that matters is money and getting your teeth fixed!" For one so passionate about literature as Schwartz, this is a singular statement. Dr. Johnson said that only a blockhead writes without the expectation of money. Well, meet one of the world's greatest blockheads. Among my recent enterprises was collecting, editing, and annotating the letters of William Goyen, a project that took five years. So far the book has not earned its advance of $1,000. Apparently it never will. That's a realization of less than $200 a year. Goyen would tell me that is big money. When one of his plays was produced off-Broadway, his total royalties were $31.

I also didn't say I write to achieve fame, although almost any writer wouldn't mind a little fame. Whitman even reviewed his own books under a pen name. Unsurprisingly, the reviews were very favorable. But fame can be tricky, especially if you have a name like Robert Phillips. I once was flown all the way to Michigan to give a poetry reading, which is flattering. When the chairperson of the English department picked me up at the airport, he said, "I admire all your books, of course. But the one I like best is the autobiography you assembled from the writings of Colette." That book, as many of you know, was assembled by Robert Phelps. On the way to the university I pondered, Should I pick up one of Phelps's books and give my reading from it? Should I inscribe his name on any books people want signed? When we got to the auditorium, fortunately, it was my books that were on sale. Only the chair had been in error.

A few years ago I was invited by Mrs. George W. Bush, then the First Lady of Texas, to participate in the annual Texas Book Fair in Austin. I was to give a reading at the state capitol, then sign my latest book under a tent. When I reached the tent, I was confronted by a mountain of books called *The Best Clean Jokes*. It was compiled by the Texas country reporter, Bob Phillips. My own books had never been ordered. The books at least could have been by Bum Phillips, the former Oilers coach. Well, even identity problems can create literature. Look at all the poems and novels about doppelgängers.

Most of what I've said here sounds terribly narcissistic: *my* renewal, *my* self-examination, *my* happiness, *my* double. Writing should not be mere self-expression. If what you have to say doesn't have implications for others, why publish it? Universality is what gives writing validity. So one of the reasons I write is to celebrate another individual, or another work of art, or a place. In my books you'll find poems of praise for Giacometti, Burchfield, Picasso, Milton Avery, Amy Jones, Isabella Gardner, as well as the unknown weavers of the Cluny unicorn tapestries in France and an anonymous chimney sweep I encountered in Germany.

I'll conclude by quoting the Master, Henry James. In "The Middle Years," James articulated, "We work in the dark—we do what we can—we give what we have. Our doubt is our passion, and our passion is our task. The rest is the madness of art."

Appendices

Grants & Awards

The following listing is based on the Grants & Awards section of *Poets & Writers Magazine*, which announces state and national prizes in poetry, fiction, and creative nonfiction of $1,000 or more, prizes of $500 or more that charge no entry fee, and prestigious nonmonetary awards. Please contact the sponsoring organizations for current deadlines and complete guidelines before submitting a manuscript. When requesting information by mail, enclose a self-addressed, stamped envelope (SASE).

ACADEMY OF AMERICAN POETS

Harold Morton Landon Translation Award

A prize of $1,000 is given annually for a translation of a poetry collection from any language into English published in the U.S. during the current year.

James Laughlin Award

A prize of $5,000 is given annually to honor a second book of poetry.

Lenore Marshall Poetry Prize

A prize of $25,000 is given annually for a book of poems published in the U.S. during the previous year.

Raiziss/de Palchi Translation Award

A prize of $20,000 and a residency at the American Academy in Rome is given biennially for a translation into English of modern Italian poetry by an American translator.

Walt Whitman Award

A prize of $5,000, publication by Louisiana State University Press, and

a one-month residency at the Vermont
Studio Center in Johnson, Vermont, is
given annually for a first poetry
collection (50 to 100 pages).

Academy of American Poets
www.poets.org
Ryan Murphy, Awards Director
588 Broadway
Suite 604
New York, NY 10012-3210

(212) 274-0343, ext. 17,
or rmurphy@poets.org

AHSAHTA PRESS

Sawtooth Poetry Prize

*A prize of $1,500 and publication by
Ahsahta Press is given annually for a
poetry collection (at least 48 pages).*

Ahsahta Press
Sawtooth Poetry Prize
ahsahtapress.boisestate.edu
Janet Holmes, Director
1910 University Drive
Boise State University
Boise, ID 83725

ahsahta@boisestate.edu

UNIVERSITY OF AKRON PRESS

Akron Poetry Prize

*A prize of $1,000 and publication by
the University of Akron Press is given*

annually for a poetry collection (60 to
100 pages).

University of Akron Press
Akron Poetry Prize
www.uakron.edu/uapress/
  poetryprize.html
Elton Glaser, Poetry Editor
374B Bierce Library
Akron, OH 44325-1703

(877) 827-7377

AMERICAN ANTIQUARIAN SOCIETY

Fellowships for Historical Research

*At least three fellowships are given
annually to poets, fiction writers, and
creative nonfiction writers for
monthlong residencies and a $1,200
stipend at the American Antiquarian
Society in Worcester, Massachusetts, to
research American history and culture
before 1877.*

American Antiquarian Society
Fellowships for Historical Research
www.americanantiquarian.org/
  artistfellowship.htm
James David Moran
185 Salisbury Street
Worcester, MA 01609-1634

(508) 363-1131
or cmcrell@mwa.org

AMERICAN LITERARY REVIEW

Poetry Contest

A prize of $1,000 and publication in American Literary Review *is given biennially for a group of poems.*

American Literary Review
Poetry Contest
www.engl.unt.edu/alr
Elizabeth Harvell, Managing
    Editor
P.O. Box 311307
University of North Texas
Denton, TX 76203-1307

americanliteraryreview@
yahoo.com

AMERICAN POETRY REVIEW

Honickman First Book Prize

A prize of $3,000 and publication in American Poetry Review *is given annually for a first book of poetry (at least 48 pages).*

American Poetry Review
Honickman First Book Prize
www.aprweb.org
Elizabeth Scanlon, Associate
    Editor
1721 Walnut Street
Philadelphia, PA 19103

(215) 496-0439

AMERICAN-SCANDINAVIAN FOUNDATION

Translation Prizes

A prize of $2,000 and publication of an excerpt in Scandinavian Review *is given annually for an English translation of a Danish, Finnish, Icelandic, Norwegian, or Swedish work of poetry, fiction, or creative nonfiction.*

American-Scandinavian
    Foundation
Translation Prizes
www.amscan.org/translation.html
Andrey Henkin
58 Park Avenue
New York, NY 10016

(212) 879-9779

ANHINGA PRESS

Prize for Poetry

A prize of $2,000 and publication by Anhinga Press is given annually for a book-length collection of poetry (48 to 80 pages).

Anhinga Press
Prize for Poetry
www.anhinga.org
Rick Campbell, Director
P.O. Box 10595
Tallahassee, FL 32302

(850) 521-9920
or info@anhinga.org

ANOTHER CHICAGO MAGAZINE

Chicago Literary Awards

Two prizes of $1,000 each and publication in Another Chicago Magazine *are given annually for an unpublished poem and short story.*

Another Chicago Magazine
Chicago Literary Awards
www.anotherchicagomag.com
Left Field Press
3709 North Kenmore
Chicago, IL 60613-2905

editors@anotherchicagomag.com

ARIZONA COMMISSION ON THE ARTS

Creative Writing Fellowships

Fellowships of $5,000 to $7,500 are given biennially to Arizona poets and fiction writers.

Arizona Commission on the Arts
Creative Writing Fellowships
www.arizonaarts.org
Paul Morris, Literature Director
417 West Roosevelt Street
Phoenix, AZ 85003

(602) 255-5882
or pmorris@arizonaarts.org

UNIVERSITY OF ARIZONA POETRY CENTER

Summer Residency Program

A monthlong residency (valued at $1,000) at the University of Arizona Poetry Center's guest house, located in Tucson, plus a stipend of $500, is given annually to a poet, fiction writer, or creative nonfiction writer who has published no more than one full-length book.

University of Arizona Poetry
    Center
Summer Residency Program
www.poetrycenter.arizona.edu
Frances Sjoberg, Assistant Director
1216 North Cherry Avenue
Tucson, AZ 85719

(520) 626-3765
or poetry@u.arizona.edu

ARROWHEAD REGIONAL ARTS COUNCIL

Individual Artist Grants

Grants of $4,500 and $2,500 are given annually to Minnesota poets, fiction writers, and creative nonfiction writers who have lived in Aitkin, Carlton, Cook, Itasca, Koochiching, Lake, or St. Louis Counties for at least six months.

Arrowhead Regional Arts Council
Individual Artist Grants
www.aracouncil.org
Robert DeArmond

101 West Second Street
Suite 204
Duluth, MN 55802

(800) 569-8134
or aracouncil@aol.com

ARTIST TRUST

Grants for Artist Projects

Grants of up to $1,400 each are given annually to Washington poets, fiction writers, and creative nonfiction writers.

Literature Fellowships

Eight to ten fellowships of $6,000 each are awarded in odd-numbered years to recognize the achievements of Washington poets, fiction writers, and creative nonfiction writers.

Artist Trust
www.artisttrust.org
Susan Myers, Program Director
1835 12th Avenue
Seattle, WA 98122

(206) 467-8734, ext. 11,
or info@artisttrust.org

ARTS COUNCIL OF INDIANAPOLIS

Creative Renewal Fellowships

Fellowships of $7,500 each are awarded biennially to Indiana poets, fiction writers, and creative nonfiction writers for the exploration of new works, research, retreats, and travel.

Arts Council of Indianapolis
Creative Renewal Fellowships
www.indyarts.org
Dave Lawrence, Director of Grants
    Services and Program
    Development
20 North Meridian Street
Suite 500
Indianapolis, IN 46204-3040

(317) 631-3301
or indyarts@indyarts.org

ARTS & LETTERS

Arts & Letters Prizes

Two prizes of $1,000 each and publication in Arts & Letters *are given annually for a group of poems and a short story.*

Arts & Letters
Arts & Letters Prizes
www.al.gcsu.edu
Martin Lammon, Editor
Campus Box 89
Georgia College and State
    University
Milledgeville, GA 31061

(478) 445-1289
or al@gcsu.edu

ASHLAND POETRY PRESS

Richard Snyder Publication Prize

A prize of $1,000 and publication by Ashland Poetry Press is given annually for a book-length poetry collection (60 to 80 pages).

Ashland Poetry Press
Richard Snyder Publication Prize
www.ashland.edu/aupoetry
Stephen Haven, Editor, English
    Department
Ashland University
Ashland, OH 44805

ASSOCIATION OF WRITERS AND WRITING PROGRAMS

Award Series

Three prizes of $2,000 each and publication by a participating university press are given annually for book-length manuscripts of poetry (at least 48 pages), short fiction (150 to 300 pages), and creative nonfiction (150 to 300 pages).

Prague Summer Program Fellowships

Fellowships to attend the Prague Summer Program in July are awarded annually to a poet, fiction writer, and creative nonfiction writer.

Association of Writers and Writing
    Programs
www.awpwriter.org

George Mason University
Mail Stop 1E3
Fairfax, VA 22030

(703) 993-4301
or awp@gmu.edu

ASTRAEA FOUNDATION

Lesbian Writers Fund

Two $10,000 grants and four $1,500 grants are given annually to emerging lesbian poets and fiction writers.

Astraea Foundation
    Lesbian Writers Fund
www.astraea.org
C. J. Griffin, Program Associate
116 East 16th Street, 7th Floor
New York, NY 10003

(212) 529-8021 or
grants@astraea.org

ATLANTA REVIEW

International Poetry Competition

A prize of approximately $2,000 and publication in the Atlanta Review *is given for an unpublished poem.*

Atlanta Review
International Poetry
    Competition
www.atlantareview.com
Dan Veach, Editor
P.O. Box 8248
Atlanta, GA 31106

contest@atlantareview.com

AUTHORS IN THE PARK

Short Story Award

A prize of $1,000 and publication in Fine Print, *the publication of Authors in the Park, a nonprofit literary organization based in Winter Park, Florida, is given annually for a short story.*

Authors in the Park
Short Story Award
David Foley
P.O. Box 85
Winter Park, FL 32790-0085

(407) 658-4520
or foley2@earthlink.net

AUTHOR'S VENUE

Writing Contest

Transportation, accommodations, and tuition to attend the Journey Conference in Lake Tahoe, Nevada, valued at $1,300, is given annually for an unpublished poem, short story, novel excerpt, excerpt of a book of creative nonfiction, or essay.

Author's Venue
Writing Contest
www.authorsvenue.com
600 Central Avenue S.E.
Suite 235
Albuquerque, NM 87102

(505) 244-9337
or info@authorsvenue.com

AUTUMN HOUSE PRESS

Poetry Prize

A prize of $1,000 and publication by Autumn House Press will be given annually for a book-length poetry collection (50 to 80 pages).

Autumn House Press
Poetry Prize
www.autumnhouse.org
Michael Simms, Executive Director
P.O. Box 60100
Pittsburgh, PA 15211

simms@duq.edu

BACKWATERS PRESS

Backwaters Prize

A prize of $1,000 and publication by Backwaters Press is given annually for a poetry collection (60 to 85 pages).

Backwaters Press
Backwaters Prize
www.thebackwaterspress.
   homestead.com
Greg Kosmicki, Publisher
3502 North 52nd Street
Omaha, NE 68104-3506

gkosm62735@aol.com

BARD COLLEGE

Bard Fiction Prize

A prize of $30,000 and a one-semester appointment as writer-in-residence at

Bard College is given annually to a fiction writer under the age of forty.

Bard College
Bard Fiction Prize
www.bard.edu/bfp
Irene Zedlacher, Manager
P.O. Box 5000
Annandale-on-Hudson, NY 12504-5000

(845) 758-7087
or bfp@bard.edu

BEAR STAR PRESS

Dorothy Brunsman Poetry Prize

A prize of $1,000 and publication by Bear Star Press is given annually for a poetry collection (50 to 65 pages) by a writer residing in a state west of the Central time zone.

Bear Star Press
Dorothy Brunsman
    Poetry Prize
www.bearstarpress.com
Beth Spencer, Editor
185 Hollow Oak Drive
Cohasset, CA 95973

(530) 891-0360
or bspencer@bearstarpress.com

BEFORE COLUMBUS FOUNDATION

American Book Awards

Approximately eighteen awards are given annually to honor books of poetry, fiction, and creative nonfiction published in the U.S. during the preceding year that make outstanding contributions to American literature.

Before Columbus Foundation
American Book Awards
Gundars Strads, Executive Director
The Raymond House
655 13th Street, Suite 302
Oakland, CA 94612

(510) 268-9775

BELLINGHAM REVIEW

Literary Awards

Three prizes of $1,000—the 49th Parallel Award for poetry, the Tobias Wolff Award for fiction, and the Annie Dillard Award for creative nonfiction—and publication in the Bellingham Review *are given annually for unpublished works.*

Bellingham Review
Literary Awards
www.wwu.edu/~bhreview
Brenda Miller, Editor
Mail Stop 9053
Western Washington University
Bellingham, WA 98225

bhreview@cc.wwu.edu

BINGHAMTON UNIVERSITY

Book Awards

Two prizes of $1,000—the Milt Kessler Poetry Book Award and the John Gardner Fiction Book Award—are given annually for books of poetry and fiction published in the previous year with a minimum print run of 500.

Binghamton University
Book Awards
english.binghamton.edu
Maria Mazziotti Gillan, Director
Creative Writing Program
P.O. Box 6000
Binghamton, NY 13902-6000

BIRMINGHAM-SOUTHERN COLLEGE

Hackney Literary Award

A prize of $5,000 is given annually for an unpublished novel.

Birmingham-Southern College
Hackney Literary Award
Annie Green, Director of Special
    Events
Box 549003
Birmingham, AL 35254

(205) 226-4921

BITTER OLEANDER PRESS

Frances Locke Poetry Award

A prize of $1,000 and publication in Bitter Oleander *is given annually for an unpublished poem.*

Bitter Oleander Press
Frances Locke Poetry Award
www.bitteroleander.com
Paul Roth, Publisher
4983 Tall Oaks Drive
Fayetteville, NY 13066-9776

info@bitteroleander.com

BLACK CAUCUS OF THE AMERICAN LIBRARY ASSOCIATION

Literary Awards

Three prizes of $500 each are given annually for a book of fiction, a first novel, and a book of creative nonfiction written by an African American and published in the U.S. during the current year.

Black Caucus of the American
    Library Association
Literary Awards
www.bcala.org
Gwendolyn Taylor Davis, Awards
    Chair
New York Public Library
112 East 96th Street
New York, NY 10128

(212) 289-0909
or gtaylor@nypl.org

BLACK WARRIOR REVIEW

Chapbook Contest

*A prize of $1,500 and publication in
Black Warrior Review is given
annually for a short collection of
unpublished poems.*

Black Warrior Review
Chapbook Contest
www.webdesol.com/bwr
Dan Kaplan, Managing Editor
P.O. Box 862936
Tuscaloosa, AL 35486

bwr@ua.edu

BLUE MOUNTAIN CENTER

Richard J. Margolis Award

*A stipend of $5,000 and a monthlong
residency at the Blue Mountain
Center, a writers and artists colony in
Blue Mountain Lake, New York, is
given annually to a creative nonfiction
writer whose work recalls that of
Richard J. Margolis, a journalist,
essayist, and poet who wrote about
those whose voices are seldom heard.*

Blue Mountain Center
Richard J. Margolis Award
www.margolis.com/award
Harry Margolis, Margolis &
    Associates
137 Newbury Street
Boston, MA 02116

harry@margolis.com

BLUESTEM PRESS

Bluestem Award

*A prize of $1,000 and publication by
Bluestem Press is given annually for a
book-length collection of poetry (at least
48 pages).*

Bluestem Press
Bluestem Award
www.emporia.edu/bluestem/
    index.htm
Philip Heldrich, Director
English Department
Box 4019, Emporia State
    University
Emporia, KS 66801-5087

(620) 341-5216

BOA EDITIONS LTD.

A. Poulin Jr. Poetry Prize

*A prize of $1,500 and publication by
BOA Editions is given annually for a
first book of poetry (48 to 100 pages).*

BOA Editions Ltd.
A. Poulin Jr. Poetry Prize
www.boaeditions.org
P.O. Box 40490
Rochester, NY 14604

BOOKMARK PRESS

John Ciardi Prize

*A prize of $1,000 and publication by
Bookmark Press is given annually for a
book-length collection of poetry (50 to
110 pages).*

G.S. Sharat Chandra Prize

A prize of $1,000 and publication by Bookmark Press is given annually for a book-length collection of short stories (50,000 to 100,000 words).

Bookmark Press
www.umkc.edu/bkmk
University of Missouri
5100 Rockhill Road
Kansas City, MO 64110-2499

(816) 235-2558
or bkmk@umkc.edu

BOSTON REVIEW

Poetry Contest

A prize of $1,000 and publication in Boston Review *is given annually for a poem.*

Short Story Contest

A prize of $1,000 and publication in Boston Review is given annually for a *short story.*

Boston Review
bostonreview.mit.edu/contests.html
E53-407 MIT
Cambridge, MA 02139

(617) 494-0708

BOULEVARD

Short Fiction Contest for Emerging Writers

A prize of $1,500 and publication in Boulevard *is given annually for a short story by a writer who has not published a book with a nationally distributed publisher.*

Boulevard
Short Fiction Contest for
    Emerging Writers
www.richardburgin.com
Richard Burgin, Editor
PMB 325
6614 Clayton Road
Richmond Heights, MO 63117

(314) 862-2643
or ballymon@hotmail.com

BREAD LOAF WRITERS' CONFERENCE

Bakeless Literary Publication Prizes

Publication by Houghton Mifflin and a fellowship to attend the Bread Loaf Writers' Conference is given annually for a first book of poems (at least 50 pages), fiction (150 to 450 pages), and creative nonfiction (150 to 300 pages).

Bread Loaf Writers' Conference
Bakeless Literary Publication Prizes
www.middlebury.edu/~blwc
Ian Pounds, Coordinator
Middlebury College
Middlebury, VT 05753

bakeless@middlebury.edu

BRIDPORT ARTS CENTRE

Bridport Prize

Two prizes of £3,000 (approximately $4,875) and publication in the Bridport Prize Anthology and a prize of £1,000 (approximately $1,625) are given annually for an unpublished poem and short story.

Bridport Arts Centre
Bridport Prize
www.bridportprize.org.uk
Frances Everitt, Prize
    Administrator
South Street
Bridport, DT6 3NR
United Kingdom

info@bridport-arts.com

BRONX WRITERS' CENTER

Fellowships

Two nine-month fellowships, each including a $5,000 grant, are given annually to poets and fiction writers under thirty who are residents of New York City.

Bronx Writers' Center
Fellowships
www.bronxarts.org
Leslie Shipman, Director
2521 Glebe Avenue
Bronx, NY 10461-1486

(718) 409-1265
or leslie@bronxarts.org

BUSH FOUNDATION

Artist Fellowships

Up to fifteen grants of $44,000 each are given biennially to poets, fiction writers, and creative nonfiction writers. Writers living in Minnesota, North Dakota, South Dakota, and northwestern Wisconsin who are twenty-five years of age or older and are not enrolled in a degree-granting program are eligible.

Bush Foundation
Artist Fellowships
www.bushfoundation.org
East 900
First National Bank Building
332 Minnesota Street
St. Paul, MN 55101

(651) 227-5222

CALIFORNIA STATE UNIVERSITY

Philip Levine Prize in Poetry

A prize of $1,500 and publication by Anhinga Press is given annually for an unpublished book of poetry (50 to 100 pages).

California State University
Philip Levine Prize in Poetry
Ruth Schwartz
Department of English
5245 North Backer Avenue
Mail Stop PB 98
Fresno, CA 93740-8001

levinepoetry@aol.com

CAMPBELL CORNER

Poetry Prize

A prize of $2,500 and publication on the Campbell Corner Web site is given annually for a poem on the themes explored in Joseph Campbell's writing.

Campbell Corner
Poetry Prize
www.slc.edu/campbellcorner
Office of Graduate Studies
Sarah Lawrence College
1 Mead Way
Bronxville, NY 10708-5999

CAVE CANEM FOUNDATION

Cave Canem Poetry Prize

A prize of $500 and publication by a participating press is given annually for an unpublished poetry collection (50 to 75 pages) by an African American poet who has not published a book.

Cave Canem Foundation
Cave Canem Poetry Prize
www.cavecanempoets.org
Carolyn Micklem, Director
P.O. Box 4286
Charlottesville, VA 22905

cavecanempoets@aol.com

CENTER FOR BOOK ARTS

Poetry Chapbook Competition

A prize of $1,000 and publication of a limited edition letterpress chapbook is given annually for a collection of poetry (20 to 24 pages).

Center for Book Arts
Poetry Chapbook Competition
www.centerforbookarts.org
28 West 27th Street
New York, NY 10001

(212) 481-0295

CHATTAHOOCHEE REVIEW

Lamar York Prize

A prize of $1,000 and publication in Chattahoochee Review *is given annually for an original essay.*

Chattahoochee Review
Lamar York Prize
Lawrence Hetrick, Editor
Georgia Perimeter College
2101 Womack Road
Dunwoody, GA 30338-4497

CHELSEA

Award for Poetry

A prize of $1,000 and publication in Chelsea *is given annually for an unpublished group of poems.*

Award for Short Fiction

A prize of $1,000 and publication in Chelsea *is given annually for an unpublished work of short fiction.*

Chelsea
Alfredo de Palchi, Editor
P.O. Box 773
Cooper Station
New York, NY 10276-0773

CLAREMONT GRADUATE UNIVERSITY

Tufts Poetry Awards

A prize of $100,000 and a one-week residence at Claremont Graduate University in California is given annually for a book of poetry by a midcareer poet. A prize of $10,000 is given annually for a first book of poetry in the Kate Tufts Discovery Award.

Claremont Graduate University
Tufts Poetry Awards
www.cgu.edu/tufts
160 East 10th Street
Harper East B7
Claremont, CA 91711-6165

(909) 621-8974

CLEVELAND FOUNDATION

Anisfield-Wolf Book Awards

A prize of $20,000 is given annually for a book of poetry, fiction, or creative nonfiction that has made "important contributions to our understanding of racism or our appreciation of the rich diversity of human cultures."

Cleveland Foundation
Anisfield-Wolf Book Awards
www.anisfield-wolf.org

Marcia Bryant
1422 Euclid Avenue
Suite 1300
Cleveland, OH 44115-2001

(216) 861-3810

CLEVELAND STATE UNIVERSITY

Poetry Center Prizes

Two prizes of $1,000 and publication in the CSU Poetry Series are given annually for unpublished book-length poetry manuscripts.

Cleveland State University
Poetry Center Prizes
www.csuohio.edu/poetrycenter
Rita Grabowski, Poetry Center
  Coordinator
2121 Euclid Avenue
Cleveland, OH 44115-2214

(216) 687-3986

COALITION FOR THE ADVANCEMENT OF JEWISH EDUCATION

David Dornstein Memorial Creative Writing Contest

A prize of $1,000 and publication in Jewish Education News *is given annually for a short story on a Jewish theme or topic by a writer aged eighteen to thirty-five.*

Coalition for the Advancement of
  Jewish Education

David Dornstein Memorial
Creative Writing Contest
www.caje.org
261 West 35th Street
Floor 12A
New York, NY 10001

(212) 268-4210
or cajeny@caje.org

COLORADO COUNCIL ON THE ARTS

Artist Fellowships

Fellowships of $5,000 are given to Colorado poets, fiction writers, and creative nonfiction writers to acknowledge outstanding achievement.

Colorado Council on the Arts
Artist Fellowships
www.coloarts.state.co.us
750 Pennsylvania Street
Denver, CO 80203

(303) 894-2617 in Colorado;
(800) 291-ARTS

COLORADO REVIEW

Colorado Prize for Poetry

A prize of $1,500 and publication by the Center for Literary Publishing is given annually for a poetry collection.

Colorado Review
Colorado Prize for Poetry
www.coloradoreview.com
David Milofsky, Director
Center for Literary Publishing

Department of English
Colorado State University
Fort Collins, CO 80523

(970) 491-5449
or creview@colostate.edu

COMMONWEALTH CLUB OF CALIFORNIA

California Book Awards

Five prizes of $2,000 each are given annually to California writers for books of poetry, fiction, first fiction, creative nonfiction, and translation published in the previous year.

Commonwealth Club of California
California Book Awards
www.commonwealthclub.org/
    bookawards.html
Barbara Lane, Book Awards
    Director
595 Market Street
San Francisco, CA 94105

(415) 597-4846
or bookawards@
commonwealthclub.org

COMSTOCK REVIEW

Muriel Craft Bailey Award

A prize of $1,000 and publication in Comstock Review *is given annually for an unpublished poem.*

Comstock Review
Muriel Craft Bailey Award
www.comstockreview.org

Peggy Flanders, Managing Editor
4956 St. John Drive
Syracuse, NY 13215

poetry@comstockreview.org

CONSTANCE SALTONSTALL FOUNDATION FOR THE ARTS

Individual Artist Grants

Grants of $5,000 are given annually to poets, fiction writers, and creative nonfiction writers who are at least twenty-one years of age and who reside in the central and western counties of New York State.

Constance Saltonstall Foundation
    for the Arts
Individual Artist Grants
www.saltonstall.org
Lee-Ellen Marvin, Program
    Manager
P.O. Box 6607,
Ithaca, NY 14851-6607

(607) 277-4933
or artsfound@clarityconnect.com

COPPER CANYON PRESS

Hayden Carruth Award

A prize of $1,000, a one-month residency at the Vermont Studio Center, and publication by Copper Canyon Press is given annually for a book-length poetry collection (at least 46 pages) by a poet who has published no more than two full-length books of poetry.

Copper Canyon Press
Hayden Carruth Award
www.coppercanyonpress.org
P.O. Box 271
Port Townsend, WA 98368

(360) 385-4925 or poetry@
coppercanyonpress.org

CRAB ORCHARD REVIEW

Crab Orchard Award Series

A first prize of $3,500 and publication by Southern Illinois University Press, and a second prize of $1,500, are given for two unpublished collections of poems (50 to 70 pages).

First Book Prize

A prize of $1,000, publication by Southern Illinois University Press, and a $1,500 honorarium to give a reading at Southern Illinois University in Carbondale is given annually for a book-length poetry collection (50 to 70 pages).

Literary Prizes

Two prizes of $1,500 each and publication in Crab Orchard Review *are given for a work of fiction and a work of creative nonfiction.*

Crab Orchard Review
www.siu.edu/~crborchd/
Jon Tribble, Series Editor
Department of English
Southern Illinois University
Carbondale, IL 62901-4503

CURBSTONE PRESS

Miguel Mármol Prize

A prize of $1,000 and publication by Curbstone Press is given annually for a first book of fiction (approximately 200 pages) in English by a Latino writer that reflects a respect for intercultural understanding, human rights, and civil liberties.

Curbstone Press
Miguel Mármol Prize
www.curbstone.org
Alexander Taylor, Codirector
321 Jackson Street
Willimantic, CT 06226

(860) 423-2998
or sandy@curbstone.org

DANA AWARDS

Literary Competition

Three prizes of $1,000 each are given annually for a group of poems, a short story, and an unpublished novel or a novel-in-progress.

Dana Awards
Literary Competition
www.danaawards.com
Mary Elizabeth Parker, Chair
7207 Townsend Forest Court
Browns Summit, NC 27214

(336) 656-7009
or danaawards@pipeline.com

DELAWARE DIVISION OF THE ARTS

Individual Artist Fellowships

Established Professional Fellowships of $5,000 and Emerging Professional Fellowships of $2,000 are given annually to Delaware poets and fiction writers who are at least eighteen years old, have lived in Delaware for at least a year prior to application, and are not enrolled in a degree program.

Delaware Division of the Arts
Individual Artist Fellowships
www.artsdel.org
Kristin Pleasanton, Coordinator
Carvel State Office Building
820 North French Street
Wilmington, DE 19801

(302) 577-8278

DORA TEITELBOIM CENTER FOR YIDDISH CULTURE

Jewish Cultural Writing Contest

A prize of $1,000 is given annually for a work of fiction or creative nonfiction.

Dora Teitelboim Center for
    Yiddish Culture
Jewish Cultural Writing Contest
www.yiddishculture.org
Liz Weintraub, Program Director
P.O. Box 14-0820
Coral Gables, FL 33114-0820

(305) 774-9244

ELIXIR PRESS

Poetry Awards

A first prize of $2,000 and a second prize of $1,000, as well as publication by Elixir Press, is given annually for two collections of poems (at least 48 pages) written in English.

Elixir Press
Poetry Awards
www.elixirpress.com
Dana Curtis, Editor
P.O. Box 18010
Minneapolis, MN 55418

info@elixirpress.com

WILLARD R. ESPY LITERARY FOUNDATION

Espy Award

A prize of $1,000 is given for an unpublished short story by a writer who has not published a book.

Willard R. Espy Literary Foundation
Espy Award
www.espyfoundation.org
Shawn Wong, Chair
Department of English
University of Washington
Box 354330
Seattle, WA 98195-4330

(360) 665-5220
or wrelf@willapabay.org

UNIVERSITY OF EVANSVILLE

Richard Wilbur Award

A prize of $1,000 and publication by University of Evansville Press is given for a book of poetry (50 to 100 pages).

University of Evansville
Richard Wilbur Award
Department of English
1800 Lincoln Avenue
Evansville, IN 47722

(812) 479-2963

FENCE BOOKS

Alberta Prize

A prize of $5,000 and publication by Fence Books is given annually for a first or second book of poetry (48 to 60 pages) by a woman.

Modern Poets Series

A prize of $1,000 and publication by Fence Books is given annually for a book (48 to 60 pages) by a poet at any stage of his or her career.

Fence Books
www.fencebooks.com
Rebecca Wolff, Editor
14 Fifth Avenue, #1A
New York, NY 10011

FINE ARTS WORK CENTER

Writing Fellowships

Fellowships for a seven-month stay at the Fine Arts Work Center in Provincetown from October 1 to May 1 with a monthly stipend of $650 are awarded to emerging poets and fiction writers.

Fine Arts Work Center
Writing Fellowships
www.fawc.org
24 Pearl Street
Provincetown, MA 02657

(508) 487-9960
or info@fawc.org

FISH PUBLISHING

Fish Short Story Prize

A prize of $1,200 and publication in a Fish Publishing anthology is given annually for an unpublished short story.

Fish Publishing
Fish Short Story Prize
www.fishpublishing.com
Clem Cairns, Editor
Durrus, Bantry
County Cork, Ireland

info@fishpublishing.com

FIVE POINTS

James Dickey Prize for Poetry

A prize of $1,000 and publication in Five Points is given annually for an unpublished group of poems.

Five Points
James Dickey Prize for Poetry
Megan Sexton, Managing Editor
Georgia State University
University Plaza
Atlanta, GA 30303-3083

FLORIDA DIVISION OF CULTURAL AFFAIRS

Individual Fellowships

Fellowships of $5,000 each are given annually to Florida poets and fiction writers.

Florida Division of Cultural Affairs
Individual Fellowships
Valerie Ohlsson
1001 DeSoto Park Drive
Tallahassee, FL 32301

(850) 487-2980

FLY ROD & REEL

Robert Traver Fly-Fishing Fiction Award

A prize of $2,500 and publication in Fly Rod & Reel will be given for a short story that "embodies an implicit love of fly-fishing" and a respect for the natural world.

Fly Rod & Reel
Robert Traver Fly-Fishing Fiction
  Award
www.flyrodreel.com
Matthew Mayo, Managing Editor
P.O. Box 370
Camden, ME 04843

FORDHAM UNIVERSITY AT LINCOLN CENTER

Poets Out Loud Prize

A prize of $1,000, publication by Fordham University Press, and an invitation to participate in the Poets Out Loud reading series is given annually for a book-length collection of poetry (50 to 80 pages).

Fordham University at Lincoln
  Center
Poets Out Loud Prize
www.fordham.edu/english/pol
Elisabeth Frost, Director
113 West 60th Street
Room 924
New York, NY 10023

(212) 636-6792
or pol@fordham.edu

THE FORMALIST

Howard Nemerov Sonnet Award

A prize of $1,000 and publication in The Formalist is given annually to a poet for an unpublished sonnet.

The Formalist
Howard Nemerov Sonnet
  Award
www2.evansville.edu/theformalist
320 Hunter Drive,
Evansville, IN 47711

FOUR WAY BOOKS

Levis Poetry Prize

A prize of $1,000, publication by Four Way Books, a reading at two or more New York City reading series, and a monthlong residency at the Fine Arts Work Center in Provincetown, Massachusetts, is given biennially for a full-length poetry collection.

Four Way Books
Levis Poetry Prize
www.fourwaybooks.com
205 North Lauderdale Drive
Kalamazoo, MI 49006

FRENCH-AMERICAN FOUNDATION

Translation Prizes

Two awards of $7,500 each are given annually for translations from French into English of a fiction and creative nonfiction book published in the previous year.

French-American Foundation
Translation Prizes
www.frenchamerican.org
Veronique Lemire, Director of
  Cultural Programs and Public
  Events

509 Madison Avenue
Suite 310
New York, NY 10022

(212) 829-8800, ext. 14,
or vlemire@frenchamerican.org

UNIVERSITY OF GEORGIA PRESS

Contemporary Poetry Series

Publication by the University of Georgia Press in its Contemporary Poetry Series is given annually for four poetry collections (at least 50 pages) by emerging and midcareer poets.

Flannery O'Connor Awards

Two prizes of $1,000 each and publication by University of Georgia Press are given annually for short story collections (200 to 275 pages).

University of Georgia Press
www.uga.edu/ugapress/pressinfo/
  guidelines.html
Erin McElroy, Competition
  Coordinator
330 Research Drive
Athens, GA 30602-4901

GLIMMER TRAIN PRESS

Fiction Open

A prize of $2,000 and publication in Glimmer Train Stories is given twice yearly for a short story. A second-place prize of $1,000 is also awarded.

Short Story Award for New Writers

A prize of $1,200 and publication in Glimmer Train Stories is given twice yearly to a writer whose fiction has not been published in a nationally distributed publication with a circulation over 5,000.

Very Short Fiction Award

A prize of $1,200 and publication in Glimmer Train Stories is given annually for an unpublished short story.

Glimmer Train Press
www.glimmertrain.com
Susan Burmeister-Brown and Linda
  Swanson-Davies, Coeditors
710 S.W. Madison Street
Suite 504
Portland, OR 97205

(503) 221-0836

GORSKY PRESS

Literary Sashimi Award

A prize of $1,000 and publication by Gorsky Press is given annually for a novella or a poetry collection or short stories by a writer who "expresses his or her talent in a concise slice of work."

Gorsky Press
Literary Sashimi Award
www.gorskypress.com
Felizon Vidad, Editor
P.O. Box 42024
Los Angeles, CA 90042

gorskypress@hotmail.com

GRAYWOLF PRESS

S. Mariella Gable Prize

A prize of $15,000 and publication by Graywolf Press is given annually for an unpublished novel.

Graywolf Press
S. Mariella Gable Prize
www.graywolfpress.org
Katie Dublinski, Editor
2402 University Avenue
Suite 203
St. Paul, MN 55114

GREAT LAKES COLLEGES ASSOCIATION

New Writers Awards

A paid reading tour is given annually to a poet and a fiction writer whose first books were published in the preceding year.

Great Lakes Colleges Association
New Writers Awards
Daniel Bourne, Director
English Department
The College of Wooster
Wooster, OH 44691

(330) 263-2332
or dbourne@wooster.edu

GREENSBORO REVIEW

Literary Awards

Two prizes of $500 and publication in the Greensboro Review *are given annually for a poem and a short story.*

Greensboro Review
Literary Awards
www.uncg.edu/eng/mfa/review/
    guidelines.htm
English Department
134 McIver Building, UNCG
P.O. Box 26170
Greensboro, NC 27402-6170

(336) 334-5459
or tlkenned@uncg.edu

GRIFFIN TRUST FOR EXCELLENCE IN POETRY

Griffin Poetry Prizes

Two prizes of $40,000 Canadian (approximately U.S. $25,500) each are given annually for published collections of poetry by a Canadian and an international poet or translator.

Griffin Trust for Excellence in
    Poetry
Griffin Poetry Prizes
www.griffinpoetryprize.com
Ruth Smith, Manager
6610 Edwards Boulevard
Mississauga, Ontario
L5T 2V6, Canada

(905) 565-5993
or info@griffinpoetryprize.com

GSU REVIEW

Writing Contest

Two prizes of $1,000 each and publication in the GSU Review, the biannual literary journal of Georgia State University, are given annually for an unpublished poem and short story.

GSU Review
Writing Contest
www.gsu.edu/~wwwrev
Katie Chaple, Editor
Campus Box 1894
Georgia State University
MSC 8R0322 Unit 8
Atlanta, GA 30303-3083

(404) 651-4804
or kchaple@emory.edu

GUADALAJARA INTERNATIONAL BOOK FAIR

Sor Juana Inés de la Cruz Prize

A prize of at least $2,000 in advances, publication in English by Curbstone Press, and travel expenses to the award ceremony at the Guadalajara International Book Fair in Mexico is given annually to a woman writer for a novel published in Spanish after 1999.

Guadalajara International Book Fair
Sor Juana Inés de la Cruz Prize
David Unger, U.S. Coordinator
Avenida Alemania 1370
Guadalajara, 44190
Jalisco, Mexico

(212) 650-7925
or premio@fil.com.mx

JOHN SIMON GUGGENHEIM MEMORIAL FOUNDATION

Fellowships to Assist Research and Artistic Creation

Annual Guggenheim fellowships averaging approximately $36,685 each are awarded to poets, fiction writers, and creative nonfiction writers "on the basis of unusually distinguished achievement in the past and exceptional promise for future accomplishment."

John Simon Guggenheim
    Memorial Foundation
Fellowships to Assist Research
    and Artistic Creation
www.gf.org
90 Park Avenue
New York, NY 10016

(212) 687-4470
or fellowships@gf.org

HADASSAH MAGAZINE

Harold U. Ribalow Prize

A prize of $1,000 and publication in Hadassah Magazine is given annually for a book of fiction on a Jewish theme published in the previous year.

Hadassah Magazine
Harold U. Ribalow Prize
www.hadassah.org/NEWS/
    magazine/ribalow.htm

Alan Tigay, Editor
50 West 58th Street
New York, NY 10019

(212) 451-6289

Hemingway Short Story Competition

A prize of $1,000 is given annually for an unpublished short story by a writer whose fiction has not appeared in a nationally distributed publication with a circulation of 5,000 or more.

Hemingway Short Story
   Competition
www.shortstorycompetition.com
Carol Shaughnessy, Codirector
P.O. Box 993
Key West, FL 33041

calico2419@aol.com

RUTH HINDMAN FOUNDATION

H.E. Francis Short Story Competition

A prize of $1,000 is given annually for an unpublished short story.

Ruth Hindman Foundation
H.E. Francis Short Story
   Competition
www.uah.edu/colleges/liberal/
   english/whatnewcontest.html
Patricia Sammon, Department of
   English
University of Alabama
Huntsville, AL 35899

HUMAN RIGHTS WATCH

Hellman/Hammett Grants

Grants of $1,000 to $10,000 each are given annually to poets, fiction writers, and creative nonfiction writers in financial need as a result of political persecution, and smaller emergency grants of $1,000 to $2,000 are given to writers who have an urgent need to leave their country, are facing a medical emergency, or are otherwise in dire financial circumstances.

Human Rights Watch
Hellman/Hammett Grants
www.hrw.org
Marcia Allina, Program Associate
350 Fifth Avenue, 34th Floor
New York, NY 10118-3299

(212) 216-1246
or allinam@hrw.org

HUMBOLDT STATE UNIVERSITY

Raymond Carver Short Story Contest

A prize of $1,000 and publication in Toyon, *Humboldt State University's literary journal, is given for an unpublished short story.*

Humboldt State University
Raymond Carver Short Story
   Contest
www.humboldt.edu/~carver
Brian Derr, Coordinator
English Department

1 Harpst Street
Arcata, CA 95521

carver@humboldt.edu

HURSTON/WRIGHT FOUNDATION

Hurston/Wright Awards

A prize of $1,000, and second- and third-place prizes of $500, are given annually to honor excellence in fiction writing by a student of African descent enrolled full-time in a U.S. college or graduate school.

Hurston/Wright Legacy Awards

Three prizes of $10,000 each are given annually to writers of African descent for a book of fiction, a first book of fiction, and a book of creative nonfiction published in the current calendar year. Two finalists in each category will also receive $5,000 each.

Hurston/Wright Foundation
www.hurston-wright.org
Clyde McElvene, Executive
    Director
6525 Belcrest Road
Suite 531
Hyattsville, MD 20782

(301) 683-2134
or info@hurston-wright.org

INDIANA REVIEW

Fiction Prize

A prize of $1,000 and publication in Indiana Review *is given annually for an unpublished short story.*

Indiana Review
Fiction Prize
www.indiana.edu/~inreview
David Daniels, Editor
Ballantine Hall 465
1020 East Kirkwood Avenue
Bloomington, IN 47405-7103

(812) 855-3439
or inreview@indiana.edu

UNIVERSITY OF IOWA PRESS

Iowa Poetry Prize

Publication by the University of Iowa Press is given annually for two unpublished poetry collections (50 to 150 pages).

Short Fiction Awards

Two publication awards are given annually by the University of Iowa Press for first collections of short fiction (at least 150 pages).

University of Iowa Press
www.uiowapress.org
100 Kuhl House
Iowa City, IA 52242-1000

IOWA REVIEW

Iowa Awards

Three prizes of $1,000 each and publication in the Iowa Review *are given annually for works of poetry, fiction, and creative nonfiction.*

Iowa Review
Iowa Awards
www.uiowa.edu/~iareview/
  mainpages/iowaaward.html
Amber Withycombe, Managing
  Editor
308 EPB
University of Iowa
Iowa City, IA 52242

(319) 335-0462
or iowa-review@uiowa.edu

IRONWEED PRESS

Fiction Prize

A prize of $2,500 and publication by Ironweed Press as part of its Discovered Voices trade paperback series is given annually for a book-length work of fiction (at least 80 pages).

Ironweed Press
Fiction Prize
Jin Soo Kang, Special Projects
  Editor
Department Four
P.O. Box 754208
Parkside Station
Forest Hills, NY 11375

CHRISTOPHER ISHERWOOD FOUNDATION

Fiction Fellowships

Three to five grants of $3,000 each are given to fiction writers to provide time for writing.

Christopher Isherwood Foundation
Fiction Fellowships
www.isherwoodfoundation.org
James White, Executive Director
P.O. Box 650,
Montrose, AL 36559

(251) 928-3711

ITALIAN AMERICANA

John Ciardi Lifetime Achievement Award in Poetry

A prize of $1,000 is given annually to an Italian American poet for lifetime achievement in poetry.

Italian Americana
John Ciardi Lifetime
  Achievement Award in Poetry
Carol Bonomo Albright, Editor
University of Rhode Island
Providence Center
80 Washington Street
Providence, RI 02903

(401) 277-5306
or bonomoal@etal.uri.edu

ALICE JAMES BOOKS

Beatrice Hawley Award

*A prize of $2,000 and publication by
Alice James Books is given annually
for an unpublished poetry collection (50
to 64 pages).*

New England/New York Prize

*A prize of $2,000, a one-month
fellowship at the Vermont Studio
Center in Johnson, Vermont, and
publication by Alice James Books is
given annually for a poetry collection
(50 to 64 pages) by a poet living in
New England or New York state.*

Alice James Books
www.alicejamesbooks.org
April Ossmann, Director
238 Main Street
Farmington, ME 04938

(207) 778-7071

JAMES JONES LITERARY SOCIETY

First Novel Fellowship

*A prize of $6,000 is given annually
for a work-in-progress of fiction (first
50 pages).*

James Jones Literary Society
First Novel Fellowship
www.wilkes.edu/humanities/
    jones.html
Jacqueline Mosher, Coordinator
Department of English

Wilkes University
Wilkes-Barre, PA 18766

english@wilkes.edu

KALLIOPE

Sue Saniel Elkind Poetry Contest

A prize of $1,000 and publication in
Kalliope *is given annually for a poem
by a woman.*

Kalliope
Sue Saniel Elkind Poetry
    Contest
www.fccj.org/kalliope
Mary Sue Koeppel, Editor
Florida Community College
3939 Roosevelt Boulevard
Jacksonville, FL 32205

(904) 381-3511

KNOXVILLE WRITERS' GUILD

Peter Taylor Prize

*A prize of $1,000 and publication by
the University of Tennessee Press is
given annually for a novel (at least
40,000 words).*

Knoxville Writers' Guild
Peter Taylor Prize
www.knoxvillewritersguild.org
P.O. Box 2565
Knoxville, TN 37901-2565

KORE PRESS

First Book Award

A prize of $1,000 and publication by Kore Press is given annually for a first book-length poetry manuscript (48 to 70 pages) by a woman.

Kore Press
First Book Award
www.korepress.org
Lisa Bowden
P.O. Box 3044
Tucson, AZ 85702

(520) 882-7542
or kore@korepress.org

THE LEDGE PRESS

Fiction Award

A prize of $1,000 and publication in The Ledge *will be given annually for an unpublished short story.*

Poetry Award

A prize of $1,000 and publication in The Ledge *is given annually for a poem of any length.*

Poetry Chapbook Competition

A prize of $1,000, publication, and fifty author copies is given annually for a chapbook-length poetry collection (16 to 28 pages).

The Ledge Press
Timothy Monaghan, Publisher

78-44 80th Street
Glendale, NY 11385

tkmonaghan@aol.com

LEEWAY FOUNDATION

Grants for Emerging and Established Artists

Grants of $2,500 to $35,000 each are given every six years to women fiction and creative nonfiction writers who have lived for at least two years in Bucks, Chester, Delaware, Montgomery, or Philadelphia Counties in Pennsylvania.

Window of Opportunity Grants

Grants of up to $2,000 are given biannually to Philadelphia-area women poets, fiction writers, and creative nonfiction writers to support literary projects.

Leeway Foundation
www.leeway.org
Pam Shropshire, Program Manager
123 South Broad Street
Suite 2040
Philadelphia, PA 19109

(215) 545-4078
or info@leeway.org

LIBRARY OF VIRGINIA

Literary Awards

Three prizes of $1,000 each are given annually for books of poetry, fiction, and creative nonfiction published in the previous year.

Library of Virginia
Literary Awards
www.lva.lib.va.us/whatwedo/
    awards/entries.htm
800 East Broad Street
Richmond, VA 23219-8000

(804) 692-3720

LITERAL LATTÉ

Ames Essay Award

A prize of $1,000 and publication in Literal Latté is given annually for an unpublished creative nonfiction essay.

K. Margaret Grossman Fiction Award

A prize of $1,000 and publication in Literal Latté is given annually for an unpublished short story.

Poetry Award

A prize of $1,000 and publication in Literal Latté is given annually for an unpublished poem.

Literal Latté
www.literal-latte.com
Jenine Gordon Bockman, Editor

61 East Eighth Street
Suite 240
New York, NY 10003

(212) 260-5532
or litlatte@aol.com

LITERARY ARTS

Literary Fellowships

Fellowships ranging from $500 to $3,000 are given annually to Oregon writers to initiate, develop, or complete literary projects in poetry, fiction, or creative nonfiction; $500 to $3,000 fellowships are given annually to Oregon women writers of poetry, fiction, or creative nonfiction whose work explores experiences of race, class, physical disability, or sexual orientation.

Oregon Book Awards

Four prizes of $500 each are given annually to honor books of poetry, fiction, and creative nonfiction by Oregon authors.

Literary Arts
www.literary-arts.org
Kristy Athens, Program
    Coordinator
219 N.W. 12th Avenue
Suite 201
Portland, OR 97209

(503) 227-2583

LOTUS PRESS

Naomi Long Madgett Poetry Award

A prize of $500 and publication by Lotus Press is given annually for a poetry collection (60 to 80 pages) by an African American poet.

Lotus Press
Naomi Long Madgett Poetry
  Award
Constance Withers, Assistant to
  the Editor
P.O. Box 21607
Detroit, MI 48221

(313) 861-1280
or lotuspress@aol.com

AMY LOWELL POETRY TRAVELLING SCHOLARSHIP

An award of approximately $37,000 is given annually to a poet for a year of travel and study abroad.

Amy Lowell Poetry Travelling
  Scholarship
Pearl Bell
Choate, Hall & Stewart
Exchange Place
53 State Street
Boston, MA 02109-2804

(617) 248-5000

LYNX HOUSE PRESS

Blue Lynx Prize

An award of $1,500 and publication by Lynx House Press is given annually for an unpublished poetry collection (at least 48 pages).

Lynx House Press
Blue Lynx Prize
Christopher Howell
P.O. Box 471
Spokane, WA 99210

(509) 624-4894

MAINE ARTS COMMISSION

Individual Artist Fellowships

Fellowships of $3,000 each are awarded biennially to Maine writers of poetry, fiction, and creative nonfiction.

Maine Arts Commission
Individual Artist Fellowships,
www.mainearts.com/artists/
  fellowships
Kathy Ann Shaw, Associate for
  Contemporary Arts
193 State Street
25 State House Station
Augusta, ME 04333-0025

(207) 287-2750
or kathy.shaw@state.me.us

MAINE COMMUNITY FOUNDATION

Martin Dibner Fellowships

Fellowships of up to $1,000 each are given in alternating years to Maine poets and fiction writers to attend writing workshops or complete writing projects.

Maine Community Foundation
Martin Dibner Fellowships
www.mainecf.org
Carl Little, Director of
    Communications
245 Main Street
Ellsworth, ME 04605

(877) 700-6800
or clittle@mainecf.org

MAIN STREET RAG

Poetry Book Award

*A prize of $1,000 and publication in
Main Street Rag is given annually
for an unpublished collection of poetry
(48 to 80 pages).*

Main Street Rag
Poetry Book Award
www.mainstreetrag.com
M. Scott Douglass, Publisher
P.O. Box 691621
Charlotte, NC 28227

(704) 573-2516
or editor@mainstreetrag.com

MANHATTANVILLE COLLEGE

Inkwell Poetry and Short Fiction Competition

*A prize of $1,500 and publication in
Inkwell, the literary journal of
Manhattanville College's Master of
Arts Writing Program, is given
annually for a short story, and a prize
of $1,000 and publication in Inkwell
is given annually for a poem.*

Manhattanville College
Inkwell Poetry and Short
    Fiction Competition
Jeremy Church, Editor
Box 1379
2900 Purchase Street
Purchase, NY 10577

(914) 323-7239

MARGIE: THE AMERICAN JOURNAL OF POETRY

Marjorie J. Wilson Award

*A prize of $2,500 and publication in
Margie is given annually for an
unpublished poem.*

Margie: The American Journal of
    Poetry
Marjorie J. Wilson Award
www.margiereview.com
P.O. Box 250
Chesterfield, MO 63006-0250

margiereview@aol.com

MARLBORO REVIEW

Prize for Poetry

*A prize of $1,000 and publication in
the Marlboro Review is given annually for a poem or group of poems.*

Marlboro Review
Prize for Poetry
www.marlbororeview.com
Ellen Dudley, Editor
P.O. Box 243
Marlboro, VT 05344

MARY ROBERTS RINEHART FUND

Rinehart Grants

Three grants of $2,000 each are given annually to an emerging poet, fiction writer, and creative nonfiction writer.

Mary Roberts Rinehart Fund
Rinehart Grants
www.gmu.edu/departments/writing
Barb Gomperts, Department of
    English
MSN 3E4
George Mason University
Fairfax, VA 22030-4444

(703) 993-1180
or bgomperts@gmu.edu

MARYLAND STATE ARTS COUNCIL

Individual Artist Awards

Grants ranging from $1,000 to $6,000 are given biennially to Maryland poets "to encourage and sustain their pursuit of artistic excellence."

Maryland State Arts Council
Individual Artist Awards
www.msac.org
175 West Ostend Street
Suite E
Baltimore, MD 21230

(410) 767-6555

UNIVERSITY OF MASSACHUSETTS PRESS

Juniper Prize

A prize of $1,000 and publication by the University of Massachusetts Press is given annually for a book of poetry (50 to 70 pages).

University of Massachusetts Press
Juniper Prize
www.umass.edu/umpress
Alice Maldonado, Assistant Editor
Amherst, MA 01003

(413) 545-2217

UNIVERSITY OF MEMPHIS

River City Writing Award in Fiction

A prize of $1,500 and publication in River City, *a biannual literary journal, is given annually for an unpublished short story.*

River City Writing Award in Poetry

A prize of $1,000 and publication in River City *is given annually for an unpublished poem.*

University of Memphis
www.people.memphis.edu/
    ~rivercity
Patrick Ryan
Department of English
Memphis, TN 38152

(901) 678-4591
or rivercity@memphis.edu

MEXICO

Juan Rulfo International Latin American and Caribbean Prize

A prize of $100,000 is given annually to honor a writer of poetry, drama, fiction, or essay who is a native of Latin America or the Caribbean and writes in Spanish, Portuguese, French, or English, or a native of Spain or Portugal who writes in Spanish or Portuguese.

Juan Rulfo International Latin
  American and Caribbean Prize
David Unger, U.S. Coordinator
Avenida Alemania 1370
Guadalajara, 44190
Jalisco, Mexico

(212) 650-7925
or premio@fil.com.mx

UNIVERSITY OF MICHIGAN PRESS

Michigan Literary Fiction Awards

Two prizes of $1,000 each and publication by the University of Michigan Press are given annually for a novel and a collection of short stories.

University of Michigan Press
Michigan Literary Fiction Awards
www.press.umich.edu/fiction

839 Greene Street
P.O. Box 1104
Ann Arbor, MI 48106-1104

ump.fiction@umich.edu

MID-LIST PRESS

First Series Awards

Two prizes of $1,000 each and publication by Mid-List Press are given annually for a collection of short stories or novellas and an essay collection or book-length work of creative nonfiction.

First Series Award for the Novel

An advance of $1,000 and publication by Mid-List Press is given annually for an unpublished novel (at least 50,000 words).

Mid-List Press
www.midlist.org
Marianne Nora, Executive Director
4324 12th Avenue South
Minneapolis, MN 55407-3218

MILTON CENTER

Award for Excellence in Poetry

A prize of $1,000 and publication in the biannual American Literary Review is given annually for an unpublished poem "that elevates the human spirit."

Milton Center
Award for Excellence in Poetry
www.newmanu.edu/miltoncenter
Essie Sappenfield, Program
  Director
Newman University
3100 McCormick Avenue
Wichita, KS 67213

(316) 942-4291, ext. 326,
or miltonc@newmanu.edu

MINNESOTA STATE ARTS BOARD

Artist Fellowships

Fellowships of $8,000 each are given annually to recognize and reward outstanding Minnesota writers of poetry, fiction, and creative nonfiction.

Minnesota State Arts Board
Artist Fellowships
www.arts.state.mn.us
Park Square Court
400 Sibley Street
Suite 200
St. Paul, MN 55101-1928

(651) 215-1600 in Minnesota;
(800) 8MN-ARTS
or msab@state.mn.us

MISSISSIPPI REVIEW

Mississippi Review Prizes

Two prizes of $1,000 and publication in the Mississippi Review are given annually for unpublished poetry and fiction by writers who are not current

or former University of Southern Mississippi students.

Mississippi Review
Mississippi Review Prizes
www.mississippireview.com
Rie Fortenberry, Managing Editor
Box 5144
Hattiesburg, MS 39406-5144

(601) 266-4321
or rief@netdoor.com

MISSOURI REVIEW

Editors' Prizes

Awards of $2,000 each for a short story and an essay are given annually in the Missouri Review *Editors' Prize competition, and an award of $2,000 is given annually in the Larry Levis Editor's Prize for poetry competition.*

Missouri Review
Editors' Prizes
www.missourireview.org
Hoa Ngo, Managing Editor
1507 Hillcrest Hall
University of Missouri
Columbia, MO 65211

MOMENT MAGAZINE

Short Story Contest

A prize of $1,000 and publication in Moment *magazine is given annually for an unpublished short story with Jewish subject matter.*

Moment Magazine
Short Story Contest

www.momentmag.com
Lisa Frydman, Managing Editor
4710 41st Street N.W.
Washington, DC 20016

(202) 362-9070

MONEY FOR WOMEN/
BARBARA DEMING
MEMORIAL FUND

Individual Artist Grants for Women

Grants of $500 to $1,500 are given twice yearly to feminist writers of poetry, fiction, and creative nonfiction.

Money for Women/Barbara
    Deming Memorial Fund
Individual Artist Grants for
    Women
Susan Pliner, Executive Director
P.O. Box 630125
Bronx, NY 10463

NATIONAL COUNCIL OF
TEACHERS OF ENGLISH

Donald Murray Prize

A prize of $500 will be given annually for the best creative essay about teaching or writing published during the previous year.

National Council of Teachers of
    English
Donald Murray Prize
John Boe, English Department
1 Shields Avenue
University of California
Davis, CA 95616

(530) 752-2257
or jdboe@ucdavis.edu

NATIONAL ENDOWMENT
FOR THE ARTS

United States/Japan Creative Artists' Program

Up to five six-month residencies, which include stipends for living and housing expenses, transportation, and language study, are awarded annually to U.S. artists (writers of poetry, fiction, and nonfiction are eligible) to live in Japan and work on independent projects that advance their artistic goals.

National Endowment for the Arts
United States/Japan Creative
    Artists' Program
Japan/U.S. Friendship
    Commission
www.jusfc.gov/commissn/
    guide.html
1110 Vermont Avenue N.W.
Suite 800
Washington, DC 20005

(202) 418-9800
or artists@jusfc.gov

NATIONAL FEDERATION OF
STATE POETRY SOCIETIES

Stevens Manuscript Competition

A prize of $1,000, publication by the National Federation of State Poetry Societies, and fifty copies of the winning book is given for an unpublished poetry manuscript (35 to 60 pages).

National Federation of State Poetry Societies
Stevens Manuscript Competition
www.nfsps.com
Doris Stengel, Chairperson
1510 South Seventh Street
Brainerd, MN 56401

dpoet@brainerd.net

NATIONAL POETRY SERIES

Open Competition

Prizes of $1,000 and publication by participating trade, university, or small press publishers are given annually for five book-length poetry manuscripts (48 to 64 pages).

National Poetry Series
Open Competition
www.nationalpoetryseries.org
Stephanie Stio, Coordinator
9 Mercer Street
Princeton, NJ 08540

(609) 430-0999

NEBRASKA ARTS COUNCIL

Literature Fellowships

Up to three $5,000 Distinguished Achievement Awards and seven to fifteen Merit Awards of $1,000 to $2,000 are given every three years to Nebraska poets, fiction writers, and creative nonfiction writers.

Nebraska Arts Council
Literature Fellowships
www.nebraskaartscouncil.org
Suzanne Wise, Program Manager
3838 Davenport Street
Omaha, NE 68131-2825

(402) 595-2122
or swise@nebraskaartscouncil.org

UNIVERSITY OF NEBRASKA PRESS

Prairie Schooner Prizes

Two prizes of $3,000 each and publication by University of Nebraska Press in the Prairie Schooner *Prize Book Series will be given annually for unpublished book-length collections of poetry (at least 50 pages) and short fiction (at least 150 pages).*

University of Nebraska Press
Prairie Schooner Prizes
www.unl.edu/schooner/psmain.htm
Erin Flanagan, Managing Editor
201 Andrews Hall
P.O. Box 880334
Lincoln, NE 68588-0334

(402) 472-0911
or eflanagan2@unl.edu

NEVADA ARTS COUNCIL

Artist Fellowship Grants

Grants of $5,000 each are given annually to Nevada poets, fiction writers, and creative nonfiction writers who have lived in Nevada for a full *year prior to the application deadline are eligible.*

Nevada Arts Council
Artist Fellowship Grants
www.nevadaculture.org
Sara Grey, Program Assistant
716 North Carson Street
Suite A
Carson City, NV 89701

(775) 687-6680

NEW ENGLAND POETRY CLUB

Daniel Varoujan Prize

A prize of $1,000 is given annually for an unpublished poem.

New England Poetry Club
Daniel Varoujan Prize
Elizabeth Crowell, Contest
  Coordinator
16 Cornell Street, #2
Arlington, MA 02474

NEW ISSUES POETRY & PROSE

Green Rose Prize in Poetry

A prize of $1,000 and publication by New Issues Press is given annually for a book-length collection of poetry (48 to 120 pages).

Poetry Prize

A prize of $1,000 and publication in the New Issues Press Poetry Series is

given annually for a first book of poems (at least 48 pages).

New Issues Poetry & Prose
  Western Michigan University
www.wmich.edu/newissues
Herbert Scott, Editor
1903 West Michigan Avenue
Kalamazoo, MI 49008-5331

(616) 387-8185
or herbert.scott@wmich.edu

NEW JERSEY STATE COUNCIL ON THE ARTS

Literary Arts Fellowships

Fellowships of $5,500 to $10,000 each are awarded biennially to support poets, fiction writers, and creative nonfiction writers.

New Jersey State Council on the
  Arts
Literary Arts Fellowships
www.njartscouncil.org
Robin Middleman
MidAtlantic Arts Foundation
22 Light Street
3rd Floor
Baltimore, MD 21202

robin@midatlanticarts.org

NEW LETTERS

Literary Awards

Three awards of $1,000 each—the New Letters Poetry Prize, the Alexander Patterson Cappon Fiction Prize, and

the Dorothy Churchill Cappon Creative
Nonfiction Prize—and publication in
New Letters *are given annually for
unpublished work.*

New Letters
Literary Awards
www.umkc.edu/newletters
Aleatha Ezra, Assistant Managing
    Editor
5101 Rockhill Road
Room 222
University of Missouri
Kansas City, MO 64110

NEW MILLENNIUM WRITINGS

New Millennium Awards

*Three prizes of $1,000 each and
publication in* New Millennium
Writings *are given for a poem, a work
of fiction, and a work of creative
nonfiction.*

New Millennium Writings
New Millennium Awards
www.mach2.com/books
Don Williams, Editor
Room A
P.O. Box 2463
Knoxville, TN 37901

(865) 428-0389
or donwilliams7@att.net

NEW YORK FOUNDATION FOR THE ARTS

Artists' Fellowships

*Alternating fellowships of $7,000 are
given to New York writers of fiction,*

poetry, *and creative nonfiction on the
basis of the excellence of their recent
work.*

New York Foundation for the Arts
Artists' Fellowships
www.nyfa.org/artists_fellowships
155 Avenue of the Americas
14th Floor
New York, NY 10013-1507

(212) 366-6900, ext. 217,
or nyfaafp@nyfa.org

NICHOLAS ROERICH MUSEUM

Poets' Prize

*A prize of $3,000 and an invitation to
read at the Nicholas Roerich Museum
in New York City is given annually
for a book of poetry published in the
preceding calendar year.*

Nicholas Roerich Museum
Poets' Prize
Daniel Entin, Director
319 West 107th Street
New York, NY 10025

(212) 864-7752

NIMROD INTERNATIONAL JOURNAL

Nimrod/Hardman Awards

*Two prizes of $2,000 (and two $1,000
runners-up) plus publication in* Nimrod
*are given annually for unpublished
works of poetry and short fiction.*

Nimrod International Journal
Nimrod/Hardman Awards
www.utulsa.edu/nimrod
Eilis O'Neal, Managing Editor
University of Tulsa
600 South College Avenue
Tulsa, OK 74104

(918) 631-3080
or nimrod@utulsa.edu

NORTH CAROLINA ARTS COUNCIL

Residency Program

A $7,500 grant for a three-month residency at the Headlands Center for the Arts in Sausalito, California, and a $2,400 grant for a monthlong residency at the Vermont Studio Center in Johnson are given annually by the North Carolina Arts Council.

North Carolina Arts Council
Residency Program
www.ncarts.org
Kirsten Mullen, Literature
    Director
Department of Cultural Resources
Raleigh, NC 27699-4632

(919) 715-1519
or kirsten.mullen@ncmail.net

UNIVERSITY OF NORTH TEXAS PRESS

Vassar Miller Prize in Poetry

A prize of $1,000 and publication by the University of North Texas Press is

given annually for an original poetry collection (50 to 80 pages).

University of North Texas Press
Vassar Miller Prize in Poetry
www.unt.edu/untpress/series/
    vassar.htm
Scott Cairns, Series Editor
English Department
Tate Hall 107
University of Missouri
Columbia, MO 65211

(573) 882-0669

NORTHEASTERN UNIVERSITY

Samuel French Morse Poetry Prize

A prize of $1,000 and publication by Northeastern University Press is given annually for a first or second book of poems (50 to 70 pages).

Northeastern University
Samuel French Morse Poetry
    Prize
www.casdn.neu.edu/~english
Guy Rotella, Editor
English Department
406 Holmes Hall
Boston, MA 02115

NORTHWOOD UNIVERSITY

Alden B. Dow Creativity Center Fellowship

Four ten-week fellowships, which provide room, board, and a $750 stipend, are offered each summer to

individuals in any field or profession to
pursue an innovative project.

Northwood University
Alden B. Dow Creativity
    Center Fellowship
www.northwood.edu/abd
Liz Drake, Assistant Director
4000 Whiting Drive
Midland, MI 48640-2398

(989) 837-4478
or creativity@northwood.edu

UNIVERSITY OF NOTRE DAME PRESS

Richard Sullivan Prize in Fiction

*A prize of $1,000, publication by the
University of Notre Dame Press, and
an invitation to read at the University
of Notre Dame is given for a collection
of short fiction.*

University of Notre Dame Press
Richard Sullivan Prize in Fiction
www.nd.edu/~alcwp
Valerie Sayers, Director
Department of English
Notre Dame, IN 46556-5639

(574) 631-7526
or english.righter.1@nd.edu

NOVELLO FESTIVAL PRESS

Novello Literary Award

*An advance of $1,000 and publication
by Novello Festival Press, a public*

library–sponsored literary publisher, is
given annually to residents of North or
South Carolina for a book-length work
of fiction or creative nonfiction.

Novello Festival Press
Novello Literary Award
www.novellopress.org
Carol Adams, Publicist
PLCMC
310 North Tryon Street
Charlotte, NC 28202

(704) 432-0153

NUCLEAR AGE PEACE FOUNDATION

Barbara Mandigo Kelly Peace Poetry Award

A prize of $1,000 and publication in
Waging Peace, *the quarterly journal
of the Nuclear Age Peace Foundation,
is given annually for an unpublished
poem.*

Nuclear Age Peace Foundation
Barbara Mandigo Kelly Peace
    Poetry Award
www.wagingpeace.org
Devon Chaffee, Research and
    Outreach Coordinator
PMB 121
1187 Coast Village Road
Suite One
Santa Barbara, CA 93108-2794

(805) 965-3443
or advocacy@napf.org

OBERLIN COLLEGE PRESS

Field Poetry Prize

A prize of $1,000 and publication by Oberlin College Press is given annually for a poetry collection (50 to 80 pages).

Oberlin College Press
Field Poetry Prize
www.oberlin.edu/~ocpress
Linda Slocum, Managing Editor
10 North Professor Street
Oberlin, OH 44074

(440) 775-8408
or oc.press@oberlin.edu

OBERON

Poetry Prize

A prize of $1,000 and publication in Oberon, a literary journal published by the Oberon Foundation, is given annually for an unpublished poem.

Oberon
Poetry Prize
Claire Nicolas White, Editor
P.O. Box 2236
St. James, NY 11780

(631) 689-3285
or oberonarts@aol.com

OHIO ARTS COUNCIL

Individual Artist Fellowships

Fellowships of $5,000 and $10,000 are awarded annually to Ohio poets and fiction writers.
Ohio Arts Council
Individual Artist Fellowships
www.oac.state.oh.us
727 East Main Street
Columbus, OH 43205-1796

(614) 466-2613

OHIO STATE UNIVERSITY PRESS

Sandstone Prize in Short Fiction

A prize of $1,500, publication by Ohio State University Press, and an invitation to direct a workshop and to give a paid reading at OSU is given annually for a collection of short fiction.

Ohio State University Press
Sandstone Prize in Short
   Fiction
www.ohiostatepress.org
Lee Martin, Fiction Editor
1070 Carmack Road
Columbus, OH 43210-1002

(614) 292-6930

OHIOANA LIBRARY ASSOCIATION

Walter Rumsey Marvin Grant

A grant of $1,000 is given annually to a fiction or creative nonfiction writer under the age of thirty who has not published a book.

Ohioana Poetry Award

A prize of $1,000 is given annually to honor an Ohio poet for his or her body of published work and contribution to poetry.

Ohioana Library Association
www.oplin.lib.oh.us/ohioana
Linda Hengst, Director
274 East First Avenue
Suite 300
Columbus, OH 43201

(614) 466-3831
or ohioana@sloma.state.oh.us

PASSAGES NORTH

Elinor Benedict Poetry Prize

A prize of $1,000 and publication in Passages North *is given annually for a group of poems.*

Passages North
Elinor Benedict Poetry Prize
Katie Hanson, Editor
Department of English
Gries Hall
Northern Michigan University
1401 Presque Isle Avenue
Marquette, MI 49855

(906) 227-1795

PAVEMENT SAW PRESS

Transcontinental Poetry Award

A prize of $1,000, publication by Pavement Saw Press, *and a $500 reading stipend is given annually for a first collection of poetry.*

Pavement Saw Press
Transcontinental Poetry Award
www.pavementsaw.org
David Baratier, Editor
P.O. Box 6291
Columbus, OH 43206

baratier@megsinet.net

PEARL EDITIONS

Pearl Poetry Prize

A prize of $1,000 and publication by Pearl Editions *is given annually for a collection of poetry (48 to 64 pages).*

Pearl Editions
Pearl Poetry Prize
www.pearlmag.com
Marilyn Johnson, Editor
3030 East Second Street
Long Beach, CA 90803

PEN AMERICAN CENTER

PEN Award for Poetry in Translation

A prize of $3,000 is given annually for a book-length translation of poetry from any language into English published in the U.S. during the current calendar year.

PEN/Martha Albrand Award for the Art of the Memoir

A prize of $1,000 is given for a memoir by a U.S. writer published in the current year.

PEN/Martha Albrand Award for First Nonfiction

A prize of $1,000 is given for a first book of creative nonfiction by a U.S. writer published in the current year.

PEN/Book-of-the-Month Club Translation Prize

A prize of $3,000 is given annually for a book-length translation of poetry or literary prose into English from any language published in the U.S. during the current calendar year.

PEN/Spielvogel-Diamonstein Award

A prize of $5,000 is given annually for a book of essays on any subject by a U.S. writer published in the current year.

PEN American Center
John Morrone, Awards Manager
568 Broadway
New York, NY 10012

(212) 334-1660, ext. 108,
or jm@pen.org

PEN CENTER USA

Literary Awards

Prizes of $1,000 are given annually to recognize outstanding books published in the current calendar year by poets, fiction writers, creative nonfiction writers, and translators living west of the Mississippi.

PEN Center USA
Literary Awards
www.penusa.org
672 South Lafayette Park Place
Suite 42
Los Angeles, CA 90057

(213) 365-8500
or awards@penusa.org

PEN CENTER USA WEST

Emerging Voices Rosenthal Fellowships

Seven to ten fellowships of $1,000 each and an eight-month mentorship in Los Angeles with a professional writer are given to poets, fiction writers, and creative nonfiction writers from minority, immigrant, or underserved communities.

PEN Center USA West
Emerging Voices Rosenthal
  Fellowships
www.penusa.org
Teena Apeles, Literary Programs
  Coordinator
672 South Lafayette Park Place,
  #42
Los Angeles, CA 90057

(213) 365-8500, ext. 15,
or ev@penusa.org

PEN NEW ENGLAND

Hemingway Foundation Award

A prize of $7,500 is given for a novel or book of short stories published in the current year by an author who has not previously published a book of fiction.

L.L. Winship Award

A prize of $3,000 is given annually for the most outstanding book of poetry, fiction, or creative nonfiction relating to New England published in the preceding year.

PEN New England
www.pen-ne.org
Catherine Parnell
P.O. Box 400725
North Cambridge, MA 02140

(617) 499-9550
or awards@pen-ne.org

PEN/FAULKNER FOUNDATION

Award for Fiction

A prize of $15,000 and four $5,000 prizes are given annually to writers for distinguished works of fiction published in the previous year.

PEN/Faulkner Foundation
Award for Fiction
www.penfaulkner.org
Janice Delaney, Executive Director
201 East Capitol Street SE
Washington, D.C. 20003

(202) 675-0345

PERUGIA PRESS

Intro Award

A prize of $1,000 and publication by Perugia Press will be given annually for a first or second poetry book (48 to 72 pages) by a woman.

Perugia Press
Intro Award
www.perugiapress.com
Susan Kan, Director
P.O. Box 60364
Florence, MA 01062

info@perugiapress.com

PIRATE'S ALLEY FAULKNER SOCIETY

William Faulkner Creative Writing Competition

A prize of $7,500 is given for a novel (50,000 to 100,000 words); $2,500 for a novella (no more than 50,000 words); $2,000 for a novel in progress (first chapter of no more than 12,500 words and an outline of a novel); $1,500 for a short story (no more than 15,000 words); and $1,000 for a personal essay (no more than 7,500 words).

Pirate's Alley Faulkner Society
William Faulkner Creative Writing
   Competition
www.wordsandmusic.org
624 Pirate's Alley
New Orleans, LA 70116-3254

(504) 586-1609
or faulkhouse@aol.com

UNIVERSITY OF PITTSBURGH PRESS

Drue Heinz Literature Prize

A prize of $15,000 and publication by the University of Pittsburgh Press is given annually for a collection of short fiction (150 to 300 pages).

Agnes Lynch Starrett Poetry Prize

A prize of $5,000 and publication by the University of Pittsburgh Press is given annually for a first poetry collection (48 to 100 pages).

University of Pittsburgh Press
www.pitt.edu/~press
Eureka Building
5th Floor
3400 Forbes Avenue
Pittsburgh, PA 15260

PLEIADES PRESS

Lena-Miles Wever Todd Poetry Series

A prize of $1,000 and publication by Pleiades Press with distribution by Louisiana State University Press is given annually for a book-length poetry collection (at least 48 pages).

Pleiades Press
Lena-Miles Wever Todd Poetry
   Series
Kevin Prufer, Director
Department of English
Central Missouri State University
Warrensburg, MO 64093

(660) 543-8106

POETRY CENTER AT PASSAIC COUNTY COMMUNITY COLLEGE

Allen Ginsberg Poetry Award

A prize of $1,000, publication in the Paterson Literary Review, *and an invitation to participate in a reading in Paterson, New Jersey, is given annually for a group of unpublished poems.*

Paterson Fiction Prize

A prize of $1,000 is given annually for a novel or collection of short fiction published in the preceding year.

Paterson Poetry Prize

A prize of $1,000 is given annually to honor a book of poetry published in the preceding year.

Poetry Center at Passaic County
   Community College
www.pccc.cc.nj.us/poetry
Maria Mazziotti Gillan, Executive
   Director
1 College Boulevard
Paterson, NJ 07505-1179

(973) 684-6555

POETRY SOCIETY OF AMERICA

Robert H. Winner Memorial Award

A prize of $2,500 is given annually to honor a poet over forty who has published no more than one book.

Poetry Society of America
Robert H. Winner Memorial
   Award
www.poetrysociety.org
15 Gramercy Park
New York, NY 10003

(212) 254-9628

POETS & WRITERS, INC.

Writers Exchange

One poet and one fiction writer from a selected state is given $500 each and a trip to New York City to give a reading and meet with writers, editors, and agents in the annual Writers Exchange Program.

Poets & Writers, Inc.
Writers Exchange
www.pw.org
Bonnie Marcus, Director
72 Spring Street
New York, NY 10012

bmarcus@pw.org

PRINCETON UNIVERSITY

Alfred Hodder Fellowship

A stipend of $51,000 is given annually to a poet, fiction writer, or creative nonfiction writer of exceptional promise to pursue an independent project in the humanities at Princeton University during the academic year.

Princeton University
Alfred Hodder Fellowship
www.princeton.edu/~humcounc
Council of the Humanities
Joseph Henry House
Princeton, NJ 08544-5264

(609) 258-4717
or humcounc@princeton.edu

PUSHCART PRESS

Editors' Book Award

A prize of $1,000 and publication by Pushcart Press is given annually for a fiction or creative nonfiction manuscript.

Pushcart Prizes

Publication in The Pushcart Prize: Best of the Small Presses *is awarded annually for the best literary works published by small presses in the current calendar year.*

Pushcart Press
Bill Henderson, Editor
P.O. Box 380
Wainscott, NY 11975

(631) 324-9300

RAGDALE FOUNDATION

Frances Shaw Fellowship

A six-week residency in the summer or fall is given annually to an emerging woman poet or fiction writer who began to write seriously after the age of fifty-five.

Ragdale Foundation
Frances Shaw Fellowship
1260 North Green Bay Road
Lake Forest, IL 60045

(847) 234-1063

RED HEN PRESS

Benjamin Saltman Poetry Award

A prize of $1,000 and publication by Red Hen Press is given annually for an unpublished poetry collection (64 to 96 pages).

Short Fiction Award

A prize of $1,000 and publication in the Los Angeles Review is given annually for a short story.

Red Hen Press
www.redhen.org
Kate Gale, Managing Editor
P.O. Box 3537
Granada Hills, CA 91394

(818) 831-0649
or editors@redhen.org

RED ROCK REVIEW

Mark Twain Award for Short Fiction

A prize of $1,000 and publication in Red Rock Review *is given annually for a short story.*

Red Rock Review
Mark Twain Award for Short
    Fiction
www.ccsn.nevada.edu/english/
    redrockreview/index.html
Richard Logsdon, Editor
Community College of Southern
    Nevada
English Department

J2A, 3200 East Cheyenne Avenue
North Las Vegas, NV 89030

(702) 651-4094
or richard_logsdon@ccsn.
nevada.edu

REED MAGAZINE

John Steinbeck Award

A prize of $1,000 and publication in
Reed *magazine is given annually for*
an unpublished short story.

Reed Magazine
John Steinbeck Award
Chris Fink, Assistant Professor of
    English
English Department
San Jose State University
1 Washington Square
San Jose, CA 95192-0090

(408) 924-4458
or cfink@email.sjsu.edu

RIVER CITY PUBLISHING

Fred Bonnie Memorial Award

A prize of $1,500 and publication
by River City Publishing is given
annually for a first novel.

River City Publishing
Fred Bonnie Memorial Award
www.rivercitypublishing.com
Tangela Parker, Publicist
1719 Mulberry Street
Montgomery, AL 36106

(334) 265-6753 or tparker@
rivercitypublishing.com

RIVER STYX

International Poetry Contest

A prize of $1,000 and publication in
River Styx *is given annually for a*
group of poems.

River Styx
International Poetry Contest
www.riverstyx.org
Melissa Gurley Bancks, Managing
    Editor
634 North Grand Boulevard
12th Floor
St. Louis, MO 63103

ROBINSON JEFFERS TOR HOUSE FOUNDATION

Poetry Prize

A prize of $1,000 is given annually
for an unpublished poem.

Robinson Jeffers Tor House
    Foundation
Poetry Prize
www.torhouse.org
Elliot Ruchowitz-Roberts
Coordinator
P.O. Box 223240
Carmel, CA 93922

(831) 624-1813
or thf@torhouse.org

ROSEBUD

X.J. Kennedy Award

A prize of $1,000 and publication in
Rosebud *is given biennially for a*
work of creative nonfiction or memoir.

Rosebud
X.J. Kennedy Award
www.rsbd.net
Roderick Clark
N3310 Asje Road
Cambridge, WI 53523

jrodclark@smallbytes.net

RUNES: A REVIEW OF POETRY

Runes Award

A prize of $1,000 and publication in
Runes: A Review of Poetry *is given*
annually for an unpublished poem.

Runes: A Review of Poetry
Runes Award
members.aol.com/runes
Arctos Press
P.O. Box 401
Sausalito, CA 94966-0401

runesrev@aol.com

SALMON RUN PRESS

National Poetry Book Award

A prize of $1,000 and publication by
Salmon Run Press is given annually
for a book-length collection of poetry
(up to 96 pages).

Salmon Run Press
National Poetry Book Award
John Smelcer, Publisher
Department of English
MSC 162
Texas A&M University
Kingsville, TX 78363

(361) 334-3373
or salmonrp@aol.com

SAN FRANCISCO FOUNDATION

Literary Awards

Three prizes of $2,000—the Joseph
Henry Jackson Award for poetry,
fiction, and creative nonfiction; the
Mary Tanenbaum Award for
nonfiction; and the James D. Phelan
Award for poetry, fiction, nonfiction
and drama—are given annually to
writers between twenty and thirty-five
years of age for unpublished works-in-
progress.

San Francisco Foundation
Literary Awards
www.theintersection.org
Intersection for the Arts
446 Valencia Street
San Francisco, CA 94103

(415) 626-2787

SARABANDE BOOKS

Poetry and Short Fiction Prizes

Two prizes of $2,000—the Kathryn A. Morton Prize in poetry and the Mary McCarthy Prize in short fiction—and publication by Sarabande Books are given annually for unpublished book-length collections.

Sarabande Books
Poetry and Short Fiction Prizes
www.sarabandebooks.org
2234 Dundee Road
Suite 200
Louisville, KY 40205

SHENANDOAH

Glasgow Prize for Emerging Writers

A prize of $2,500, rotating yearly between the genres of poetry, short fiction, and creative nonfiction, is given triennially to a writer who has published one book.

Shenandoah
Glasgow Prize for Emerging
    Writers
shenandoah.wlu.edu
Lynn Leech, Managing Editor
Washington and Lee University
Troubadour Theater
2nd Floor
Lexington, VA 24450-0303

(540) 458-8765

SILVERFISH REVIEW PRESS

Gerald Cable Book Award

A prize of $1,000 and publication by Silverfish Review Press is given annually for a first poetry collection (at least 48 pages).

Silverfish Review Press
Gerald Cable Book Award
Rodger Moody, Series Editor
P.O. Box 3541
Eugene, OR 97403

(541) 344-5060
or sfrpress@earthlink.net

SLIPSTREAM PRESS

Poetry Chapbook Competition

A prize of $1,000 and publication by Slipstream Press is given annually for an unpublished poetry collection (up to 40 pages).

Slipstream Press
Poetry Chapbook Competition
www.slipstreampress.org
Box 2071
Niagara Falls, NY 14301

SLOPE EDITIONS

Book Prize

A prize of $1,000 and publication by Slope Editions, a nonprofit press associated with the online literary journal Slope, *is given annually for a* *book-length collection of poetry (40 to 70 pages).*

Slope Editions
Book Prize
www.slope.org
Ethan Paquin, Editor
2350 Kensington Avenue
Amherst, NY 14226

ethan@slope.org

SMALLMOUTH PRESS

Andre Dubus Novella Award

A prize of $1,000 and electronic publication on the Smallmouth Press Web site is given annually for a novella (75 to 150 pages).

Smallmouth Press
Andre Dubus Novella Award
www.smallmouthpress.com
P.O. Box 661
New York, NY 10185

info@smallmouthpress.com

SOCIETY OF AMERICAN HISTORIANS

James Fenimore Cooper Prize

A prize of $2,500 is given biennially for a historical novel on an American theme that "significantly advances the historical imagination."

Society of American Historians
James Fenimore Cooper Prize
Ene Sirvet, Administrative Secretary
603 Fayerweather MC 2538

Columbia University
New York, NY 10027

(212) 854-5943
or es28@columbia.edu

SONIA RAIZISS-GIOP

Charitable Foundation Bordighera Poetry Prize

A prize of $2,000 and bilingual publication by Bordighera, Inc., is given annually for a collection of poetry written in English to be translated into Italian.

Sonia Raiziss-Giop Charitable
    Foundation
Bordighera Poetry Prize
www.italianamericanwriters.com/
    prize.html
Daniela Gioseffi and Alfredo de
    Palchi, Contest Coordinators
57 Montague Street, 8G
Brooklyn, NY 11201

daniela@garden.net

SOUTH CAROLINA ARTS COMMISSION

South Carolina Fiction Project

Up to twelve prizes of $500 each are given annually for short stories by South Carolina fiction writers.

South Carolina Arts Commission
South Carolina Fiction Project
www.state.sc.us/arts

Sara June Goldstein, Program
   Director
1800 Gervais Street
Columbia, SC 29201

(803) 734-8694
or goldstsa@arts.state.sc.us

UNIVERSITY OF SOUTHERN CALIFORNIA

Ann Stanford Poetry Prize

A prize of $1,000 and publication in the Southern California Anthology, *an annual publication of USC's Master of Professional Writing Program, is given annually for an unpublished poem.*

University of Southern California,
Ann Stanford Poetry Prize
James Ragan, Director
Master of Professional Writing
   Program
WPH 404
Los Angeles, CA 90089-4034

(213) 740-3252
or mpw@mizar.usc.edu

SOUTHERN POETRY REVIEW

Guy Owen Prize

A prize of $1,000 and publication in Southern Poetry Review *is given annually for an unpublished poem.*

Southern Poetry Review
Guy Owen Prize
www.spr.armstrong.edu

Robert Parham, Editor
Department of Languages,
   Literature, and Philosophy
Armstrong Atlantic State
   University
Savannah, GA 31419-1997

(912) 927-5289 or parhamro@
mail.armstrong.edu

SOUTHERN REVIEW/LSU
Short Fiction Award

A prize of $500 is given annually to a U.S. citizen to honor a first published collection of short stories.

Southern Review/LSU
Short Fiction Award
www.lsu.edu/thesouthernreview
John Easterly, Associate Editor
43 Allen Hall
Louisiana State University
Baton Rouge, LA 70803-5005

(225) 578-5108
or jeaster@lsu.edu

SOUTHWEST REVIEW

Morton Marr Poetry Prize

A prize of $1,000 and publication in Southwest Review *is given annually for a poem or a group of poems in a traditional form (such as a sonnet, sestina, or villanelle) by a writer who has not yet published a book.*

Southwest Review
Morton Marr Poetry Prize

www.southwestreview.org
P.O. Box 750374
Dallas TX 75275-0374

SOW'S EAR PRESS

Chapbook Competition

*A prize of $1,000 and publication by
Sow's Ear Press with distribution to*
Sow's Ear Poetry Review *subscribers
is given annually for a poetry collection
(22 to 26 pages).*

Poetry Prize

A prize of $1,000 and publication in
Sow's Ear Poetry Review *is given
annually for an unpublished poem of
any length.*

Sow's Ear Press
Larry Richman, Managing Editor
19535 Pleasant View Drive
Abingdon, VA 24211-6827

(276) 628-2651
or richman@preferred.com

SPOON RIVER POETRY REVIEW

Editors' Prize

A prize of $1,000 and publication in
Spoon River Poetry Review *is given
annually for a group of unpublished
poems.*

Spoon River Poetry Review
Editors' Prize
www.litline.org/spoon

Lucia Getsi, Editor
4241 Department of English
Illinois State University
Normal, IL 61790- 4241

(309) 438-7906

ST. LOUIS POETRY CENTER

National Poetry Contest

A prize of $2,000 and publication in
Margie: The American Journal of
Poetry *is given annually for a single
poem.*

St. Louis Poetry Center
National Poetry Contest
www.stlouispoetrycenter.org
Robert Nazarene, Contest Chair
567 North and South Road, #8
St. Louis, MO 63130

margiereview@aol.com

STANFORD UNIVERSITY

Wallace Stegner Fellowships

*Two-year fellowships, five in poetry
and five in fiction, are given annually
to allow emerging writers to develop
their craft in workshops with senior
faculty members at Stanford
University.*

Stanford University
Wallace Stegner Fellowships
www.stanford.edu/dept/english/cw
Gay Pierce, Program Coordinator
Creative Writing Program

Department of English
Stanford, CA 94035-2087

(650) 723-2637
or gpierce@stanford.edu

STANFORD UNIVERSITY LIBRARIES

William Saroyan International Prize

A prize of $12,500 is awarded annually for a book of fiction or a memoir published during the previous year.

Stanford University Libraries
William Saroyan International
  Prize
saroyanprize.stanford.edu
Gay Pierce, Program Coordinator
Green Library
Stanford, CA 94305

gpierce@stanford.edu

STATE UNIVERSITY OF NEW YORK, FARMINGDALE

Paumanok Poetry Award

A prize of $1,000 and travel expenses to read in the SUNY Farmingdale poetry series is awarded annually for a group of poems.

SUNY Farmingdale
Paumanok Poetry Award
Margery Brown, Director
Visiting Writers Program
Knapp Hall

Route 110
Farmingdale, NY 11735

(631) 420-2645
or brownml@farmingdale.edu

STORY LINE PRESS

Nicholas Roerich Poetry Prize

A prize of $1,000, publication by Story Line Press, and a reading at the Nicholas Roerich Museum in New York City is given annually for a poetry manuscript (at least 48 pages) by a writer who has not published a full-length collection.

Three Oaks Prize

An advance of $1,500 and publication by Story Line Press is given annually for a novel, novella, or collection of short stories.

Story Line Press
www.storylinepress.com/projects/
  threeoak.htm
Three Oaks Farm
P.O. Box 1240
Ashland, OR 97520-0055

(541) 512-8792

SUMMER LITERARY SEMINARS

Fiction and Poetry Contest

Two prizes, which include plane fare, accommodations, and tuition to attend the Summer Literary Seminars program in St. Petersburg, Russia, and publication in Tin House, *are given annually for an unpublished poem and a novel excerpt or short story. Second prize in each category is tuition, valued at $2,650.*

Summer Literary Seminars
Fiction and Poetry Contest
www.sumlitsem.org
Jeff Parker, Assistant Director
P.O. Box 1358
Schenectady, NY 12301

(518) 388-6041
or parker@sumlitsem.org

UNIVERSITY OF TAMPA PRESS

Tampa Review Prize for Poetry

A prize of $1,000 and publication by University of Tampa Press is given annually for an unpublished collection of poetry (60 to 100 pages).

University of Tampa Press
Tampa Review Prize for Poetry
tampareview.ut.edu
Richard Mathews, Editor
401 West Kennedy Boulevard,
  #19F
Tampa, FL 33606

(813) 253-6266

TEXAS CHRISTIAN UNIVERSITY PRESS

Texas Book Award

A prize of $5,000 is given biennially for the best book of fiction or creative nonfiction about Texas.

Texas Christian University Press
Texas Book Award
Judy Alter, Director
Box 298300
Fort Worth, TX 76129

(817) 257-7822
or j.alter@tcu.edu

TEXAS INSTITUTE OF LETTERS

Literary Awards

The Texas Institute of Letters gives seven awards annually to honor outstanding books on a Texas subject or books by authors who were born in Texas or have spent at least two consecutive years living in the state.

Texas Institute of Letters
Literary Awards
www.stedwards.edu/newc/marks/til
Paula Marks, Secretary
Box 935
St. Edward's University
3001 Congress Avenue
Austin, TX 78704-6489

paulam@admin.stedwards.edu

UNIVERSITY OF TEXAS/ TEXAS INSTITUTE OF LETTERS

Dobie Paisano Fellowships

A stipend of $12,000 and a six-month residency at a retreat west of Austin is given annually to a writer of poetry or fiction who is a native Texan, who has lived in Texas for at least two years, or who has used Texas as the subject of his or her published work.

University of Texas/Texas Institute
    of Letters
Dobie Paisano Fellowships
www.utexas.edu/ogs/Paisano
Audrey Slate, Director
J. Frank Dobie House
702 East Dean Keeton Street
Austin, TX 78705

(512) 471-8542
or aslate@mail.utexas.edu

THURBER HOUSE

Writers-in-Residence

A stipend of $6,000 and a residency in a furnished apartment in James Thurber's boyhood home is offered annually to a poet, fiction writer, or creative nonfiction writer.

Thurber House
Writers-in-Residence
www.thurberhouse.org/
    writersinresidence.htm
Trish Houston, Program Director

77 Jefferson Avenue
Columbus, OH 43215

(614) 464-1032

TRUMAN STATE UNIVERSITY PRESS

T. S. Eliot Prize

A prize of $2,000 and publication by Truman State University Press is given annually for an unpublished book-length poetry collection (60 to 100 pages).

Truman State University Press
T. S. Eliot Prize
tsup.truman.edu
Nancy Rediger, Coordinator
100 East Normal Street
Kirksville, MO 63501-4221

(800) 916-6802
or tsup@truman.edu

TUPELO PRESS

Dorset Prize

A prize of $3,000, publication by Tupelo Press, and a two-week residency at the Dorset Writers Colony in Dorset, Vermont, is given for an unpublished poetry collection (50 to 80 pages).

Poetry Prizes

A Judge's Prize of $3,000 and an Editors' Prize of $1,000 are given *annually for first poetry collections (48 to 80 pages) and include publication by Tupelo Press.*

Tupelo Press
www.tupelopress.org
P.O. Box 539
Dorset, VT 05251

editors@tupelopress.org

UNITED STATES CIVIL WAR CENTER

Michael Shaara Award

A prize of $1,500 is given annually for a novel about the Civil War published in the current calendar year to "encourage fresh approaches to Civil War fiction."

United States Civil War Center
Michael Shaara Award
www.cwc.lsu.edu/cwc/mshaara.htm
Leah Wood Jewett, Director
Raphael Semmes Drive
Louisiana State University
Baton Rouge, LA 70803

(225) 578-3151
or lwood@lsu.edu

UNIVERSITIES WEST PRESS

Emily Dickinson Award in Poetry

A prize of $1,200 and publication in an anthology by Universities West Press is given annually for an unpublished poem.

Universities West Press
Emily Dickinson Award in
  Poetry
www.popularpicks.com
Glenn Reed, Editor
P.O. Box 0788
Flagstaff, AZ 86002-0788

glenn@usa.net

UNTERBERG POETRY CENTER

"Discovery"/*The Nation* Prizes

Four prizes of $300 each, publication in The Nation, *and an expenses-paid trip to read at the 92nd Street Y Unterberg Poetry Center in New York City are given annually for a group of unpublished poems.*

Unterberg Poetry Center
"Discovery"/*The Nation* Prizes
www.92ndsty.org/content/
  discovery_nation_poetry_
  contest.asp
92nd Street Y
1395 Lexington Avenue
New York, NY 10128

(212) 415-5759

UTAH STATE UNIVERSITY PRESS

May Swenson Poetry Award

A prize of $1,000 and publication by Utah State University Press is given annually for a poetry collection (50 to 100 pages).

Utah State University Press
May Swenson Poetry Award
www.usu.edu/usupress
7800 Old Main Hill
Logan, UT 84322-7800

(435) 797-1362

VERMONT STUDIO CENTER

Fellowship Competition

Monthlong residencies at the Vermont Studio Center, valued at $3,300 each, are given to approximately eight poets, fiction writers, and creative nonfiction writers three times a year.

Vermont Studio Center
Fellowship Competition
www.vermontstudiocenter.org
Kevin Cummins, Writing Program
    Coordinator
P.O. Box 613
Johnson, VT 05656

(802) 635-2727 or writing@
vermontstudiocenter.org

VERSE PRESS

Verse Prize

A prize of $1,000 and publication by Verse Press is given annually for an unpublished book-length collection of poetry.

Verse Press
Verse Prize
www.versepress.org
Lori Shine, Managing Editor

221 Pine Street
Studio 2A3
Florence, MA 01062

(413) 219-9024

VIRGINIA CENTER FOR THE CREATIVE ARTS

Goldfarb Family Fellowship

A two-week residency, valued at $1,400, is given annually to a creative nonfiction writer.

Virginia Center for the Creative
    Arts
Goldfarb Family Fellowship
www.vcca.com
Craig Pleasants, Program Director
154 San Angelo Drive
Amherst, VA 24521

(434) 946-7236
or pleasants@vcca.com

VIRGINIA COMMISSION FOR THE ARTS

Artist Fellowships

Fellowships of up to $5,000 are given biennially to Virginia poets and fiction writers to support projects that will advance the art form or the writers' careers.

Virginia Commission for the Arts
Artist Fellowships
www.arts.state.va.us
Donna Champ Banks, Program
    Coordinator

223 Governor Street
Lewis House
2nd Floor
Richmond, VA 23219-2010

dbanks.arts@state.va.us

VIRGINIA COMMONWEALTH UNIVERSITY

Levis Reading Prize

A prize of $1,000 and an invitation to travel, expenses paid, to give a public reading in Richmond, Virginia, is given annually to honor a first or second book of poetry published in the current calendar year.

Virginia Commonwealth
   University
Levis Reading Prize
www.has.vcu.edu/eng/grad/
   Levis_Prize.htm
Department of English
P.O. Box 842005
Richmond, VA 23284-2005

(804) 828-1331
or eng_grad@vcu.edu

WASHINGTON CENTER FOR THE BOOK

Washington State Book Awards

Ten prizes of $1,000 each are given annually for books of poetry, fiction, and creative nonfiction.

Washington Center for the Book
Washington State Book Awards

www.spl.org/wacentbook/
   centbook.html
Christine Higashi, Associate
   Director
Seattle Public Library
800 Pike Street
Seattle, WA 98101

(206) 386-4650
or chris.higashi@spl.org

WESTERN STATES ARTS FEDERATION

Western States Book Awards

Prizes of $1,000 each are given by the Western States Arts Federation for books of poetry, fiction, creative nonfiction, and translation by writers living in the West, published by presses that have their principal offices in these states.

Western States Arts Federation
Western States Book Awards
www.westaf.org
Ryan Blum, Director of Programs
1543 Champa Street
Suite 220
Denver, CO 80202

(303) 629-1166
or ryan.blum@westaf.org

WHITE PINE PRESS

Poetry Prize

A prize of $1,000 and publication by White Pine Press is given annually for an unpublished poetry collection (no more than 90 pages).

White Pine Press, Poetry Prize
Elaine LaMattina
P.O. Box 236
Buffalo, NY 14201

(716) 627-4665
or wpine@whitepine.org

WICK POETRY PROGRAM

Stan and Tom Wick Poetry Prize

A prize of $2,000 and publication by Kent State University Press is given annually for a first book of poems (48 to 68 pages).

Wick Poetry Program
Stan and Tom Wick Poetry
    Prize
dept.kent.edu/wick
Maggie Anderson, Coordinator
Department of English
Kent State University
P.O. Box 5190
Kent, OH 44242-0001

(330) 672-2067

UNIVERSITY OF WISCONSIN

Institute for Creative Writing Fellowships

A stipend of $25,000 and an academic year in residence at the Wisconsin Institute for Creative Writing in Madison is given annually to six

writers working on their first books of poetry or fiction.

Brittingham and Felix Pollak Prizes

Two prizes of $1,000 each and publication by the University of Wisconsin Press are given annually for collections of poetry (50 to 80 pages).

University of Wisconsin
www.wisc.edu/wisconsinpress/
    poetryguide.html
Department of English
600 North Park Street
University of Wisconsin
Madison, WI 53706

WISCONSIN ARTS BOARD

Artist Fellowship Awards

Eight fellowships of $8,000 each are given biennially to Wisconsin writers to support continued artistic achievement. Poets, fiction writers, and creative nonfiction writers living in Wisconsin who are not full-time students pursuing a fine arts degree are eligible.

Wisconsin Arts Board
Artist Fellowship Awards
www.arts.state.wi.us
101 East Wilson Street
1st Floor
Madison, WI 53702

(608) 266-0190

WORD PRESS

First Book Prize

A prize of $1,000 will be given annually for a first collection of poetry (at least 48 pages).

Poetry Prize

A prize of $1,000 and publication by Word Press is given annually for an unpublished poetry collection (at least 48 pages).

Word Press
Poetry Prize
www.word-press.com
Lori Jareo
P.O. Box 541106
Cincinnati, OH 45254-1106

(513) 474-3761
or ljareo@wordtechweb.com

WORD WORKS

Washington Prize

A prize of $1,500 and publication by Word Works, a nonprofit literary organization, is given annually to a poet for an unpublished poetry manuscript (48 to 64 pages).

Word Works
Washington Prize
www.wordworksdc.com
Karren Alenier, President
P.O. Box 42164
Washington, DC 20015

editor@wordworksdc.com

WRITER'S DIGEST

Short Short Story Competition

A prize of $1,500 is given annually for an unpublished short story.

Annual Writing Competition

A prize of $1,500 and either an expenses-paid trip to New York City to meet with editors and agents or a trip to the Maui Writers Conference is given annually for poems, short stories, and personal essays.

Writer's Digest
www.writersdigest.com
Terri Boes
4700 East Galbraith Road
Cincinnati, OH 45236

(513) 531-2690, ext. 1328,
or competitions@fwpubs.com

WRITERS AT WORK

Fellowship Competition

Three prizes of $1,500 and publication in Quarterly West *are given annually to a poet, fiction writer, and creative nonfiction writer who have not published a book.*

Writers at Work
Fellowship Competition
www.writersatwork.org
Joan Coles, Fellowship
    Competition Chair

P.O. Box 540370
North Salt Lake, UT 84054-0370

(801) 292-9285

WRITERS' CENTER OF INDIANA

Maize Prize for Poetry

A prize of $1,000 plus publication in the literary journal Maize *and in* Literally, *the Writers' Center of Indiana's newsmagazine, is given annually for a group of poems.*

Writers' Center of Indiana
Maize Prize for Poetry
www.indianawriters.org
Christina Williams, Program
  Manager
P.O. Box 30407
Indianapolis, IN 46230-0407

(317) 255-0710
or mail@indianawriters.org

WRITERS' LEAGUE OF TEXAS

Fellowships in Literature

In cooperation with the Texas Commission on the Arts, the Writers' League of Texas distributes literary fellowships totaling $18,000 among poets, fiction writers, and creative nonfiction writers to "support the growth and deepening excellence of the literary arts in Texas."

Writers' League of Texas
Fellowships in Literature
www.writersleague.org

1501 West Fifth Street
Suite E-2
Austin, TX 78703

(512) 499-8914
or awl@writersleague.org

YALE UNIVERSITY PRESS

Yale Series of Younger Poets

Publication of a first book of poetry (48 to 64 pages) by a poet under forty years of age is given annually by Yale University Press.

Yale University Press
Yale Series of Younger Poets
www.yale.edu/yup
P.O. Box 209040
New Haven, CT 06520-9040

ZENPRINT

Black Zinnias First Book Award

A prize of $2,000 and publication by the publisher Zenprint is given annually for a first poetry collection (50 to 100 pages).

Zenprint
Black Zinnias First Book Award
www.blackzinnias.com
Jeff Munnis
345 Forest Avenue #202
Palo Alto, CA 94301

(650) 326-5588
or jeff@zenprint.com

ZOETROPE: ALL-STORY

Short Fiction Contest

A first prize of $1,000 is given annually for a short story (up to 5,000 words).

Zoetrope: All-Story
Short Fiction Contest
www.all-story.com
Paul Kramer, Associate Editor
916 Kearny Street
San Francisco, CA 94133

contests@all-story.com

ZOO PRESS

Kenyon Review Prize

A prize of $3,500 and publication by Zoo Press is given annually for a first book of poems (50 to 100 pages).

Paris Review Prize

A prize of $5,000 and publication by Zoo Press is given annually for a book of poems (50 to 100 pages).

Prize for Short Fiction

A prize of $5,000 and publication by Zoo Press is given annually for a collection of short stories (at least 40,000 words).

Zoo Press
www.zoopress.org
P.O. Box 22990
Lincoln, NE 68542

editors@zoopress.org

Conferences & Residencies

The following listing is based on the Conferences & Residencies section of *Poets & Writers Magazine*, which announces application information for writers conferences, literary festivals, residencies, and colonies of interest to poets, fiction writers, and creative nonfiction writers. Some conferences and festivals have rolling, first-come, first-served admission; others accept registration on the date of the event. Please contact the sponsoring organizations for current dates, deadlines, and complete guidelines. When requesting information by mail, enclose a self-addressed, stamped envelope (SASE).

EDWARD F. ALBEE FOUNDATION

The Edward F. Albee Foundation provides one-month residencies from June through October to poets, fiction writers, and creative nonfiction writers at the William Flanagan Memorial Creative Persons Center in Montauk, Long Island.

Edward F. Albee Foundation
www.pipeline.com/~jtnyc/
   albeefdtn.html
Jacob Holder, Foundation
   Secretary,

14 Harrison Street
New York, NY 10013

(212) 226-2020

ANDERSON CENTER RESIDENCY PROGRAM

The Anderson Center offers two-week to one-month residencies from May through October to poets, fiction writers, and creative nonfiction writers on 330 acres of farmland and forestland in Red Wing, Minnesota.

Anderson Center
Residency Program
www.andersoncenter.com
163 Tower View Drive
P.O. Box 406
Red Wing, MN 55066

(651) 388-2009
or acis@pressenter.com

ANTIOCH WRITERS' WORKSHOP

*The annual Antioch Writers'
Workshop, held for a week in July in
Yellow Springs, Ohio, features lectures,
panel discussions, and workshops in
poetry, fiction, and creative nonfiction.*

Antioch Writers' Workshop
www.antiochwritersworkshop.com
Jordis Ruhl, Director
P.O. Box 494
Yellow Springs, OH 45387

(937) 475-7357 or info@
antiochwritersworkshop.com

UNIVERSITY OF ARIZONA POETRY CENTER

*The Poetry Center provides a $500
stipend and a one-month residency to a
poet, fiction writer, or creative
nonfiction writer each summer.*

University of Arizona Poetry
    Center
Summer Residency Program
www.coh.arizona.edu/poetry
Frances Sjoberg, Assistant Director

1216 North Cherry Avenue
Tucson, AZ 85719

(520) 626-3765
or poetry@u.arizona.edu

ART & SOUL CONFERENCE

*The annual Art & Soul Conference,
held concurrently with an
international scholarly conference on
religion and the arts in March at
Baylor University in Waco, Texas,
features readings, lectures, workshops,
and panel discussions.*

Art & Soul Conference
www.baylor.edu/~Rel_Lit
Baylor University
P.O. Box 97270
Waco, TX 76798

(254) 710-4805

ART WORKSHOP INTERNATIONAL

*The annual Art Workshop
International, held in June in Assisi,
Italy, offers two-week workshops in
poetry, fiction, memoir, and publishing.*

Art Workshop International
www.artworkshopintl.com
Kali Lopez Huffman, Coordinator
463 West Street, #1028H
New York, NY 10014

(866) 341-2922
or kali@artworkshopintl.com

ARTS & LETTERS WORKSHOPS

The annual Arts & Letters Creative Writing Workshop for poets, fiction writers, and creative nonfiction writers is held for a week in May at Georgia College and State University in Milledgeville, Georgia.

Arts & Letters Workshops
al.gcsu.edu
Martin Lammon
Campus Box 89
Georgia College and State
    University
Milledgeville, GA 31061

(478) 445-1289
or al@gcsu.edu

ASPEN SUMMER WORDS

The annual Aspen Summer Words Writing Retreat and Literary Festival, held in June in Aspen, Colorado, offers workshops in poetry, fiction, and creative nonfiction, as well as lectures, readings, panel discussions, and the opportunity to meet with agents and editors.

Aspen Summer Words
Aspen Writers' Foundation
www.aspenwriters.org
Julie Comins, Executive Director
110 East Hallam Street
Suite 116
Aspen, CO 81611

(970) 925-3122
or info@aspenwriters.org

ASSOCIATION OF WRITERS AND WRITING PROGRAMS CONFERENCE

AWP's annual conference, held in March, features meetings and caucuses for teachers, writers, publishers, and arts administrators; a book fair; readings; panel discussions on a wide range of literary issues; and forums on the teaching of creative writing.

Association of Writers and Writing
    Programs
www.awpwriter.org
Matt Scanlon, Conference Director
George Mason University
Mail Stop 1E3
Fairfax, VA 22030

(703) 993-4301
or awp@gmu.edu

THE BANFF CENTRE WRITING STUDIO

The Banff Centre Writing Studio offers five-week residencies during April through July on the Banff campus in Alberta, Canada, to published poets, fiction writers, and creative nonfiction writers who are working on a book-length manuscript.

The Banff Centre Writing Studio
www.banffcentre.ca/arts
Greg Hollingshead, Director
Office of the Registrar
Box 1020, Station 28
107 Tunnel Mountain Drive
Banff, Alberta
Canada T1L 1H5

(403) 762-6187
or arts_info@banffcentre.ca

BEAR RIVER WRITERS' CONFERENCE

The annual Bear River Writers' Conference, held in May or June at Camp Daggett, near Petoskey, Michigan, offers workshops in poetry, fiction, and creative nonfiction, as well as readings, discussions, nature walks, and time for writing.

Bear River Writers' Conference
www.lsa.umich.edu/bearriver
Richard Tillinghast, Director
3187 Angell Hall
Department of English Language
   & Literature
University of Michigan
Ann Arbor, MI 48109-1003

(734) 764-4139
or beariver@umich.edu

BREAD LOAF WRITERS' CONFERENCE

The annual Bread Loaf Writers' Conference, held in August in the Green Mountains of Ripton, Vermont, features lectures, craft classes, meetings with editors and agents, readings by faculty and guests, and workshops in poetry, fiction, and creative nonfiction.

Bread Loaf Writers' Conference
www.middlebury.edu/blwc
Noreen Cargill, Administrative
   Manager

Middlebury College
Middlebury, VT 05753

(802) 443-5286
or blwc@middlebury.edu

CALDERA

Located on a ninety-acre site in the Central Cascades, seventeen miles west of Sisters, Oregon, Caldera offers residencies of up to five weeks to poets, fiction writers, creative nonfiction writers, musicians, and visual artists during the fall, winter, and spring.

Caldera
www.calderaarts.org
Miriam Feuerle, Director of Adult
   Programs
224 NW 13th Avenue
Portland, OR 97209

(503) 937-7563
or miriam.feuerle@wk.com

CAPE COD WRITERS' CONFERENCE

The annual Cape Cod Writers' Conference, held in August in Craigville Beach, a Cape Cod village that overlooks Nantucket Sound, offers workshops for poets, fiction writers, and creative nonfiction writers; manuscript evaluations; and personal conferences with faculty.

Cape Cod Writers' Conference
www.capecodwriterscenter.com

Jacqueline Loring, Executive
    Director
P.O. Box 186
Barnstable, MA 02630

(508) 375-0516
or ccwc@capecod.net

CATHOLIC WRITERS CONFERENCE AND RETREAT

The annual Catholic Writers Conference and Retreat, held in January at the Redemptorist Retreat and Renewal Center at Picture Rocks, near Tucson, Arizona, offers readings, lectures, opportunities to meet with publishing professionals, and roundtable discussions for "established and new writers sharing a common Catholic spiritual base and tradition."

Catholic Writers Conference and
    Retreat
Thomas Santa, CSSR
Picture Rocks Retreat Center
P.O. Box 569
Cortaro, AZ 85652

(520) 744-3400, ext. 12

CENTRUM'S PORT TOWNSEND WRITERS' CONFERENCE

Centrum's annual Port Townsend Writers' Conference, held in July at Fort Worden State Park on Washington's Olympic Peninsula, features workshops, lectures, and open-mike readings.

Centrum's Port Townsend Writers'
    Conference
www.centrum.org
Carla Vander Ven, Conference
    Coordinator
P.O. Box 1158
Port Townsend, WA 98368

(360) 385-3102
or carla@centrum.org

CHICAGO HUMANITIES FESTIVAL

The annual Chicago Humanities Festival, held in October or November, features panel discussions and readings at numerous venues in Chicago, including Alliance Française, the Art Institute of Chicago, the Chicago Cultural Center, the Chicago Historical Society, the Chicago Shakespeare Theater, the Field Museum, and the Museum of Contemporary Art.

Chicago Humanities Festival
www.chfestival.org
Eileen Mackevich, Executive
    Producer
500 North Dearborn Street
Suite 1028
Chicago, IL 60610

(312) 661-1028
or eileen@chfestival.org

CONFERENCE ON SOUTHERN LITERATURE

The biennial Conference on Southern Literature, held in April in

Chattanooga, features workshops, lectures, and open-mike readings.

Conference on Southern
    Literature
www.artsedcouncil.org
Laurel Eldridge, Administrative
    Coordinator
Arts & Education Council
P.O. Box 4203
Chattanooga, TN 37405-0203

(800) 267-4232
or leldridge@artsedcouncil.org

CONSTANCE SALTONSTALL ARTS COLONY

The Constance Saltonstall Arts Colony awards monthlong residencies in a rural setting five miles from Ithaca, New York, to poets, fiction writers, and creative nonfiction writers who are residents of New York State.

Constance Saltonstall Arts Colony
www.saltonstall.org
Lee-Ellen Marvin, Program
    Manager
P.O. Box 6607
Ithaca, NY 14851-6607

(607) 277-4933
or artsfound@clarityconnect.com

DEEP SOUTH FESTIVAL OF WRITERS

The annual Deep South Festival of Writers, held in October at the University of Louisiana in Lafayette,

features workshops in poetry and fiction, panel discussions, craft lectures, and readings.

Deep South Festival of Writers
www.louisiana.edu/Academic/
    LiberalArts/ENGL/Creative/
    DeepSouth.htm
Reggie Young, Director
University of Louisiana
English Department
Griffin Hall
Lafayette, LA 70504-4691

(337) 482-5481
or reggiey@louisiana.edu

DINGLE WRITING COURSES

The Dingle Writing Courses, offered in September and October at the Lios Dána Centre in Inch, Ireland, on the Dingle Peninsula, include weekend workshops, lectures, writing exercises, individual tutorials, and manuscript critiques for poets, fiction writers, and creative nonfiction writers.

Dingle Writing Courses
www.dinglewriting.com
Ballyneanig, Ballyferriter
Tralee, County Kerry, Ireland

(353) 66 915-4990
or info@dinglewriting.com

DJERASSI RESIDENT ARTISTS PROGRAM

The Djerassi Resident Artists Program offers residencies of four and five weeks

*to poets, fiction writers, creative
nonfiction writers, and other creative
artists on a 580-acre ranch south of
San Francisco.*

Djerassi Resident Artists Program
www.djerassi.org
Judy Freeland, Residency
    Coordinator
2325 Bear Gulch Road
Woodside, CA 94062

(650) 747-1250
or drap@djerassi.org

EARLY SPRING IN CALIFORNIA CONFERENCE

*The annual Early Spring in
California Conference, held in March
in Santa Cruz, California, offers
workshops and lectures for women
poets, fiction writers, and creative
nonfiction writers.*

Early Spring in California
    Conference
www.iwwg.com
Hannelore Hahn, Executive
    Director
International Women's Writing
    Guild
P.O. Box 810
Gracie Station
New York, NY 10028-0082

(212) 737-7536

ENVIRONMENTAL WRITING INSTITUTE

*The annual Environmental Writing
Institute for environmental essayists,
journalists, scientists, and natural
historians is held in May or June at
the Teller Wildlife Refuge in Corvallis,
Montana.*

Environmental Writing Institute
www.umt.edu/ewi
Phil Condon, Director
Environmental Studies Program
University of Montana
Missoula, MT 59812

(406) 243-2904
or phil.condon@mso.umt.edu

WILLARD R. ESPY LITERARY FOUNDATION

*The Willard R. Espy Literary
Foundation offers one-month
residencies in February, June, and
October to emerging and established
writers of poetry, fiction, and creative
nonfiction in Oysterville, Washington,
a village located on Willapaba Bay.*

Willard R. Espy Literary
    Foundation
Writers Residency Program
www.espyfoundation.org
P.O. Box 614
Oysterville, WA 98641

(360) 665-5220
or wrelf@willapabay.org

FINE ARTS WORK CENTER SUMMER WORKSHOP PROGRAM

The Fine Arts Work Center's annual Summer Workshops, held in June through August in Provincetown, Massachusetts, offers eighty-six weekend and weeklong workshops in poetry, fiction, creative nonfiction, and visual arts, as well as readings and private meetings with faculty members.

Fine Arts Work Center Summer
   Workshop Program
www.fawc.org
Dorothy Antczak, Programs
   Administrator
24 Pearl Street
Provincetown, MA 02657

(508) 487-9960, ext. 103,
or workshops@fawc.org

FLATHEAD RIVER WRITERS CONFERENCE

The Flathead River Writers Conference, held in October at Grouse Mountain Lodge in Whitefish, Montana, a resort community twenty-five miles west of Glacier National Park, offers panel discussions, workshops, and personal meetings with an editor or agent.

Flathead River Writers Conference
Jake How, Conference Chairman
P.O. Box 7711
Kalispell, MT 59904

hows@centurytel.net

FLORIDA SUNCOAST WRITERS' CONFERENCE

The annual Florida Suncoast Writers' Conference, held in Tampa during February, offers lectures, readings, workshops, and consultations with faculty for poets, fiction writers, and creative nonfiction writers.

Florida Suncoast Writers'
   Conference
Florida Center for Writers
University of South Florida
Department of English
4202 East Fowler Avenue MHH-
   116,
Tampa, FL 33620

(813) 974-1711

GEMINI INK SUMMER LITERARY FESTIVAL

The annual Gemini Ink Summer Literary Festival, held in July in the Southtown Arts District of San Antonio, offers workshops and readings in poetry, fiction, and creative nonfiction, as well as the opportunity to meet with editors and agents.

Gemini Ink Summer Literary
   Festival
www.geminiink.org
Jennifer Hamilton
513 South Presa
San Antonio, TX 78205

(877) 734-9673
or jenh@geminiink.org

GREEN MOUNTAIN WRITERS' CONFERENCE

The Green Mountain Writers' Conference, held annually during August in Tinmouth, Vermont, includes workshops for poets, fiction writers, and creative nonfiction writers; individual conferences; and faculty readings.

Green Mountain Writers'
  Conference
www.vermontwriters.com
Yvonne Daley, Director
47 Hazel Street
Rutland, VT 05701

(802) 775-5326
or ydaley@sbcglobal.net

HEADLANDS CENTER FOR THE ARTS

Headlands Center for the Arts, located in the Marin Headlands outside San Francisco, offers extended live-in residencies of four weeks to eleven months to poets, fiction writers, creative nonfiction writers, and other artists from California, New Jersey, North Carolina, and Ohio.

Headlands Center for the Arts
Artists-in-Residence Program
www.headlands.org
Holly Blake, Residency Manager
944 Fort Barry
Sausalito, CA 94965

(415) 331-2787, ext. 24,
or hblake@headlands.org

HEDGEBROOK

Hedgebrook offers residencies of one week to two months to women writers of poetry, fiction, and creative nonfiction on a forty-eight-acre farm located on Whidbey Island, twenty-seven miles northwest of Seattle.

Hedgebrook
www.hedgebrook.org
2197 East Millman Road
Langley, WA 98260

(360) 321-4786

HURSTON/WRIGHT WRITERS' WEEK

The annual Hurston/Wright Writers' Week, held in July at Howard University in Washington, D.C., offers workshops in fiction and creative nonfiction for published and unpublished African American writers.

Hurston/Wright Writers' Week
www.hurston-wright.org
Clyde McElvene, Coordinator
6525 Belcrest Road
Suite 531
Hyatsville, MD 20782

(301) 683-2134
or info@hurston-wright.org

INTERNATIONAL FESTIVAL OF AUTHORS

The annual International Festival of Authors, held during the fall at

Harbourfront Centre in Toronto, offers readings, discussions, and interviews.

International Festival of Authors
Harbourfront Reading Series
www.readings.org
Vicky Cheng, Publicist
235 Queens Quay West
Toronto, Ontario
Canada M5J 2G8

(416) 973-4760
or readings@harbourfront.on.ca

IOWA SUMMER WRITING FESTIVAL

The annual Iowa Summer Writing Festival, held in June and July in Iowa City, offers week- and weekend-long noncredit workshops for poets, fiction writers, and creative nonfiction writers over eighteen.

Iowa Summer Writing Festival,
www.uiowa.edu/~iswfest
Amy Margolis, Director
100 Oakdale Campus W310
Iowa City, IA 52242

(319) 335-4160
or iswfestival@uiowa.edu

ISLAND INSTITUTE

The annual Sitka Symposium and Celebration, held in June at the Island Institute in Sitka, Alaska, features panel discussions, optional manuscript critiques, and readings in poetry, fiction, and creative nonfiction.

Island Institute
Sitka Symposium and Celebration
www.islandinstitutealaska.org
Carolyn Servid, Codirector
P.O. Box 2420
Sitka, AK 99835

(907) 747-3794
or island@ak.net

JOURNEY CONFERENCE

The annual Journey Conference, held in April at the Hyatt Regency Resort & Casino in Lake Tahoe, Nevada, offers consultations with editors and agents, banquets, readings, discussion groups, and workshops for poets, fiction writers, and creative nonfiction writers.

Journey Conference
Author's Venue
www.authorsvenue.com
600 Central Avenue S.E.
Suite 235
Albuquerque, NM 87102

(505) 244-9337
or info@authorsvenue.com

KENTUCKY WOMEN WRITERS CONFERENCE

The annual Kentucky Women Writers Conference, held in March in Lexington, Kentucky, features workshops, readings, panel discussions, and individual consultations in poetry, fiction, and creative nonfiction.

Kentucky Women Writers
  Conference
www.uky.edu/conferences/kywwc
Brenda Weber, Director
113 Bowman Hall
University of Kentucky
Lexington, KY 40506-0059

(859) 257-8734
or brweber@uky.edu

KENYON REVIEW WRITERS WORKSHOP

The annual Kenyon Review *Writers Workshop for poets, fiction writers, and creative nonfiction writers is held during June at Kenyon College in Gambier, Ohio.*

Kenyon Review
Writers Workshop
www.kenyonreview.org
Ellen Sheffield, Summer Programs
  Coordinator
Walton House
Gambier, OH 43022

(740) 427-5207

LEAGUE OF UTAH WRITERS CONFERENCE

The annual League of Utah Writers Conference, held in September at the Airport Hilton in Salt Lake City, includes workshops in poetry, fiction, and creative nonfiction.

League of Utah Writers
  Conference

www.luwrite.com
Charlene Hirschi, Chairperson
736 West 470 North
Logan, UT 84321

chirschi1@attbi.com

MACDOWELL COLONY

MacDowell Colony offers residencies from one to two months to poets, fiction writers, and creative nonfiction writers on a 450-acre estate near Mount Monadnock in Peterborough, New Hampshire.

MacDowell Colony
www.macdowellcolony.org
Admissions Coordinator
100 High Street
Peterborough, NH 03458

(603) 924-3886
or info@macdowellcolony.org

MIAMI BOOK FAIR INTERNATIONAL

The annual Miami Book Fair International, held in November at the Wolfson Campus of Miami-Dade Community College in downtown Miami, Florida, offers readings, workshops, outdoor exhibits by booksellers and publishers, and opportunities to buy rare and antiquarian books.

Miami Book Fair International
www.miamibookfair.com
Miami-Dade Community College

300 N.E. Second Avenue
Miami, FL 33132

(305) 237-3258

311 Brantly Hall
University of Montana
Missoula, MT 59812

(406) 243-6022
or kanders@selway.umt.edu

MID-ATLANTIC CREATIVE NONFICTION WRITERS' CONFERENCE

The annual Mid-Atlantic Creative Nonfiction Writers' Conference, held in August at Goucher College in Baltimore, offers workshops, lectures, panel discussions, and readings for creative nonfiction writers.

Mid-Atlantic Creative Nonfiction
    Writers' Conference
www.goucher.edu/conference/
    writers
Noreen Mack
Goucher College
1021 Dulaney Valley Road
Baltimore, MD 21204-2794

(800) 697-4646
or center@goucher.edu

MONTANA FESTIVAL OF THE BOOK

The annual Montana Festival of the Book, held in September in Missoula, offers readings, panels, workshops, and performances.

Montana Festival of the Book
www.bookfest-mt.org
Kim Anderson, Festival
    Coordinator
Montana Center for the Book

NEW YORK STATE SUMMER WRITERS INSTITUTE

The annual New York State Summer Writers Institute, held during June and July at Skidmore College in Saratoga Springs, features two- and four-week workshops in poetry, fiction, and creative nonfiction.

New York State Summer Writers
    Institute
Jodie Phaneuf, Program
    Coordinator
Office of the Dean of Special
    Programs
Skidmore College
815 North Broadway
Saratoga Springs, NY 12866-1632

(518) 580-5590
or jphaneuf@skidmore.edu

NORTH CAROLINA WRITERS' NETWORK SPRING CONFERENCE

The North Carolina Writers' Network Spring Conference, held annually in May at Meredith College in Raleigh, is a daylong program of workshops in poetry, fiction, and creative nonfiction, as well as readings and book signings.

North Carolina Writers' Network
Spring Conference
www.ncwriters.org
Carol Henderson, Program
Coordinator
P.O. Box 954
Carrboro, NC 27510

(919) 967-9540
or mail@ncwriters.org

UNIVERSITY OF NORTH DAKOTA WRITERS CONFERENCE

The University of North Dakota's annual conference, held during March in Grand Forks, North Dakota, includes panel discussions, readings, a film festival, book signings, and open mike readings.

University of North Dakota
Writers Conference
www.undwritersconference.org
James McKenzie, Director
Box 7209
Department of English
Grand Forks, ND 58202-7209

(701) 777-3321

NORTHERN ARIZONA BOOK FESTIVAL

The annual Northern Arizona Book Festival, held in April in Flagstaff, Arizona, features readings, panel discussions, and writing workshops.

Northern Arizona Book Festival
www.flagstaffcentral.com/
bookfest
Rick Swanson, Director
4046 Nicholas Street
Flagstaff, AZ 86001

(928) 774-9118
or bookfest@flagstaffcentral.com

OJAI VALLEY POETRY FESTIVAL

The Ojai Valley Poetry Festival, held in May at the Libbey Bowl in Ojai, California, features readings and discussions for poets.

Ojai Valley Poetry Festival
www.ojaipoetryfestival.org
Claudia Reder
P.O. Box 1581
Ojai, CA 93023

(805) 289-0487
or claudia@poetryroom.com

PARIS WRITERS' WORKSHOP

The annual Paris Writers' Workshop, held in June and July, offers workshops in poetry, the novel, short fiction, and creative nonfiction, as well as readings, lectures, a guided literary walking tour, and individual conferences with faculty members.

Paris Writers' Workshop
www.wice-paris.org

Rose Burke and Marcia Lebre,
    Codirectors
20, boulevard du Montparnasse
75015 Paris, France

pww@wice-paris.org

PRAIRIE SCHOOL OF WRITING

The annual Prairie School of Writing, held in July in Bushnell, a town on the Illinois prairie near Macomb, features seminars in poetry and publishing.

Prairie School of Writing
www.prairieschoolofwriting.com
Jane Hertenstein
920 West Wilson Avenue
Chicago, IL 60640

(773) 989-2087
or janeh@jpusa.org

RAGDALE FOUNDATION

The Ragdale Foundation offers residencies of two weeks to two months to poets, fiction writers, creative nonfiction writers, and visual artists on a historic estate attached to fifty-five acres of prairie in Lake Forest, Illinois, thirty miles north of Chicago.

Ragdale Foundation
www.ragdale.org
Melissa Mosher, Director of
    Admissions
1260 North Green Bay Road
Lake Forest, IL 60045

(847) 234-1063, ext. 206,
or mosher@ragdale.org

SACATAR FOUNDATION

The Sacatar Foundation, located on the island of Itaparica in the Bay of All Saints, near the city of Salvador, Brazil, offers residencies of six weeks to three months to poets, fiction writers, creative nonfiction writers, and other artists.

Sacatar Foundation
www.sacatar.org
Admissions
P.O. Box 2612
Pasadena, CA 91102-2612

info@sacatar.org

SAGE HILL WRITING EXPERIENCE

The Sage Hill Writing Experience offers a Canadian retreat for published poets during October at St. Peter's College in Muenster, Saskatchewan.

Sage Hill Writing Experience
www.lights.com/sagehill
Steven Ross Smith, Executive
    Director
Box 1731
Saskatoon, Saskatchewan
Canada S7K 3S1

(306) 652-7395
or sage.hill@sasktel.net

SAINTS AND SINNERS LITERARY FESTIVAL

Saints and Sinners, an annual literary festival for gay, lesbian, bisexual, and transgender writers of poetry, fiction, and creative nonfiction, is held in May in the French Quarter of New Orleans.

Saints and Sinners Literary Festival
Paul Willis, Director
5500 Prytania Street
PMB 215
New Orleans, LA 70115

saintandsinnola@aol.com

SAN MIGUEL POETRY WEEK

The annual San Miguel Poetry Week, held in January in San Miguel de Allende, Mexico, offers lectures, readings, and workshops.

San Miguel Poetry Week
www.sanmiguelpoetry.com
P.O. Box 171
Cooper Station
New York, NY 10276

(212) 439-5104
or info@sanmiguelpoetry.com

SEWANEE WRITERS' CONFERENCE

The annual Sewanee Writers' Conference, held in July at the University of the South in Sewanee, Tennessee, *offers lectures, panel discussions, and workshops for poets and fiction writers.*

Sewanee Writers' Conference
www.sewaneewriters.org
Wyatt Prunty, Director
310 St. Luke's Hall
735 University Avenue
University of the South
Sewanee, TN 37383-1000

(931) 598-1141

SITKA CENTER FOR ART AND ECOLOGY

The Sitka Center for Art and Ecology, located on the central Oregon coast, offers residencies of one week to four months from October to May for poets, fiction writers, and creative nonfiction writers, as well as naturalists and visual artists.

Sitka Center for Art and Ecology
www.sitkacenter.org
P.O. Box 65
Otis, OR 97368

(541) 994-5485
or info@sitkacenter.org

SOUTH CAROLINA BOOK FESTIVAL

The annual South Carolina Book Festival, held in February at the State Fairgrounds in Columbia, offers panel discussions, book signings, readings, antiquarian book vendors, and master classes for writers of poetry, fiction, and creative nonfiction.

South Carolina Book Festival
www.scbookfestival.org
Bruce Lane, Director
Humanities Council of South
    Carolina
P.O. Box 5287
Columbia, SC 29250

bookfest@schumanities.org

SOUTHERN CALIFORNIA WRITERS' CONFERENCE LOS ANGELES

The annual Southern California Writers' Conference Los Angeles, held in October at the Radisson Hotel in Oxnard on California's Strawberry Coast, offers workshops in poetry, fiction, and creative nonfiction; readings; individual critiques; and discussions with editors and agents.

Southern California Writers'
    Conference Los Angeles
www.writersconference.com
Michael Steven Gregory, Executive
    Director
4406 Park Boulevard
Suite E
San Diego, CA 92116

(619) 233-4651 or wewritela@
writersconference.com

SOUTHERN CALIFORNIA WRITERS' CONFERENCE SAN DIEGO

The annual Southern California Writers' Conference San Diego, held in February at the Holiday Inn Hotel and Suites in Old Town, San Diego, offers readings, individual critiques, discussions with editors and agents, and workshops in poetry, fiction, and creative nonfiction.

Southern California Writers'
    Conference San Diego
www.writersconference.com
Michael Steven Gregory, Executive
    Director
4406 Park Boulevard
Suite E
San Diego, CA 92116

(619) 233-4651
or msg@writersconference.com

SOUTHERN FESTIVAL OF BOOKS

The annual Southern Festival of Books, held in October in Nashville, offers readings, panel discussions, and book signings.

Southern Festival of Books
www.tn-humanities.org/
    sfbmain.htm
Humanities Tennessee
1003 18th Avenue South
Nashville, TN 37212

(615) 320-7001
or serenity@tn-humanities.org

SPLIT ROCK ARTS PROGRAM

The annual Split Rock Arts Program, held in the summer at the University of Minnesota's Duluth campus, offers thirty-eight weeklong workshops in poetry, fiction, creative nonfiction, and visual arts.

Split Rock Arts Program
www.cce.umn.edu/splitrockarts
Andrea Gilats, Program Director
University of Minnesota
360 Coffey Hall
1420 Eckles Avenue
St. Paul, MN 55108-6084

(612) 625-8100
or srap@cce.umn.edu

SQUAW VALLEY COMMUNITY OF WRITERS

The Squaw Valley Community of Writers, located near the north shore of Lake Tahoe in the Sierra Nevada mountains, offers craft talks, faculty readings, and daily workshops in poetry in July and fiction in August.

Squaw Valley Community of
    Writers
www.squawvalleywriters.org
Brett Hall Jones, Executive
    Director
P.O. Box 1416
Nevada City, CA 95959

(530) 470-8440
or svcw@oro.net

STEAMBOAT SPRINGS WRITERS CONFERENCE

The annual Steamboat Springs Writers Conference is held in July in Steamboat Springs, Colorado.

Steamboat Springs Writers
    Conference
Harriet Freiberger, Conference
    Director
P.O. Box 774284
Steamboat Springs, CO 80477

(970) 879-8079
or mshfreiberger@cs.com

SUMMER WRITING PROGRAM AT NAROPA UNIVERSITY

The Summer Writing Program at Naropa University, held in June or July in Boulder, Colorado, features workshops in poetry, fiction, translation, and letterpress printing.

Summer Writing Program at
    Naropa University
www.naropa.edu/swp
Lisa Birman, Assistant Director
2130 Arapahoe Avenue
Boulder, CO 80302

(303) 245-4600
or lisab@naropa.edu

TEXAS BOOK FESTIVAL

The annual Texas Book Festival, held in November in Austin, includes panel discussions, readings, and book signings.

Texas Book Festival
www.texasbookfestival.org
P.O. Box 13143
Austin, TX 78711

(512) 477-4055
or bookfest@worldnet.att.net

TRUCKEE MEADOWS COMMUNITY COLLEGE WRITERS' CONFERENCE

The annual Truckee Meadows Community College Writers' Conference, held in March at John Ascuaga's Nugget, a luxury resort in Reno, Nevada, offers a panel discussion, lectures on craft and marketing, and critique sessions.

Truckee Meadows Community
    College Writers' Conference
commserv.tmcc.edu/
    WritersConf.html
Kathy Berry, Marketing
    Coordinator
TMCC Community Services
7000 Dandini Boulevard
RTM A1
Reno, NV 89512

(775) 824-8626
or kberry@tmcc.edu

VASTO WRITERS & ARTISTS RETREAT

The Vasto Writers & Artists Retreat is held in June in Vasto, Italy, in the Abruzzo region on the Adriatic Sea.

Vasto Writers & Artists Retreat
www.vasto.splinder.it
Syed Haider
517 Sherman Avenue
Evanston, IL 60202

retreat@luigimonteferrante.com

VERMONT COLLEGE FALL FOLIAGE LITERARY FESTIVAL

The annual Vermont College Fall Foliage Literary Festival, held in October at Vermont College in Montpelier, offers readings and lectures for poets and fiction writers.

Vermont Fall Foliage Literary
    Festival
www.tui.edu/vermontcollege
Louise Crowley, Administrative
    Director
MFA in Writing
Vermont College
Montpelier, VT 05602

(802) 828-8840
or louise.crowley@tui.edu

VERMONT STUDIO CENTER

The Vermont Studio Center offers four-week residencies to poets, fiction writers, and creative nonfiction writers in Johnson, a village in the Green Mountains.

Vermont Studio Center
www.vermontstudiocenter.org
Kevin Cummins, Writing Program
   Coordinator
P.O. Box 613
Johnson, VT 05656

(802) 635-2727
or writing@vermontstudiocenter.
org

VIRGINIA CENTER FOR THE CREATIVE ARTS

The Virginia Center for the Creative Arts offers residencies of two weeks to two months to writers, visual artists, and composers for a working retreat on a 450-acre estate at the foothills of the Blue Ridge Mountains, approximately 60 miles south of Charlottesville.

Virginia Center for the Creative
   Arts
www.vcca.com
Mount San Angelo
Sweet Briar, VA 24595

(434) 946-7236
or vcca@vcca.com

VIRGINIA FESTIVAL OF THE BOOK

The annual Virginia Festival of the Book, held in March in Charlottesville, Virginia, to celebrate books and pro-

mote literacy, offers readings, panels, and discussions with writers and publishing professionals.

Virginia Festival of the Book
www.vabook.org
Virginia Foundation for the
   Humanities
145 Ednam Drive
Charlottesville, VA 22903

(434) 924-6890

WALLOON WRITERS' RETREAT

The annual Walloon Writers' Retreat, held in September on Walloon Lake in Michigan, offers readings, workshops, and panel discussions.

Walloon Writers' Retreat
www.springfed.org
John Lamb, Director
P.O. Box 304
Royal Oak, MI 48068-0304

(248) 589-3913
or johndlamb@ameritech.net

WESLEYAN WRITERS CONFERENCE

The annual Wesleyan Writers Conference, held in June at Wesleyan University in Middletown, Connecticut, offers workshops in poetry, fiction, and creative nonfiction, as well as seminars, readings, lectures, and manuscript consultations.

Wesleyan Writers Conference,
www.wesleyan.edu/writing/
  conferen.html
Anne Greene, Conference
  Director
Wesleyan University
279 Court Street
Middletown, CT 06459

(860) 685-3604
or agreene@wesleyan.edu

WHIDBEY ISLAND WRITERS' CONFERENCE

The Whidbey Island Writers' Conference, held in February or March on Whidbey Island in Washington's Puget Sound, one hour north of Seattle, offers workshops, individual consultations with editors and agents, and fireside chats with published authors.

Whidbey Island Writers'
  Conference
www.whidbey.com/writers
Celeste Mergens
P.O. Box 1289
Langley, WA 98260

(360) 331-6714
or writers@whidbey.com

WILLIAM PATERSON UNIVERSITY SPRING WRITER'S CONFERENCE

The annual Spring Writer's Conference, held in April on the WPU campus in Wayne, New Jersey, twenty miles from New York City, offers lectures, readings, and workshops in poetry, fiction, and creative nonfiction.

William Paterson University
  Spring Writer's Conference
euphrates.wpunj.edu/
  writersconference
John Parras
English Department
300 Pompton Road
Wayne, NJ 07640

(973) 720-3067
or parrasj@wpunj.edu

WINTER POETRY & PROSE GETAWAY

The annual Winter Poetry & Prose Getaway is held in January at the Grand Hotel in Cape May, New Jersey.

Winter Poetry & Prose Getaway
www.wintergetaway.com
Peter Murphy
18 North Richards Avenue
Ventnor, NJ 08406

(609) 823-5076
or info@wintergetaway.com

WITTER BYNNER POETRY TRANSLATOR RESIDENCY

The Witter Bynner Foundation and the Santa Fe Art Institute offers two residencies of up to four weeks for poetry translators in May and June at the Ricardo Legoretta facility in Santa Fe, New Mexico.

Witter Bynner Poetry Translator
  Residency
www.sfai.org
Joe Girandola, Assistant Director
Santa Fe Art Institute
1600 St. Michael's Drive
Santa Fe, NM 87505

(505) 424-5050

WOODSTOCK GUILD'S BYRDCLIFFE ARTS COLONY

The Byrdcliffe Arts Colony in the Catskill Mountains offers four-week residencies to approximately forty literary and visual artists between June and September.

Woodstock Guild
Byrdcliffe Arts Colony
34 Tinker Street
Woodstock, NY 12498

(845) 679-2079
or wguild@ulster.net

WRITERS CONFERENCE AT PENN

The annual Writers Conference at Penn, held in November at the University of Pennsylvania in Philadelphia, offers workshops in fiction and creative nonfiction.

Writers Conference at Penn
www.upenn.edu/writconf
Nadia Daniel, Administrative
  Coordinator
College of General Studies

University of Pennsylvania
3440 Market Street
Suite 100
Philadelphia, PA 19104

(215) 898-6479
or writconf@sas.upenn.edu

WRITERS STUDIO AT UCLA EXTENSION

The Writers Studio at UCLA Extension, held in February in Westwood, California, offers intensive four-day workshops for prose writers.

Writers Studio at UCLA
  Extension
www.uclaextension.org/writers
Rick Noguchi, Program Manager
UCLA Extension Writers'
  Program
10995 Le Conte Avenue
Room 440
Los Angeles, CA 90024

(800) 388-UCLA

WRITING THE WEST

The annual Writing the West Writer's Conference, held in July in Gunnison, Colorado, a historic cattle and mining community in the Rocky Mountains, offers workshops in poetry, fiction, and creative nonfiction, as well as meetings with editors and classes in editing and marketing.

Writing the West
www.writingthewest.com

Corinne Brown, Chair
48 Cherry Lane Drive
Englewood, CO 80110

(303) 753-6353
or corinnejb@aol.com

YADDO

*Yaddo offers residencies of two weeks to
two months to poets, fiction writers,
and creative nonfiction writers on a
400-acre estate in Saratoga Springs,
New York.*

Yaddo
www.yaddo.org
Candace Wait, Program
    Coordinator
Admissions
P.O. Box 395
Saratoga Springs, NY 12866

(518) 584-0746
or chwait@yaddo.org

YOKNAPATAWPHA SUMMER WRITERS' WORKSHOP

*The Yoknapatawpha Summer Writers'
Workshop, held in June at the
University of Mississippi in Oxford,
features panel discussions, readings,
and workshops in poetry and fiction.*

Yoknapatawpha Summer Writers'
    Workshop
www.outreach.olemiss.edu/
    ProfDev
Shirley Prather, Senior Project
    Administrator
University of Mississippi
Office of Professional
    Development
P.O. Box 879
University, MS 38677-0879

(662) 915-7036
or sprather@olemiss.edu

Resources for Writers

THE ACADEMY OF AMERICAN POETS

588 Broadway, Suite 604
New York, NY 10012-3210
(212) 274-0343
www.poets.org
academy@poets.org

A nonprofit organization founded in 1934 to support American poets at all stages of their careers and to foster the appreciation of contemporary poetry. The largest organization in the country dedicated to the art of poetry, the Academy sponsors annual awards, a national series of poetry readings and poets' residencies, and the American Poets Fund and the Atlas Fund, which provide financial assistance to poets and noncommercial publishers of poetry. The Academy also sponsors National Poetry Month (April), an annual celebration of American poetry; the Online Poetry Classroom, an educational resource and online teaching community for high school teachers; and the Poetry Audio Archive, a collection of audio recordings of poetry readings.

AMERICAN LITERARY TRANSLATORS ASSOCIATION

The University of Texas at Dallas
Box 830688, Mail Station MC35
Richardson, TX 75083-0688
(972) 883-2093
www.utdallas.edu/research/cts/alta.htm

ALTA was founded in 1978 to provide services to literary translations from all languages and to create a professional forum for the exchange of ideas on the art and craft of literary translation. Through its annual conference, its publications, collaboration with other professional organizations, and lobbying efforts, ALTA works to enhance the quality and status of literary translation and to improve the market for the publication of works in English translation.

AMERICANS FOR THE ARTS

Washington Office
1000 Vermont Avenue N.W.,
    6th Floor

Washington, DC 20005
(202) 371-2830
New York Office
1 East 53rd Street
New York, NY 10022
(212) 223-2787
www.artsusa.org
webmaster@artsusa.org

A nonprofit organization seeking to advance the arts in America by representing and serving local communities and creating opportunities for every American to participate in and appreciate all forms of the arts. Americans for the Arts partners with local, state, and national arts organizations; government agencies; business leaders; educators; and funders throughout the country to provide arts industry research, information, and professional development opportunities for community arts leaders.

ARTJOB ONLINE

1743 Wazee Street, Suite 300
Denver, CO 80202
(303) 629-1166
(888) JOBS-232
www.artjob.org
artjob@westaf.org

A source for professional opportunities and career information in all areas of the arts, including visual arts, arts nonprofits, performing arts, commercial art and design firms, film, public arts agencies, academic arts positions, galleries, internships, fellowships, conferences, and commissions.

ARTS MIDWEST

2908 Hennepin Avenue
Suite 200
Minneapolis, MN 55408-1954
(612) 341-0755
www.artsmidwest.org
general@artsmidwest.org

A nonprofit organization connecting the arts to audiences throughout the nine-state region of Illinois, Indiana, Iowa, Michigan, Minnesota, North Dakota, Ohio, South Dakota, and Wisconsin. Cultural programs initi..ted by Arts Midwest include performances by theater, dance, and music ensembles; arts educational activities; visual arts exhibitions; and conferences.

ASSOCIATION OF AUTHORS' REPRESENTATIVES, INC.

P.O. Box 237201, Ansonia Station
New York, NY 10003
www.aar-online.org

A nonprofit organization serving independent literary and dramatic agents.

ASSOCIATION OF WRITERS AND WRITING PROGRAMS

George Mason University
Mail Stop 1E3
Fairfax, VA 22030
(703) 993-4301
www.awpwriter.org
awp@gmu.edu

A nonprofit organization for teachers and students in creative writing programs. AWP's mission is to foster literary talent and achievement, to advance the art of writing as essential to a good education, and to serve the makers, teachers, students, and readers of contemporary writing.

THE AUTHORS GUILD, INC.

31 East 28th Street, 10th Floor
New York, NY 10016
www.authorsguild.org
staff@authorsguild.org

An advocacy group for freelance writers offering legal services, health insurance, and information.

THE AUTHORS LEAGUE OF AMERICA

31 East 28th Street, 10th Floor
New York, NY 10016

A national organization representing authors on copyright, taxes, and freedom of expression. Membership is restricted to authors who are members of the Authors Guild.

BLACK WRITERS ALLIANCE

www.blackwriters.org

An online forum for networking and fellowship opportunities among the black writing community. BWA sponsors local, regional, and online

writing and discussion groups, chats with writing and publishing experts and other industry professionals, message boards, classifieds, and a periodic Web-based newsletter that offers BWA and member news, industry news, articles, upcoming events, calls for submissions, contests, tips, and poetry.

CENTER FOR BOOK CULTURE

200 North Michigan Avenue
Suite 404
Chicago, IL 60601
(312) 263-7710
www.centerforbookculture.org
mcriker@centerforbookculture.org

A nonprofit organization consisting of Dalkey Archive Press, Context *magazine, and the* Review of Contemporary Fiction. *The Center for Book Culture also offers high school, undergraduate, and graduate internship programs in cooperation with the Illinois Arts Council.*

CONSORTIUM FOR PACIFIC ARTS AND CULTURES

1580 Makaloa Street, Suite 930
Honolulu, HI 96814-3220
(808) 946-7381
www.pixi.com/~cpac/index.html
cpac@pixi.com

A nonprofit regional arts organization serving the U.S. jurisdictions of American Samoa, Guam, and the

Commonwealth of the Northern Mariana Islands (CNMI).

COUNCIL OF LITERARY MAGAZINES AND PRESSES

154 Christopher Street, Suite 3C
New York, NY 10014
(212) 741-9110
www.clmp.org
info@clmp.org

A service organization for independent literary publishers, CLMP guides literature through the business of publishing. Services and resources are designed to develop each member's publishing capacity through increased marketing and organizational skills.

CREATORS FEDERATION

P.O. Box 756
New York, NY 10033
www.creatorsfederation.org

An international coalition of writers and artists working in all media and the organizations that represent them.

ELECTRONIC LITERATURE ORGANIZATION

Department of Design/Media Arts
UCLA
11000 Kinross Avenue, Suite 245
Los Angeles, CA 90095
(310) 206-1863
www.eliterature.org
jesspres@ucla.edu

A nonprofit organization founded in 1999 to promote and facilitate the writing, publishing, and reading of electronic literature.

ELECTRONIC POETRY CENTER

Poetics Program
Department of Media Study
231 Center for the Arts
State University of New York
Buffalo, NY 14260-6020
www.epc.buffalo.edu

A list of resources centered on digital and contemporary poetry, new media writing, and literary programming, compiled by the poetics program at the University of Buffalo. EPC offers links to literary magazines, presses, and poetry organizations.

THE FOUNDATION CENTER

Atlanta: (404) 880-0094
Cleveland: (216) 861-1933
New York City: (212) 620-4230
San Francisco: (415) 397-0902
Washington, DC: (202) 331-1400
www.fdncenter.org

A center founded in 1956 that supports and improves institutional philanthropy by promoting public understanding of the field and helping grant seekers succeed. The Center collects, organizes, and communicates information on U.S. philanthropy; conducts and facilitates research on trends in the field; provides education and training; and ensures public access to information and services through its print and electronic publications, five library/learning centers, and a national network of over 200 cooperating collections.

THE HURSTON/WRIGHT FOUNDATION

6525 Belcrest Road, Suite 531
Hyattsville, MD 20782
(301) 683-2134
www.hurston-wright.org
info@hurston-wright.org

A nonprofit organization that aims to develop, nurture, and sustain the world community of writers of African descent. Programs and services are designed to preserve the legacy and ensure the future of black writing.

THE INTERNATIONAL DIRECTORY OF LITERARY MAGAZINES AND PRESSES (DUSTBOOKS)

P.O. Box 100
Paradise, CA 95967
(530) 877-6110
www.dustbooks.com
publisher@dustbooks.com

An annual reference guide providing descriptions, contact information, and relevant information for submissions to literary magazines and book publishers.

INTERNATIONAL WOMEN'S WRITING GUILD

Box 810, Gracie Station
New York, NY 10028-0082
(212) 737-7536
www.iwwg.com
dirhahn@aol.com

A membership organization for the personal and professional empowerment of women through writing.

LIBRARY OF CONGRESS

101 Independence Avenue S.E.
Washington, DC 20540
(202) 707-5000
www.loc.gov

The largest library in the world, with more than 120 million items on approximately 530 miles of bookshelves. The collections include more than 18 million books, 2.5 million recordings, 12 million photographs, 4.5 million maps, and 54 million manuscripts.

LITERARY MARKET PLACE (INFORMATION TODAY, INC.)

www.literarymarketplace.com

An annual reference guide providing descriptions, contact information, and relevant information for submissions to book publishers.

MID-AMERICAN ARTS ALLIANCE

912 Baltimore, Suite 700
Kansas City, Missouri 64105
(816) 421-1388
info@maaa.org
www.maaa.org

A nonprofit organization founded in 1972 to stimulate cultural activity in the states of Arkansas, Kansas, Missouri, Nebraska, Oklahoma, and Texas. M-AAA creates and manages regional, national, and international programs to transform lives and build communities by uniting people through the power of art.

MID-ATLANTIC ARTS FOUNDATION

201 North Charles Street, Suite 401
Baltimore, MD 21201
(410) 539-6656
www.charm.net/~midarts/

A nonprofit organization dedicated to promoting access to all artistic disciplines and providing opportunities for artists in the region and beyond to advance their craft.

MODERN LANGUAGE ASSOCIATION

26 Broadway, 3rd Floor
New York, NY 10004-1789
(646) 576-5000
www.mla.org

A membership organization founded in 1883 to provide opportunities for members to share their scholarly findings and teaching experiences with colleagues and to discuss trends in the academy in an effort to strengthen the study and teaching of language and literature.

NATIONAL ASSEMBLY OF STATE ARTS AGENCIES

1029 Vermont Avenue N.W.
2nd Floor
Washington, DC 20005
(202) 347-6352
www.nasaa-arts.org
nasaa@nasaa-arts.org

A membership organization that unites, represents, and serves the nation's state and jurisdictional arts agencies. NASAA's mission is to advance and promote a meaningful role for the arts in the lives of individuals, families, and communities throughout the United States by empowering state arts agencies through strategic assistance that fosters leadership, enhances planning and decision making, and increases resources.

NATIONAL ENDOWMENT FOR THE ARTS

1100 Pennsylvania Avenue N.W.
Washington, DC 20506
(202) 682-5400
www.nea.gov
webmgr@arts.endow.gov

An independent agency of the federal government, the NEA awards grants to arts organizations and artists in all fifty states. The NEA is the largest single funder of the nonprofit arts sector in the United States.

NATIONAL WRITERS UNION

113 University Place, 6th Floor
New York, NY 10003
(212) 254-0279
www.nwu.org
nwu@nwu.org

A labor union working for equitable payment and fair treatment for freelance writers through collective action.

NEW ENGLAND FOUNDATION FOR THE ARTS

266 Summer Street, 2nd Floor
Boston, MA 02210
(617) 951-0010
www.nefa.org
info@nefa.org

A nonprofit organization providing funding, advocacy, and networking to promote the creation and distribution of the full range of artistic expression. NEFA functions as a grantmaker, program initiator, regional laboratory, project coordinator, developer of resources, and builder of creative partnerships among artists, arts organizations, and funders.

NEW YORK FOUNDATION FOR THE ARTS

155 Avenue of the Americas
14th Floor
New York, NY 10013-1507
(212) 366-6900NYFA
www.nyfa.org
NYFAweb@NYFA.org

A nonprofit organization founded in 1971 to provide the time and resources for the creative mind and the artistic spirit to think, work, and prosper. NYFA offers grants and fellowships, information services, and Web site development to New York State writers and artists.

NEW YORK STATE COUNCIL ON THE ARTS

175 Varick Street
New York, NY 10014
(212) 627-4455
www.nysca.org
helpdesk@nysca.org

A state funding agency that provides support for activities of nonprofit arts and cultural organizations in New York State.

PEN AMERICAN CENTER

568 Broadway, 4th Floor
New York, NY 10012
(212) 334-1660
www.pen.org
pen@pen.org

A membership organization of prominent literary writers and editors that seeks to defend the freedom of expression wherever it may be threatened, and promote and encourage the recognition and reading of contemporary literature.

PEN CENTER USA WEST

672 South Lafayette Park Place
Suite 42
Los Angeles, CA 90057
(213) 365-8500
www.penusa.org
pen@penusa.org

A nonprofit organization founded in 1943 to protect the rights of writers around the world, to stimulate interest in the written word, and to foster a vital literary community among the diverse writers living in the western United States. Among PEN's activities are public literary events, a mentorship project, literary awards, and international human rights campaigns on behalf of writers who are censored or imprisoned.

PEN/FAULKNER FOUNDATION

201 East Capital Street S.E.
Washington, DC 20003
(202) 675-0345
www.penfaulkner.org

A nonprofit organization that confers an annual national prize for the best work of fiction by an American author, brings literary programs of quality to the citizens of the Washington metropolitan area, and extends its programs to young people at a time when they are forming their literary tastes and contemplating their future vocations.

THE POETRY CENTER

San Francisco State University
1600 Holloway Avenue
San Francisco, CA 94132
(415) 338-2227
www.sfsu.edu/~poetry/

A literary arts organization founded in 1954 offering readings series' and an audio archive.

POETRY SOCIETY OF AMERICA

15 Gramercy Park
New York, NY 10003
(212) 254-9628
www.poetrysociety.org

A nonprofit organization founded in 1910 to place "poetry at the crossroads of American life" with a variety of interconnected programs and readings series, including Poetry in Motion, Poetry in the Schools, the Favorite Poem Project, Crossroads: The Journal of the Poetry Society of America, *and poetry events across the country.*

POETS HOUSE

72 Spring Street, 2nd Floor
New York, NY 10012
(212) 431-7920
www.poetshouse.org
info@poetshouse.org

A nonprofit organization and poetry archive featuring a 40,000-volume library.

POETS & WRITERS, INC.

72 Spring Street
New York, NY 10012
(212) 226-3586
www.pw.org

A nonprofit organization founded in 1970 to foster the professional development of poets, fiction writers, and creative nonfiction writers. Programs and services—including Poets & Writers Magazine, A Directory of American Poets and Fiction Writers, *readings/workshops, and publishing seminars—introduce writers to the larger literary community and connect them to audiences.*

PUBLISHERS WEEKLY

360 Park Avenue South
13th Floor
New York, NY 10010
(646) 746-6400
www.publishersweekly.com

An international newsmagazine covering the $23 billion book industry, serving all segments involved in the creation, production, marketing, and sale of the written word in book, audio, video, and electronic formats.

THE PUBLISHING TRIANGLE

17 East 47th Street, 3rd Floor
New York, NY 10017
www.publishingtriangle.org

A nonprofit organization founded in 1988 to create and support a sense of community for lesbian and gay people in the publishing industry by offering forums, as well as networking and social opportunities, for members.

SMALL PRESS CENTER

20 West 44th Street
New York, NY 10036
(212) 764-7021
www.smallpress.org
info@smallpress.org

A nonprofit organization that provides information and draws public awareness of small, independent, literary presses through its sponsorship of Small Press Month (March), an annual book fair, and a publishing workshop series.

SMALL PRESS DISTRIBUTION

1341 Seventh Street
Berkeley, CA 94710-1409
(510) 524-1668
(800) 869-7553
www.spdbooks.org
spd@spdbooks.org

A nonprofit literary arts organization providing wholesaling services to independent presses through public programs and advocacy efforts.

SOUTHERN ARTS FEDERATION

1800 Peachtree Street N.W.
Suite 808
Atlanta, GA 30309
(404) 874-7244
www.southarts.org

A nonprofit regional arts organization that creates partnerships and collaborations; assists in the professional development of artists, arts organizations, and arts professionals; presents, promotes and produces Southern arts and cultural programming; and advocates for the arts and art education. The organization works in partnership with the state arts agencies of Alabama, Florida, Georgia, Kentucky, Louisiana, Mississippi, North Carolina, South Carolina, and Tennessee.

TEACHERS & WRITERS COLLABORATIVE

5 Union Square West
New York, NY 10003-3306
(212) 691-6590
(888) BOOKS-TW
www.twc.org
info@twc.org

A nonprofit organization offering workshops for students in the New York tri-state region. It publishes a catalogue of creative writing books and sponsors an educational radio show, a spoken word program, and a literacy initiative for teen mothers.

VOLUNTEER LAWYERS FOR THE ARTS

1 East 53rd Street, 6th Floor
New York, NY 10022-4201
(212) 319-2787
www.vlany.org

A nonprofit organization providing pro bono legal services, education, and advocacy to the New York arts community. VLA frequently acts on issues vitally important to the arts community—freedom of expression and the First Amendment being areas of special expertise and concern. The Web site includes a national directory of the organization's offices in twenty-six states.

WESTERN STATES ARTS FEDERATION

1743 Wazee Street, Suite 300
Denver, CO 80202
(303) 629-1166
(888) 562-7232
www.westaf.org
staff@westaf.org

A nonprofit arts service organization dedicated to the creative advancement and preservation of the arts. Based in Denver, WESTAF fulfills its mission to strengthen the financial, organizational, and policy infrastructure of the arts by providing innovative programs and services to artists and arts organizations in the West and nationwide.

WRITER'S MARKET AND POET'S MARKET (WRITER'S DIGEST BOOKS)

Annual reference guides providing descriptions, contact information, and relevant information for submissions to literary and trade magazines, agents, and book publishers.

Notes on Contributors

Scott Bane, a writer, is a manager of the Community Justice Program at the JEHT Foundation in New York City.

Helen Benedict is the author of three novels, *A World Like This* (Dutton, 1990), *Bad Angel* (Plume, 1997), and *The Sailor's Wife* (Zoland, 2000), as well as four books of nonfiction. She is a professor of journalism at Columbia University.

Tom Bradley is a novelist living in Nagasaki, Japan. His work has appeared in *McSweeney's, Exquisite Corpse, Nthposition,* as well as on the Web sites Salon.com and Arts & Letters Daily. Excerpts and reviews of his books, plus recordings of his rousing readings, can be found at tombradley.org.

Melvin Jules Bukiet is the author of seven books of fiction, most recently *Strange Fire* (W.W. Norton, 2001) and *A Faker's Dozen* (Norton, 2003). He teaches at Sarah Lawrence College.

Julie Checkoway is the author of two books, *Little Sister: Searching for the Shadow World of Chinese Women* (Viking, 1996) and *Creating Fiction* (Story Press, 1999). A recipient of a fellowship from the National Endowment for the Arts, Checkoway has published work in the *New York Times,* on NPR, and in many anthologies. She lives in Houston with her husband and daughter.

C. Michael Curtis is a senior editor at the *Atlantic Monthly,* where he has edited fiction and nonfiction articles for more than thirty years.

Natalie Danford is coeditor of the *Best New American Voices* series (Harvest/Harcourt). Her reviews and articles have appeared on the Web site Salon.com as well as in the *Washington Post*, *Boston Globe*, and *Publishers Weekly*, among other publications.

Michael Depp writes for Reuters and has contributed to *The Chronicle of Higher Education*, *Food & Wine*, *Time Out*, *The Dictionary of Literary Biography*, and many other publications, as well as public radio. He teaches at Tulane University.

Jacqueline Deval, publisher of Hearst Books, formerly worked as director of publicity for several publishing houses, including William Morrow, Villard, Doubleday, and the Book-of-the-Month Club. She is the author of *Publicize Your Book!* (Perigee, 2003), from which her article in *The Practical Writer* was excerpted. To read more about her book, or to contact her, visit www.publicizeyourbook.com.

Fran Gordon is the author of the novel *Paisley Girl* (St. Martin's, 1999), a finalist for Quality Paperback Book Club's New Voices Award in 2000. She directs the National Arts Club's PAGE reading series and teaches creative writing at the New School and Fairleigh Dickinson.

David Hamilton is the author of *Deep River: A Memoir of a Missouri Farm* (University of Missouri Press, 2001) and the chapbook *The Least Hinge* (Frith Press, 2002). Other poems and essays have appeared from time to time in various magazines. Since 1978, he has been the editor of the *Iowa Review*.

Amy Holman has taught more than 700 writers how to publish, pitch, and promote their poetry, fiction, and creative nonfiction in her position as director of Publishing Seminars at Poets & Writers, Inc. She is also a contributor to "The Artist's Toolbox" on the National Endowment for the Arts Web site and to *Making the Perfect Pitch* (The Writer Books, 2004). Her poetry has been in *The Best American Poetry 1999* and twice nominated for a Pushcart Prize.

Betsy Lerner has an MFA in poetry from Columbia University. She worked as an editor for twelve years at various trade publishing houses before becoming an agent with the Gernert Company. She is the author of *The Forest for the Trees: An Editor's Advice to Writers* (Riverhead, 2000) and *Food and Loathing: A Lament* (Simon & Schuster, 2003).

David Long's most recent novel is *The Daughters of Simon Lamoreaux* (Scribner, 2000). He lives in Tacoma, Washington.

Noah Lukeman is a New York–based literary agent and author of the best-sellers *The First Five Pages* (Simon & Schuster, 1999) and *The Plot Thickens* (St. Martin's Press, 2002), recently published in paperback. To read a sample chapter, or to contact him, visit www.lukeman.com/the plotthickens.

Robert McDowell, a poet, is the publisher of Story Line Press.

Kay Murray is general counsel and assistant director of the Authors Guild, the nation's largest organization of published authors. She is also the executive editor of the *Authors Guild Bulletin*, a quarterly publication of business and legal advice.

Gregory Orr teaches at the University of Virginia. He is the author of eight books of poetry, the most recent of which is *The Caged Owl: New and Selected Poems* (Copper Canyon Press, 2002). He is also the author of a memoir, *The Blessing* (Council Oak Books, 2002), and a book on lyric poetry, *Poetry as Survival* (University of Georgia, 2002).

R. Eirik Ott was recently featured on national television as part of HBO's showcase *Def Poetry* and as part of Black Entertainment Television's comedy/variety show *The Way We Do It*. His chapbook series *The Wussy Boy Chronicles* was nominated to the Utne Reader's Best of the Alternative Press Awards 2000. He was a member of the 1999 San Francisco Poetry Slam Team, which was a cochampion of the 1999 Poetry Slam in Chicago.

Robert Phillips is the author and editor of more than thirty-two books of poetry, fiction, and criticism. His honors include an Award in Literature from the American Academy of Arts and Letters. He has been director of the Creative Writing Program at the University of Houston, where he is currently the John & Rebecca Moores Professor of English. Most recently he published *The Madness of Art: Interviews with Poets and Writers* (Syracuse University Press, 2003).

Joanna Smith Rakoff is a contributing editor of *Poets & Writers Magazine*. She writes frequently on books and authors for the *New York Times, Vogue, Newsday,* and many other publications.

M.J. Rose (www.mjrose.com) is the author of *Flesh Tones* (Ballantine Books, 2002) and *Sheet Music* (Ballantine Books, 2003) and more than 150 articles on the publishing industry.

Guy Shahar is the editor in chief of the *Cortland Review* (www.cortland review.com), an online literary magazine founded in 1997. He works as the sole Interactive Project Engineer at OgilvyInteractive, where he leads the display technology team in the development of Web sites. He lives in New York City.

Jeffrey Skinner's latest collection of poems, *Gender Studies*, was published by Miami University Press in 2002.

Sol Stein was publisher and editor in chief of Stein and Day for twenty-seven years. Two of the books he edited and published were chosen for inclusion in Modern Library's list of *The 100 Best Books of the Century*. He is the author of *Stein on Writing* (St. Martin's, 1995), nine novels, and the computer programs for writers WritePro® and FictionMaster® (www.writepro.com). His article "*Midlist* and Other Fictions" is derived in part from *How to Grow a Novel*, published by St. Martin's Press in 1999.

Michael Taeckens received his MFA from the Iowa Writers' Workshop. He currently works as publicity director at Algonquin Books of Chapel Hill, a division of Workman Publishing.

Catherine Wald is the author of *The Resilient Writer: Tales of Rejection and Triumph from 20 Top Authors* (Persea Books, 2004). She can be contacted through www.writerwald.com and www.rejectioncollection.com.

Nicholas Weinstock's writing has been featured on National Public Radio and in the *New York Times Magazine, Vogue, Glamour, US, Elle, Out*, and *Ladies' Home Journal*, among other publications. He is the author most recently of the novel *As Long as She Needs Me* (Harper-Collins, 2001). Weinstock lives in New York City with his wife, the writer Amanda Beesley, and their two children.

Kate Whouley works with booksellers across the U.S. and abroad on a variety of projects, from designing new stores and store expansions to advising bookstore owners on operational and financial matters. A frequent contributor to book industry publications, Whouley edited the fifth edition of *Manual on Bookselling* (American Booksellers Association, 1996) and is the series editor for the American Booksellers Association's *Fundamentals of Bookselling*.

Rebecca Wolff is the editor and publisher of *Fence* and Fence Books. She is the author of two books of poems, *Manderley* (University of Illinois Press, 2001) and *Figment* (W.W. Norton, 2004).

Hilma Wolitzer has written several novels, including *Ending* (William Morrow & Company, 1974), *Hearts* (FSG, 1980), and *Silver* (FSG, 1988), and a book on the craft of fiction, *The Company of Writers: Fiction Workshops and Thoughts on the Writing Life* (Penguin, 2001). She has taught at the Bread Loaf Writers Conference, Columbia University, the University of Iowa Writers Workshop, and many other universities.

About Poets & Writers, Inc.

Founded in 1970, Poets & Writers believes in contemporary literature's indispensable value to our national culture. Its mission is to foster the professional development of poets and writers, to promote communication throughout the U.S. literary community, and to help create an environment in which literature can be appreciated by the widest possible public.

P&W is unique among national literary organizations in that it focuses on the *source* of literature, providing information, support, and guidance to writers at all stages in their careers. Each year, over 100,000 poets and fiction writers benefit from P&W's publications, programs, and services, which introduce writers to the larger literary community and connect them to audiences, making today's writing visible and accessible across the country.

Poets & Writers Magazine, the organization's flagship publication, is the leading journal of its kind for creative writers. Along with essays on the literary life and interviews with contemporary writers of poetry, fiction, and creative nonfiction, the magazine publishes articles with practical applications for both emerging and established writers. In addition, it provides the most comprehensive listing of literary grants and awards, deadlines, and prizewinners available in print.

Poets & Writers Online includes a searchable directory of over 5,000 listings of American poets and fiction writers; links to over 1,000 Web sites of interest to writers; advice on topics such as copyright, publishing, and finding a writers conference; along with weekly news updates about the literary community. Another popular feature is the **Speakeasy Message Forum,** which serves as a central meeting place and community center for writers.

Each year, through its **Readings/Workshops Program,** P&W sponsors more than 1,000 literary events throughout New York and California, as well as in Chicago and Detroit. P&W makes matching grants (restricted to the payment of writers' fees) to a variety of organizations—from grassroots to nationally acclaimed presenters and distributes more than $170,000 annually to some 700 writers from 35 states.

In 1984, the **Writers Exchange Contest** was established to introduce emerging writers to literary communities outside their home states. Each year one poet and one fiction writer are selected from one state to participate in the program. Writers are selected based on manuscripts they submit to P&W and flown to New York City for an all-expenses-paid, weeklong trip, at which time they meet with literary agents, editors, publishers, and writers. To date, more than sixty-five writers from twenty-five states have participated in this program.

As a cofounder of **The Literary Network,** Poets & Writers continues to champion the cause of freedom of expression and advocates on behalf of writers for public funding of literature and the arts.

For more information about Poets & Writers, Inc., contact us at Poets & Writers, 72 Spring Street New York, NY 10012; (212) 226-3586. Or visit us at www.pw.org.

Index

FOR THE BEST IN PAPERBACKS, LOOK FOR THE

In every corner of the world, on every subject under the sun, Penguin represents quality and variety—the very best in publishing today.

For complete information about books available from Penguin—including Penguin Classics, Penguin Compass, and Puffins—and how to order them, write to us at the appropriate address below. Please note that for copyright reasons the selection of books varies from country to country.

In the United States: Please write to *Penguin Group (USA) Inc., P.O. Box 12289 Dept. B, Newark, New Jersey 07101-5289* or call 1-800-788-6262.

In the United Kingdom: Please write to *Dept. EP, Penguin Books Ltd, Bath Road, Harmondsworth, West Drayton, Middlesex UB7 0DA.*

In Canada: Please write to *Penguin Books Canada Ltd, 10 Alcorn Avenue, Suite 300, Toronto, Ontario M4V 3B2.*

In Australia: Please write to *Penguin Books Australia Ltd, P.O. Box 257, Ringwood, Victoria 3134.*

In New Zealand: Please write to *Penguin Books (NZ) Ltd, Private Bag 102902, North Shore Mail Centre, Auckland 10.*

In India: Please write to *Penguin Books India Pvt Ltd, 11 Panchsheel Shopping Centre, Panchsheel Park, New Delhi 110 017.*

In the Netherlands: Please write to *Penguin Books Netherlands bv, Postbus 3507, NL-1001 AH Amsterdam.*

In Germany: Please write to *Penguin Books Deutschland GmbH, Metzlerstrasse 26, 60594 Frankfurt am Main.*

In Spain: Please write to *Penguin Books S. A., Bravo Murillo 19, 1° B, 28015 Madrid.*

In Italy: Please write to *Penguin Italia s.r.l., Via Benedetto Croce 2, 20094 Corsico, Milano.*

In France: Please write to *Penguin France, Le Carré Wilson, 62 rue Benjamin Baillaud, 31500 Toulouse.*

In Japan: Please write to *Penguin Books Japan Ltd, Kaneko Building, 2-3-25 Koraku, Bunkyo-Ku, Tokyo 112.*

In South Africa: Please write to *Penguin Books South Africa (Pty) Ltd, Private Bag X14, Parkview, 2122 Johannesburg.*